Missouri

To Dr. Eric Turner

"Illegitimi non carborundum"

Missouri

FAMOUS (AND INFAMOUS) MISSOURIANS WHO LED THE WAY IN THEIR FIELD

PAUL W. BASS

Paul W Bass

6/24/19

AℙP™

Acclaim Press

MORLEY, MISSOURI

Acclaim Press
—— *Your Next Great Book* ——

P.O. Box 238
Morley, MO 63767
(573) 472-9800
www.acclaimpress.com

Book Design: Rodney Atchley
Cover Design: Kevin Williamson, *Kevin Williamson Design*

ISBN: 978-1-948901-14-7 | 1-948901-14-5
Library of Congress Control Number: 2018962054

First Printing: 2019
Printed in the United States of America
10 9 8 7 6 5 4 3 2 1

This publication was produced using available information.
The publisher regrets it cannot assume responsibility for errors or omissions.

Contents

Acknowledgments

Much thanks is given to Dr. Jerry Plunkett of Dixon, Missouri. He gave me the original idea for a book of Missouri Innovators, dealing with scientific inventors and entrepreneurs of national significance. Although a book could be written about the two hundred such persons, it was felt that a book including some of those persons and others from Missouri in an expanded range of categories would be of more general interest. After reading some of the preliminary writing, Dr. Plunkett readily agreed and was very supportive of the book concept.

My gracious publisher, Doug Sikes of Acclaim Press, was interested from the very beginning. He saw the opportunity for statewide promotion. His editor, Randy Baumgardner, and the Acclaim Press staff were very helpful in bringing this book to creation and providing the great design ideas to help me look like I am a much better writer.

My wife, Jan, provided her usual and very capable proofreading expertise. Others assisting in the proofreading assistance were Gaytha Suits, Cecelia Chittenden, and Jerry Plunkett.

Several friends have offered suggestions for persons to be included in the book. Thanks goes to Steve Weigenstein, Joe Driscoll, and Doug Sikes.

This is the twelfth book that I have had published. I certainly want to somehow thank the state of Missouri for providing me with a good education and the inspiration to accomplish seemingly impossible personal goals. It is a great place to be from and a great place to retire.

Author's Notes

In December 2016, I received a phone call from Dr. Jerry Plunkett of Dixon, Missouri. I had met him at the annual meeting of the Sustainable Ozarks Partnership in Waynesville, Missouri, in 2015. He had read my book on *The History of Fort Leonard Wood* and liked it very much. He wanted to meet with me to discuss writing a book on innovators from Missouri. It sounded interesting to me, and I agreed to meet with him.

In January 2017, we met in Springfield and had several additional meetings plus other correspondence. At the first meeting, I became aware of his unique life in the scientific and technological fields and government service. He had just turned ninety years old and still had a sharp mind. Besides being a creative innovator himself, he has several patents on business and government-related projects. He also had helped other local authors in getting a very popular book published. I agreed to begin a preliminary search of the topic and see what was available.

I was surprised and pleased at the number of innovators from Missouri that were quickly discovered. Several books for children had been written, but there were no extensive books published for older teens or adults. I had ongoing book promotion events for *The History of Fort Leonard Wood* book and was competing the first draft of a three-year project on the history of the early churches in Springfield, Missouri. I had also agreed to teach two sections of Old Testament History for the Mercy School of Nursing program sponsored by Southwest Baptist University. In March 2017, I had completed the first draft of *Pioneer Churches in Springfield, Missouri* and prepared to get the final draft to the publisher by late April. That would free me to get more active in pursuing research for the Missouri innovators book.

The major theme of my past published books was of people, events, and places of great significance about which no book had been written. Although the subject of innovators in Missouri was written in limited areas, a major work had not been written. Plus, I must admit, as a Missourian, the topic was of genuine interest to me. So the adventure began in earnest in April 2017.

Through early research, a larger number than expected (about 300!) of famous Missouri Innovators was discovered. It became necessary to limit the number of persons to be examined in greater detail for a reasonable-sized book to be printed. The selection of these individuals was the decision of the author. It in no way discounts the contributions and significance of those not selected, but it does offer a good selection of significant Missourians.

I love research. It's like trying to find all of the pieces of a big picture puzzle. To me, the writing is like trying to fit the puzzle pieces collected into a beautiful, clear picture. The proofreading and editing are painful but always necessary. The publication process for me has been too easy, with publishers committing to publish before the book was even finished. My Missouri publisher, Doug Sikes of Acclaim Press, is a great gentleman who fortunately, for me, thrives on sales and promotion. The promotion of the published book is inevitable, enjoyable, and everlasting. With the completion of this book, I now have three Missouri-related books that can be shared in promotional events. It is my desire that all three of these books provide Missourians with education, pride, and motivation of creativity in their own pursuits.

Introduction

What is the difference between an innovator and an inventor? Defining terms may offer some insight. An "inventor" is defined as one who "originates or creates as a product of one's own ingenuity, experimentation, or contrivance." An innovator is one who "introduces something new; makes changes in anything established." An inventor may create a product, but an innovator may make it better. Hence the subtitle, "Show Me a Better Way."

There are a few books written about famous Missourians. These are written on an older children's level by talented elementary school teachers. It is also necessary to consider the difference between a "famous Missourian" and a "Missouri innovator." Famous Missourians may not be innovators, and Missouri innovators may not be famous. An attempt will be made to consider those famous Missourians who were or are innovators.

The use of the word "innovator" in this book is used to describe individuals who have made significant contributions in various fields of life. These individuals all have some connection with Missouri. They were either born in Missouri or chose to live in Missouri. They are recognized as sources of great pride for our state. Many of them, sadly, had to leave our state to find implementation of their innovations. Regrettably, those making their way into actual production of innovative technology usually found outlets outside of our state.

This book has several purposes. First, is to educate Missourians about our proud individual heritage and accomplishments. Second, is to encourage our state leaders to provide more business and economic incentives in helping the innovators to remain in Missouri for research and production purposes. Third, is to inspire our youth to be challenged by their fellow Missourians who have succeeded in their innovations.

As our state begins to look ahead to our third century of existence, it would be great to see this listing of respected innovators grow exponentially statewide because of increased awareness of the importance of education, research, and industry. With the advances of technology and communication, Missourians have every opportunity to continue to "show the world a better way."

Missouri

INNOVATORS
THE STATE BY STATE SERIES

FAMOUS (AND INFAMOUS) MISSOURIANS WHO LED THE WAY IN THEIR FIELD

Chapter One

Entertainers

Josephine Baker
St. Louis
Singer

The first decade of the 1900s, only two generations removed from the tragedy of the Civil War, was an especially difficult time for blacks in the United States. This was apparent in a border state like Missouri. Racial prejudice and mob rule were common. In 1906, three young black men were lynched by a large mob in the central square of Springfield, Missouri. They had been accused of molesting a white woman. The accusations were later proven false. The impact on the sizeable black community was immediate. Over half of the black population left Springfield overnight, going mainly to Kansas City and St. Louis. Word of the Springfield calamity arrived with the migrants. In that same year in St. Louis, Carrie McDonald and Eddie Carson, former vaudeville performers, produced a child—Freda Josephine McDonald.

Eddie quickly abandoned the family, and Carrie was left to find support for her child. The slums of St. Louis offered minimal opportunity for meaningful employment. Carrie worked as a laundress. At age eight, Baker quit school and helped with the family income through services as a maid and a babysitter. She was constantly subjected to discrimination by the white people who hired her. She had an opportunity to watch dancers at a nearby vaudeville show. She even had the chance to dance part time in a chorus line.

She experienced the race riots of St. Louis in 1917. Tired of the blatant discrimination and dangerous racial climate, she left for Philadelphia with a vaudeville troupe at age thirteen. She performed in the popular musical comedy *Shuffle Along*. When she was fifteen years old, she married a Philadelphian named Willie Baker. Soon after, she was offered a job in New York City and left Willie behind but kept his name. At the age of nineteen, she was offered a job in Paris, France. The decision to leave the United States was not difficult. The proposed salary of $250 a week was far better than any other offer. She also was growing tired and angry over the discrimination she faced even on the East Coast.

Europe in the 1920s was an exciting location. World War I had concluded. Americans were welcomed as heroes, and blacks faced little racial prejudice. Baker gained prominence as a popular dancer and national star in France. She danced freely, bare-breasted or with very skimpy costumes. Her reputation grew throughout Europe but received negative opinion in Austria. One Austrian parliamentarian complained that the issue was not one of race but that she "dressed only in a postage stamp."

Baker made a world tour from 1928-1930, covering twenty-five countries in Europe and the Americas. She was able to return to the United States briefly in 1935, to perform with the Ziegfeld Follies in New York. She also visited with her mother in St. Louis. She was still haunted by the experiences of racial prejudice, commenting, "If I want to make a telephone call in the street, I am still a Negress."

Returning to France, she married a French industrialist, Jean Lyon, becoming an official citizen of France. Her continuation of dance and a film career were halted at the beginning of World War II. Baker worked as a Red Cross volunteer and served in the French underground. In spite of a year-long battle with bronchitis, she entertained the French troops in North Africa and the Middle East. For her services, the nation of France awarded her the Legion of Honor and the Rosette of the Resistance decoration.

After the war, Baker bought a very large 300-acre estate in southwestern France. She cared for a large menagerie of various pets on her estate. She also "began adopting orphaned babies of different races, nationalities, and religious backgrounds and raising them." Financial obligations for her estate and dependents caused her to continue her performances throughout France. In 1940, she married Jo Bouillon, a French orchestra leader. She continued her life caring for pets and adopted children and expanding her estate to include a restaurant, motel, and museum.

In 1951, she visited New York City. She was refused service in the Stork Club because she was black. She challenged the popular columnist Walter Winchell for his segregationist ideas. Her outspokenness on American racial prejudice found her caught in the "Red Scare," and she was falsely accused of being a communist sympathizer.

In 1952, she returned briefly for a visit to St. Louis. She told an audience at Kiel Auditorium, "To me, for years, St. Louis represented a city of fear, humiliation, misery and terror—a city where in the eyes of the white man, a Negro should know his place, and had better stay in it."

She became an active participant in the Civil Rights Movement in the United States in the 1960s. She participated in the 1963 March on Washington for Jobs and Freedom and spoke alongside Dr. Martin Luther King, Jr.

Fulfilling the financial responsibilities of her estate was now beyond her ability. Forced to sell the estate, she found assistance from Grace Kelly, then the Princess of Monaco. Baker continued limited performances in Monaco, France, and the United States. On April 8, 1975, she premiered a tour in Paris at the Bobino Theater. Celebrities and Parisians honored her life and career by their attendance. Four days later, April 12, after a cerebral hemorrhage, she slipped into a coma and died.

The streets of Paris were crowded with over 20,000 paying respects as Baker's funeral procession passed. The French government honored her with a 21-gun salute, "making her the first American woman buried in France with military honors." She was buried in the Cimitiere de Monaco, Monaco.

Josephine Baker, known by some as the "Black Venus," was an international star. She overcame early financial and racial challenges to become an effective proponent of civil rights and freedom of expression. Her creativity and talents were used to support her causes. She indeed was a unique innovator in the field of entertainment.

Linda Bloodworth-Thomason
Poplar Bluff
Producer/author

If women had challenges in Hollywood acting and dancing, then the challenge was even greater for a screenwriter and producer. Linda Bloodworth-Thomason was up to the challenge. She was born in Poplar Bluff, Missouri, April 15, 1947, to Ralph Bloodworth and his wife Claudia. She graduated from Poplar Bluff High School. She graduated from the University of Missouri with a Bachelor of Arts degree. She helped to found the Alpha Pi Phi sorority. In 1970, she left Missouri and traveled to Los Angeles, California. There she taught English at Jordan High School in the south Los Angeles suburb of Watts.

After the challenging teaching career ended, she worked for the *Wall Street Journal* in advertising. She changed jobs to work as a reporter for the *Los Angeles Daily Journal*. She began to also work as a freelance writer for television. She developed acclaimed scripts written for *M*A*S*H** and several short-lived sitcoms. Succeeding in scriptwriting, she began to consider other television production avenues.

In 1980, she met Harry Thomason. He had been an Arkansas high school science teacher and football coach. He had also an interest in television production and moved to Los Angeles. In July 1983, they created Mozark Productions. It combined the origins of their state roots and culture — Harry from Arkansas and Linda from Missouri.

The two worked together to create their first major comedy series, *Filthy Rich* (1982–83). This was followed by *Lime Street* (1985) and the highly successful *Designing Women* (1986–1992). Their success led to spinoffs and new series, such as *Evening Shade* (1990–1992), *Hearts Afire* (1992–1994), *Women of the House* (1995), *Emeril* (2000–2001), and *Twelve Miles of Bad Road* (2008).

During this successful professional period, Linda and Harry became involved in the national political campaign of longtime friend Bill Clinton for the presidency. They produced an effective film, *The Man from Hope*, which introduced Clinton at the 1992 Democratic Convention. They worked with the Clintons during other aspects of election activities. They also suffered through the challenges of Whitewater investigations and the Clinton impeachment process.

In 2004, Linda wrote her first novel, *Liberating Paris*. The pair worked together to produce a screen adaptation of the book. They also worked on a screen adaptation of a documentary called *Southern Comfort*.

Remembering her Missouri roots, Linda founded the Claudia Foundation in Poplar Bluff, in the Bloodworth House. The organization supports young people with "scholarships and opportunities for community services and positions in the art industry." While receiving current peer recognition for her accomplishments, time will only serve to increase the innovations provided by Linda Bloodworth-Thomason.

In 1994, Linda was awarded the Women in Film Industry Award "in recognition of her excellence and innovation in her creative works that have enhanced perception of women through the medium of television."

Molly Brown
St. Louis
Actress/activist

Sometime titles and acclaim come after one's life on earth. Such was the case with Margaret Tobin. Never known in her lifetime as "Molly," Margaret (or "Maggie") was born in Hannibal, Missouri, on July 18, 1867. Her parents, John Tobin and Johanna Collins, migrated to Missouri from Europe. Maggie had several siblings from her mother's previous marriages. She led a rather quiet life in Hannibal, attending a grammar school run by her aunt until she was thirteen. She then went to work at Garth's Tobacco Factory in Hannibal. Several of her siblings had gone west to Colorado in search of gold. Tired of Hannibal and seeking adventure, she joined her brother Daniel in the mining town of Leadville, Colorado, in 1886. She found work at a mercantile store. Shortly after arrival, she met James Joseph (J.J.) Brown, a mining superintendent. After a brief courtship, they married in September 1886 and moved close to the mines in nearby Stumpftown.

In 1887, they had their first child, a son, Lawrence Palmer Brown. Even though the family struggled economically, Maggie found time to establish soup kitchens for the miners' families and became involved with the growing women's suffrage movement. In 1889, she gave birth to a daughter, Catherine Ellen. While J.J. was climbing in the ranks of the mining company, Brown continued her community interests, helping families to improve the town's schools.

With the discovery of gold in the mine in 1893, J.J. received a partnership at the Ibex Mining Company. With finances more secure, the family moved to Denver, Colorado. Brown continued her community activism and founded the Denver Women's Club. In an unusual act, Brown ran for a Colorado state senate seat, eventually withdrawing from the race. She also helped to establish the first juvenile court in the country. Brown enjoyed her newfound wealth and found excitement in world travel. She studied languages at the Carnegie Institute. Her interest in drama and stage led her to participate in the Sarah Bernhardt studies in Paris and New York. Though Maggie and J.J. did travel together at times, it became apparent that J.J. was not in sympathy with his wife's activities. The couple separated in 1909, though never officially divorced. The agreement provided for Brown to receive a cash settlement, the house in Denver, and a monthly payment of $700 for her travels and activities.

Gaining newfound freedom, Brown departed for a trip to Egypt, Rome, and Paris in 1912 with her daughter and friends. While on the trip she received word that her grandson was very ill. She sought to immediately return to the United States. She traveled to Cherbourg, France, and boarded the first available ship home, the newest British luxury liner, the RMS *Titanic*. The ill-fated trip tragically ended with the ship striking an iceberg. She recalled, "I stretched on the brass bed, at the side of which was a lamp. So completely absorbed in my reading I gave little thought to the crash that struck at my window overhead and threw me to the floor." She then began the heroic efforts to help other passengers to the lifeboats. After she was physically forced into lifeboat #6, she continued her assistance to others. The lifeboat was designed for sixty-five passengers. Upon leaving the ship, only twenty-one women, two men, and a twelve-year-old boy were on board. All passengers helped with the rowing for many hours. Early in the morning the ship *Carpathia* was sighted. The lifeboat came alongside, and the passengers went aboard one at a time. Once on board, Brown took charge of helping the many survivors. Her knowledge of languages helped her comfort the foreign passengers. She found extra blankets and supplies and placed the survivors in the relative safety of halls and dining rooms. Realizing the great losses suffered by the mostly women survivors, Brown began soliciting donations from the passengers. It is said that "before the *Carpathia* reached New York, $10,000 had been raised."

Several legends have been created attributing to her eventual title, "the unsinkable Molly Brown." One was that after stepping off the *Carpathia* in New York, she said, "Typical Brown luck. I'm unsinkable." More realistic was the snide comment made by a Denver gossip columnist calling Brown "the unsinkable Mrs. Brown." The gossip columnist had been upset because she was not able to publish the first printed account of Brown's story. The name "Molly" was never used while she was alive. It was a nickname that just became popular.

Her life after the adventure with the *Titanic* continued in typical Maggie Brown style. Maggie returned to Colorado as a celebrity. She tried to use that to her advantage to again run for a U.S. Senate seat in 1914. Failing to win once again, she became active in support of the miners in Ludlow, Colorado, in their strike against the Rockefeller-owned facility. Physical violence erupted, and two dozen people were killed. Brown brought national attention to the event and raised funds for support of the victims' families. Her efforts were rewarded when the Rockefeller company eventually made concessions for the mine workers.

Brown found more time and enjoyment at her rental home in Newport, Rhode Island. She fit in immediately with high society and found a common ally in Alva Vanderbilt. Brown traveled the country in support of women's and labor issues. In July 1914, Brown worked with Alva Vanderbilt to organize the Conference of Great Women. Her third attempt to run for a U.S. Senator from Colorado was interrupted with the outbreak of World War I. Brown focused her attention on war relief efforts in France. Her activities earned her the French Legion of Honor.

Her life would again undergo great changes in interest and direction. World War I ended, women's suffrage was finally passed in 1920 and J. J. Brown died in 1922. Brown renewed her interest in the stage and acting, most famously remembered for her portrayal as Sarah Bernhardt in *L'Aiglon*, performed in Paris and New York. Her health began to fail in her last few years. At the Barbizon Hotel in New York City, she died in her sleep on October 26, 1932 at the age of sixty-five. She was buried next to J. J. in the Cemetery of the Holy Rood in Westbury, New York.

Margaret "Maggie" Tobin Brown became known as the "unsinkable Molly Brown." She was a trailblazer in the causes of humanitarianism, benevolence, and fairness for all people. She once said, "It isn't who you are, nor what you have, but what you are that counts." Her life counted as an innovator for the common good of all people.

Walt Disney
Marceline
Producer

There are those rare people whose accomplishments were not only praised during their lifetime but will also be remembered by an international audience for generations to come. Such an innovator is to be recognized and honored by the public, national leaders, and, especially, by peers in their industry. One of the greatest examples is Walt Disney.

Walter Elias Disney was born on December 5, 1901, in the Hermosa section of Chicago, Illinois, to parents Flora Call and Elias Disney. His father had a quick temper while his mother was the peacemaker and comforter. He had three older brothers and later a younger sister. When Disney was four years old, the family moved to Marceline, Missouri, in the north-central part of the state to live on a forty-eight acre farm. The open, natural setting was enjoyed by Disney with its abundance of animals, trees, and idyllic scenes. Disney discovered on the farm what he called the "Dream Tree." Underneath the tree, Disney observed all nature around him. He said, "I drew whatever we saw. I could always count on rabbits and squirrels and field mice. And on a good day, sometimes Bambi came by." In 1938, he wrote to the *Marceline News*, "More things of importance happened to me in Marceline than have happened since—or are likely to in the future." It is said in that town Disney "found his magic."

Disney was also fascinated early in his life by railroads. Tracks ran near the farm, and a family member was an engineer. Farm work proved to be too hard for his two older brothers who ran away from home and their father's temper. The farm lost money and had to be sold.

When Disney was nine, the family moved to Kansas City. His father bought a large route of one thousand Kansas City newspaper subscribers. Disney's job was to deliver fifty papers each morning and evening. In addition, Disney was enrolled in Benton Grammar School where he developed an interest in art. He was not otherwise a very good student. He also found time to take Saturday morning classes at the Kansas City Art Institute. On his paper route was Bert Hudson's barbershop. He also enrolled in correspondence school cartooning classes. Disney's early cartoons were a hit with Bert, who proudly displayed them in his store window, even offering to buy a few of them.

The family moved back to Chicago when Disney was sixteen. He found work on a train selling candy, sandwiches, magazines, etc. He grew in his love for trains. His schooling was disrupted, but he continued his art training at the Chicago Art Institute. With the outbreak of World War I in 1918, Disney tried to enlist but was turned down because of his young age. He volunteered with the Red Cross and found an assignment in France as an ambulance driver. He covered his ambulance with his cartoon characters and entertained the troops with his talks.

After the war, Disney moved back to Kansas City, working as an advertising cartoonist with the Kansas City Slide Company. He developed a unique style of animated films for local businesses. He met a valued associate named Ub Iwerks. He created a company, Laugh-O-Grams, with his creation of the Alice Comedies. He ran out of money and had to leave Kansas City.

Undiscouraged, Disney set out for California in 1923, where his older brother, Roy, was settled. With borrowed money, they bought camera equipment and began to develop an animated movie character, *Oswald the Lucky Rabbit*. It was a very popular and profitable venture. His earlier work with the Alice Comedies found an interested buyer in New York. They now had money to invest in additional projects.

On July 23, 1925, Disney married one of his first employees, Lillian Bounds, in Lewiston, Idaho. Universal Studios stole the rights to *Oswald* and also most of the Disney collaborators except for Ub Iwerks.

Disney began to develop a new character. In Kansas City, he had a former pet mouse named Mortimer. He began to sketch this new character, and fortunately, his wife persuaded him to change the name to Mickey. The new character made his film debut November 18, 1928, in the first synchronized and sound cartoon, *Steamboat Willie*. The success was immediate and profitable. It also earned Disney a special Oscar from the Academy of Motion Picture Arts and Sciences. The League of Nations endorsed Mickey Mouse as a symbol of international goodwill. This was the launching pad for many additional characters and future full-length animated films. In 1937, *Snow White and the Seven Dwarfs* premiered and made an unprecedented $1.5 million dollars and won eight Oscars. Throughout the early 1940s, a number of popular and profitable films were made. They provided good family entertainment in the midst of another world war. Disney productions also assisted with the national war effort by creating training and propaganda films and short subject entertainment. After the war, Disney productions had grown to fill a new facility in Burbank, California, employing many new creative assistants.

In the 1950s, Disney began to expand his horizons in entertainment. He was the first to use the new technology of television for family entertainment with the Mickey Mouse Club and featured serials. He pioneered the medium with his popular *Walt Disney's Wonderful World of Color*. After taking his daughters to run-down, dirty amusement parks, he began to develop a plan for a clean amusement park for family entertainment. This would result in the opening of Disneyland in July 17, 1955. The seventeen-million-dollar investment was paid back tenfold in just a few years.

In 1956, Disney and his brother Roy returned to Marceline. They bought a 300-acre lot that included the old original farm and Dream Tree. On a Disney celebration day in Marceline that year, Disney said to the children, "You are lucky to live in Marceline. My best memories are the years I spent here." The site for a proposed theme park, regrettably, was never developed.

In 1964, President Lyndon Johnson presented him with the Presidential Medal of Freedom. His work continued, and his films and theme parks were now experienced internationally. A chronic smoker, he developed lung cancer. He died in a hospital on December 15, 1966.

Walt Disney never finished high school and failed in business attempts at least four times but never gave up on his dreams. He has been called "the most significant figure in the creative arts since Leonardo Da Vinci." He said, "I believe in being an innovator." He also modestly concluded, "I only hope that we don't lose sight of one thing—that it was all started by a mouse."

Emmett Kelly
Houston
Clown

Only a few people achieve the pinnacle of their profession as the acknowledged master of their trade. Such recognition is more unusual in that it was directed to a clown. Emmett Kelly was acknowledged as "a king among kings" in the entertainment business. His experiences reached beyond the circus tents to the theater, television, movies, and even ballparks.

Emmett Kelly was born on December 9, 1898, in Sedan, Kansas. He was named after the famous Irish patriot Robert Emmett. His father worked as a section foreman for the Missouri-Pacific railroad. In 1905, his family moved to the small rural town of Houston, Missouri. Here, Kelly grew up working on a farm and received a limited, academic education. He developed an interest in art and cartooning. Tiring of the hard life of farming, he moved to Kansas City after his schooling.

He found work in an advertising agency that produced advertising in print and silent films. He also enjoyed presenting creative chalk talks in various local theaters. One of his characters created in the "chalk talks" and introduced later into his print ads was Weary Willie. The character was described as "a mournful tramp dressed in tattered clothes and made up with a growth of beard and a bulbous nose." He would eventually bring this character to life with his effective acting and pantomime skills.

During this time, he had associations with several local circuses, painting sideboards, kewpie dolls, circus wagons and merry-go-rounds. His interest with the circus developed beyond his painting talents. With his own savings, he bought a high wire rigging and taught himself the art of a trapeze performer.

In the early 1920s, Kelly moved to the winter quarters of five major circuses in Peru, Indiana. There he met and married Eva Moore in 1923. She was a trapeze artist, and the two created an act called the "Aerial Kellys." They joined with the John Robinson Circus and performed what was called "lightning fast Double Trapeze Act." He also began to develop his clown career character, Weary Willie. In the difficult Depression era of the 1930s, the trapeze act folded, and his marriage with Eva ended. Kelly continued traveling with various circuses and perfecting his clown act. The audiences identified with the Weary Willie character during this economically distressed time.

In 1938, Kelly joined the London Olympia Circus at Bertram Mills. The British audiences fell in love with the sad clown from America. He kept perfecting his character and his clown act in Europe. When the circus season concluded in Europe, Kelly returned to the United States and joined with the Cole Brothers Circus. His now popular clown act received many favorable reviews. He was recognized among his peers for his unique and creative performances.

In 1942, he joined with the renowned Ringling Brothers' Barnum & Bailey Circus. He was the very first to perform a solo act as a clown in the main ring. At the request of some of the other performers, he often interacted with them in the ring. He would stay with Barnum & Bailey for fourteen years. In 1955, he married a circus gymnast from Germany, Evi Gebhardt. She was beautiful and talented and part of an act called "The Whirlwinds." The two moved to Sarasota, now a winter headquarters for the circus, and purchased a house. Kelly, now fifty-seven years old, had an official home for the first time in his life. The couple had two children, Stasia and Monika.

An unusual career shift happened to him in 1957 as he became the official mascot for the popular Brooklyn Dodgers. He entertained the crowds as he strolled around the ballpark and on the baseball field.

He also expanded his activities, appearing on stage, in movies, and in television guest appearances. In addition, he made commercials that seemed to cycle his career back to his early professional life.

Kelly said, "Willie and I will never retire." But eventually on March 28, 1979, he passed away. His lifelong friend Red Skelton said, "I guess those in heaven needed a laugh." He was acclaimed as "the master of pathos and pantomime, best remembered for his sweeping up the spotlight routine." Still recognized today as the master of clowns, he was unique and a true innovator in entertainment.

Sally Rand
Cross Timbers
Dancer

There are some circumstances where an innovator can be seen as a great benefit for society while also being seen as a great evil. That was the case for a woman known as Sally Rand. She was acknowledged as an innovator in the field of burlesque entertainment. But there was much more to see in the life of this multi-talented woman.

Sally Rand was born as Harriet Helen Gould Beck, near Cross Timbers, Missouri, on April 3, 1904. Her mother, Mary Annette "Nettie" Grove, was a Pennsylvania Dutch Quaker, schoolteacher, and a part-time newspaper correspondent. Her father, Colonel William Beck, was a graduate of West Point and veteran of the Spanish-American War.

While in grade school, the family moved to Jackson County, Missouri, close to Kansas City. Helen continued her formal education and developed an early interest in dancing. At age thirteen, she worked part time as a chorus girl at Kansas City's Empress Theater. She also appeared in several local nightclubs. She was then known as "Billy Beck," receiving very favorable reviews for her talent. She realized her career opportunities were limited in Kansas City and desired to move to Hollywood, California. With that goal in mind, she left home and joined with a traveling carnival group. She found work in nightclubs as a cigarette girl, artist's model, and cafe dancer. In her travels, she worked for the Adolph Bohm Chicago Ballet Company, the Ringling Brothers Circus, and Will Seabury's Repertory Theatre Company. Her talents expanded beyond dancing to stage productions. In the 1920s, the Seabury Company arrived in Los Angeles and soon disbanded.

"Billy" made contact with the new studios in the area. Her experiences and talent helped her to land work on stage productions and appearances in silent films. She caught the attention of Cecil B. DeMille, who was forming a stock company. He hired her and changed her name to "Sally Rand," supposedly inspired by a Rand McNally road map. Rand increased her appearances in silent films as a supporting actor and even occasionally as a lead. She was becoming popular with movie fans.

When talking films began to grow in popularity in the late 1920s and early 1930s, Sally's career hit a snag. She had a very pronounced lisp and what was called "a distinct Ozark twang." She did make appearances in several talking films but found the prospects limited. It now seemed her career, after twenty movies, had ended.

She returned to nightclubs, dance, and stage productions. In 1932, she traveled to Chicago with a stage show, "Sweethearts on Parade." While appearing at the Paramount Club, she developed her famous "fan dance" act. Using two large ostrich feather fans purchased at a local second-hand shop, Rand performed the exotic dance with the appearance of nudity. She actually wore a flesh-colored body stocking or a thick layer of body paint. While many admired her sensual dance, others found her act indecent. She found great notoriety in 1933 with her appearances at the Chicago World's Fair.

Rand promoted the fair and her act with a controversial ride through Chicago as Lady Godiva, riding a horse in an apparent state of nudity. Her fan dance act at the fair created further controversy to the extent that she was arrested as often as four times in one day. The ensuing publicity only served to increase her attendance and popularity. She was charged with "lewd, lascivious, and acts degrading to public morals." The judge gave his reply to the charges,

There is no harm and certainly no injury to public morals when the human body is exposed, some people would want to put pants on a horse…. When I go to the fair, I go to see the exhibits and perhaps to enjoy a little beer. As far as I'm concerned, all these charges are just a lot of old stuff to me. Case dismissed for want of equity.

All of this "exposure" increased the popularity of Sally Rand. Twenty-two million visitors attended the 1933 Chicago World's Fair, spreading Sally's reputation around the country and the world. When the fair reopened in 1934, Rand created a new dance act known as the "bubble dance." She held "a large, translucent plastic bubble between herself and the audience." The act blossomed into a full-scale production with twenty-four dancers and sixteen showgirls. It was another big hit.

After the fair closed, Rand and cast traveled with their act. They met with success and faced continued attacks of immorality. She was also becoming a celebrity in her own right. She made public appearances giving interviews and even attended church services. People were discovering a real person beyond the public image. In 1936, Sally was able to purchase the Music Box, a popular burlesque house in San Francisco. In the following years, she created a troupe known as "Sally Rand's Nude Ranch." It was a collection of "women dressed in cowboy hats, boots, gun belts, and little else." The successful act continued for many years but not without the usual controversy. In 1946, Rand was again arrested in San Francisco during her bubble dance. The judge made the unusual decision to view her performance at the Savoy Club and reach his conclusion. He cleared her of all charges and stated, "Anyone who could find something lewd about the dance as she puts it on has to have a perverted sense of morals."

Rand was making appearances at state and county fairs. She also visited several military bases to speak to the troops. She would become a popular guest on several new television shows, as well. In addition, she also hosted a weekly television program in 1954 while in Las Vegas. In 1956, she resumed her education and received her college degree. She worked for a while as a speech therapist. She shared her intellectual side by speaking about Shakespeare. She appeared before 1,300 Harvard freshmen and lectured on the evils of communism.

She continued to perform her dance acts well into her sixties and seventies. She famously said, "I haven't been out of work since the day I took my pants off." She married four times in her career and mothered several children. At the age of seventy-five, she died of congestive heart failure at the Foothills Presbyterian Hospital in Glendora, California. She was buried at Oakdale Memorial Park in Glendora next to her mother. At her death, she was rumored to be in debt in spite of her many successes. It is reported that Sammy Davis, Jr. wrote a large check to cover her final expenses.

Sally Rand was indeed a creative innovator in the field of entertainment. Her actions as an independent woman were unusual, and her challenge of the public sense of morality was also daring. But to many who can objectively view her life, she was innovative in her career choice.

Ginger Rogers
Independence
Dancer/actress

Another female actress and dancer, a contemporary of Sally Rand, took her talents and creativity in an entirely different professional direction. She proved to be an effective force in what was described as "a man's world." She became the highest paid actress in the mid-1940s. She found fame in a dance partnership but also found success in her own talent as an actress. Her name was Ginger Rogers.

Born Virginia Katherine McMath in Independence, Missouri, on July 16, 1911, "Ginger" was a child of a very troubled marriage relationship. Her mother, Lela Imogene Owens, known as "Lelee," moved to Independence to have her child, away from her husband. Ginger's father, William Edie McMath, an electrical engineer, separated from Lelee soon after Ginger's birth. A vicious custody dispute arose. Her father actually kidnapped Ginger twice before custody was awarded to Lelee. Lelee's parents, Walter and Saphrona Owens, lived nearby in Kansas City and had the primary duty of raising Ginger and several other cousins in their home. One cousin had difficulty in saying the name Virginia with the sound of "Jinja." After that the child was called Ginger.

Lelee left Kansas City to become a scriptwriter in Hollywood, California. She later moved to New York City to continue her scriptwriting. Earning enough income, Lelee sent for Ginger to live with her in New York City. With the outbreak of World War I, Lelee joined the Marines in 1918 in the publicity department. Ginger returned to Kansas City to again live with her grandparents. While in the Marines, Lelee met John Logan Rogers, an insurance salesman. After leaving the Marines, they returned to the Kansas City area and married in Liberty, Missouri, in May 1920. Ginger found John to be the absent father figure she needed and took his last name, although she was never officially adopted.

The family was transferred to the Dallas-Fort Worth area for John's new job. Ginger had developed an early interest in dancing and performing. It was said that she could dance before she could walk. At the age of ten she appeared at local charity shows, celebrations, and lodge meetings with her stepfather. Her mother was happy to give her personal guidance toward a career.

Described as a "freckle-faced young tomboy," Rogers attended Central High School in Fort Worth. Lelee began work as theater critic for the *Fort Worth Record*. Ginger was given access to the theatre experience. She quickly learned songs and dances from the performers while waiting for her mother. One night at the theatre, a unique opportunity came for Ginger. The very popular vaudeville dance team of Eddie Foy and his children needed a quick substitute. Rogers had already learned the Charleston dance routine from Eddie Foy, Jr., and filled in immediately. In 1925, at the age of fourteen, Ginger entered the Texas state Charleston contest and won a prize for a four-week vaudeville tour. She quit school, and the four weeks turned into over twenty-one weeks, having created an act, with her mother's help, "Ginger and the Redheads." Returning to Fort Worth, Ginger and her mother prepared for a four-year national tour of vaudeville shows.

Rogers, at age seventeen, sought separation from her mother by marrying a fellow vaudeville dancer, Jack Culpepper, on March 29, 1929. The marriage lasted only several months before Rogers found her way back to her mother's care and continued the vaudeville circuit. Her mother had also divorced John by then. In New York City, Rogers made radio appearances, short films, and a Broadway debut on December 25, 1929. Several months later she starred in Gershwin show, *Girl Crazy*, singing songs designed for her, such as "Embraceable You." She was a big hit and, in 1930, signed a seven-year contract with Paramount Pictures. She "made movies in the morning and hit the Broadway boards at night." She got released from the Paramount contract and signed a three-year contract with Pathe, moving to California to make movies.

Rogers and her mother moved to Hollywood. Her film career was not successful, and she found herself returning to vaudeville and do freelance film work.

Her big break came in 1933, when she performed in Warner Brothers' *42ⁿᵈ Street*. She sang "Shuffle Off to Buffalo." With another success in *Gold Diggers*, she was signed by RKO Films. She performed in several films, but in the film *Flying Down to Rio*, she found her association with a dancer named Fred Astaire to be a lasting legacy.

The dancing pair teamed up in ten musical films from 1933–1939. The two were mutually complimentary and off screen led very separate lives. Rogers made from one to six films a year on her own during that time. In 1940, a film she starred in, *Kitty Foyle*, won an Academy Award. She continued in her film career being very selective of the films she chose. She refused to be a part of films that had lurid love scenes. She found continued success in comedies and war-time patriotic films. By 1945, Rogers was the highest-paid performer in all of Hollywood. After that year, her film career began to decline. In 1950, at the Academy Awards ceremony, she was chosen to present Fred Astaire with an honorary Oscar "for his unique artistry and his contributions to the technique of musical pictures." Later, when asked about her own contributions, she commented, "I did everything Fred did, only backwards and in high heels."

After 1950, Rogers found other avenues of entertainment and enjoyment. She was described as a keen artist and did many paintings, sculptures, and sketches but never sold any of them. She was also a near-champion tennis player and loved going fishing. She did find time for guest appearances on television shows. She made a return to Broadway and continued a limited film career in Hollywood. Rogers kept up a busy pace of stage and screen productions throughout the 1960s and 1970s. She created her own musical stage show, "The Ginger Rogers Show," and toured for four years. Her mother died in 1977.

In the 1980s, Rogers made public appearances and received countless honorary awards. In 1991, she published her autobiography, *Ginger, My Story*. She acknowledged her five failed marriages, all ending in divorce. She also described her involvement with the Christian Science faith. She stated, "When two people love each other, they don't look at each other, they look in the same direction." In 1992, she received the Kennedy Center Honors Lifetime Achievement Award. During the last few years of her life, she moved to Oregon and bought a ranch. She became active in community causes. She moved back to her home in Rancho Mirage, California. On April 25, 1995, at the age of eighty-three, she died of a heart attack. She was buried at Oakwood Memorial Park Cemetery in Chatsworth, California, next to her mother and near the grave of Fred Astaire.

Ginger Rogers was an innovator on stage and screen. Her talents in acting and dancing listed her among the top in her profession. She appeared in seventy-three films and numerous Broadway shows. Fred Astaire commented about her, "Ginger was brilliantly effective. She made everything work fine for her. Actually she made things very fine for both of us and she deserves most of the credit for our success."

Dick Van Dyke
West Plains
Actor/dancer

He was 6' 1" by the time he was eleven years old. He was a dancer, singer, stand-up comedian, movie star, television star, Broadway performer, philanthropist, and author. He received a Screen Actors Guild Life Achievement Award, a People's Choice Award, a Tony Award, two Grammy Awards, two Golden Globe Awards, and nine Emmy Awards. He was also an alcoholic and a chain smoker and found success after the age of thirty-seven. This is Dick Van Dyke.

Richard Wayne Van Dyke was born in West Plains, Missouri, on December 13, 1925. His parents were Hazel Victoria (McCord), a stenographer, and Loren Wayne Van Dyke, a salesman. As a child, Dick was influenced by his community and mother. His mother taught a Sunday School class in the local Presbyterian church. Later, Van Dyke would also be a Sunday School teacher and Presbyterian elder and seriously considered becoming a minister. It was only after a high school drama class and experiencing the life of a professional entertainer that he felt his true calling. He stated, "I suppose that I never completely gave up my childhood idea of being a minister. Only the medium and the message changed. I still have endeavored to touch people's souls, to raise their spirits and put smiles on their faces."

Later in his childhood, the family moved to Danville, Illinois. He found joy and identity in clowning and making people laugh. He became captivated by the antics of Laurel and Hardy at the local cinema.

He was active in his high school's drama performances. He found employment at a local station, WDAN, as an announcer.

In 1942, Van Dyke enlisted in the U.S. Air Force as a radio announcer and ended up in the special services unit, entertaining troops stateside. In 1945, after the war, Van Dyke returned to Danville and tried to set up an advertising agency. Not enjoying the work, he teamed up with friend, Philip Erickson, in a record-pantomime act, The Merry Mutes. The team was able to travel from coast to coast.

In 1948, while in Los Angeles, he met Margerie Willett. They were married February 12, 1948, on the radio show *Bride and Groom* because the show paid for the wedding rings, a honeymoon, and household appliances. But the couple was so poor that for a while they had to live in their car. Their marriage would last for thirty years before a long separation and ultimate divorce in 1984. They parented four children.

In 1953, the touring comedy team broke up. Van Dyke appeared on tour alone until he was offered a job from a television station in Atlanta, Georgia, as master of ceremonies for two programs, *The Merry Mutes Show* and *The Music Shop*. Two years later he moved to New Orleans, where he hosted his own television variety show, *The Dick Van Dyke Show*. The show was very successful and caught the attention of CBS officials in New York City. They offered him a seven-year contract. He accepted and moved to New York City. He hosted the popular *The Morning Show*. They now wanted him to move to a nighttime position, and he asked to withdraw from his contract. With growing popularity, he made numerous guest appearances on nationally broadcast shows. He began a career on Broadway in the production of *The Girls Against the Boys*. He later accepted a role in the production of *Bye Bye Birdie*. He won his first Tony Award for his performance in 1961.

That year would be a hallmark in his career. He was offered the lead role in a new television sitcom, *The Dick Van Dyke Show*. The show, with an all-star cast, grew in popularity, winning four Emmy Awards as an Outstanding Comedy Series. Van Dyke won three Emmy Awards as Outstanding Lead in a Comedy Series. The series lasted for five years.

He began a very successful movie career with the film version of *Bye, Bye, Birdie* in 1963. Teaming up with Disney Productions, he made two popular films, *Mary Poppins* in 1965 and *Chitty Chitty Bang Bang* in 1968. In 1969, working again with Carl Reiner, Dick starred in *The Comic*, a somewhat autobiographical film about the successes and tragedies in a comic's life. In 1968, he left Hollywood and bought a ranch in Arizona.

In the 1970s, Van Dyke worked on several television and film productions. He came to grips with his alcoholism as depicted in the television movie, *The Morning After*. He made several guest appearances on national television shows. He also found time for and therapeutic comfort in writing two books, *Faith, Hope and Hilarity: A Child's View of Religion* and *Those Funny Kids: A Treasury of Classroom Laughter*.

The 1980s found Van Dyke embroiled in family matters. He had a long separation from his wife, eventually divorcing in 1984. He admitted his closeness with lifelong friend, Michelle Triola. Michelle had failed in her suit against Lee Marvin for palimony. Van Dyke admitted to giving her a six-figure amount he felt she was due. The two lived together until Michelle's death in 2009.

In 1993, Van Dyke found renewed television popularity, after twenty-seven years, with his series, *Diagnosis Murder*. He appeared often with his sons in supporting roles. He found time for involvement in an a capella music quartet. In September 2000, he formed "Dick Van Dyke and the Vantastix." The group toured the nation and appeared on several television shows.

In 2011 he wrote his autobiography, *My Lucky Life In and Out of Show Business*. In March 2012, he married forty-year-old makeup artist, Arlene Silver. In 2013, at the age of eighty-seven, he was presented with Screen Actors Guild Life Achievement Award.

Still very active in appearances, national politics, and philanthropic activities, he reflects on a full life. He said, "I've retired so many times now it's getting to be a habit." He summed up his life and career stating, "I never wanted to be an actor and to this day I don't. I can't get a handle on it. An actor wants to be someone else. I am a song and dance man and I enjoy being myself, which is all I can do." Such is the mindset of this Missouri-born innovator.

Other Missouri Innovators in Entertainment

Ed Asner • *Kansas City* • actor
Bob Barker • *Springfield* • television host
Wallace Berry • *Smithville* • actor
Joan Crawford • *Kansas City* • actress
Robert Cummings • *Joplin* • actor
Phyllis Diller • *Webster Groves* • comedienne
Redd Foxx • *St. Louis* • comedian
John Goodman • *Affton* • actor
Betty Grable • *St. Louis* • model
Jean Harlow • *Kansas City* • actress
John Huston · *Nevada* · director
Kevin Kline • *Clayton* • actor
Agnes Moorehead • *St. Louis* • actress
Steve McQueen • *Slater* • actor
Geraldine Page • *Kirksville* • actress
Brad Pitt • *Springfield* • actor/producer
William Powell • *Kansas City* • actor
Vincent Price • *St. Louis* • actor
Kathleen Turner • *Springfield* • actress
Jane Wyman • *St. Joseph* • actress
Dennis Weaver • *Joplin* • actor

Chapter Two

Fine Arts (music, art, media)

Thomas Hart Benton
Neosho
Artist

When researching information about Thomas Hart Benton, it is confusing that two identical names pop up as famous Missourians. One is an important politician, and the other is a nationally acclaimed artist. Both are related and lived about a century apart. For this category, the artist is more correctly identified as an innovator in his field.

Thomas Hart Benton was born April 15, 1889, in Neosho, Missouri. Very little is written about his mother's background, even though she had a significant influence on his choice of profession. His father, Colonel Maecenas Benton, was a four-term U.S. Congressman and U.S. Attorney. His great-uncle Benton was a prominent U.S. Senator from Missouri who served in the Senate for thirty years. Thomas was named after him and expected to follow in the family tradition of service through politics.

Benton spent much of his childhood in Washington, D. C., while his father served in Congress. Very early in his life, Benton demonstrated a love and talent for art. He even drew creative scenes on the walls of their house, much to the displeasure of his mother. After having moved back to Neosho, Benton spent much time in the woods, observing nature from an artist's perspective. At seventeen, he quit school to work on a survey crew in Joplin. He was very talented at drawing caricatures of local residents. His talents helped him land a job with the *Joplin American* as a cartoonist.

His father was determined his only son should pursue a law degree as a means for a political career. In 1905, Benton was sent to attend the Western Military Academy in Alton, Illinois. He lasted only one year. Benton would rebel and, with the encouragement of his mother, pursue his interest in art at the Art Institute of Chicago in 1907. The next year he traveled to Paris, France, to study at the famed Academie Julian. In 1913, he traveled to New York City and set up an office studio for his artwork. His work was attracting attention and growing in popularity. Tragically, a fire in his studio destroyed much of his early artwork.

With the outbreak of World War I and the United States' involvement, Benton joined the U.S. Navy in 1918. He was stationed at Norfolk Naval Base. He used his art talent in drawing camouflage on ships and as an architectural draftsman. A year after the war, he returned to New York City. In 1920, he began teaching at the New York Art Students League. One of his most famous students was Jackson Pollock. He found time to travel in the Midwest and South, exploring people and landscapes that became subjects of his paintings. The mural became his favorite art form. He was creating his own unique style and attracted widespread acclaim. In 1922, he married an Italian immigrant, Rita Piacenza, a former student. Their marriage lasted over fifty years.

In the 1930s he won several commissions to paint murals. One of these was for New York's famed New School of Social Research. In 1930, he painted a suite of murals entitled *American Today*. Another commission in 1932 was to paint for the state of Indiana a mural of Indiana life, entitled *The Cultural and Industrial Progress of Indiana*, to be displayed at the 1933 World's Fair in Chicago. He was featured in the December 1934 issue of *Time* magazine. The newfound success was brought to the attention of his home state, Missouri. In 1934, he was commissioned by the state to paint a mural designed for the state capitol in Jefferson City, entitled *A Social History of the State of Missouri*. His painting during the Depression years always focused on the workingman and his struggles. He completed his work in 1936, and it remains as an important interest of congressmen and tourists. He later declared that the mural was his best work.

In 1935, he accepted a teaching position at the Kansas City Art Institute, serving until 1941. He had an opportunity to work for Walt Disney at Disney Studios but declined because of limited artistic freedom. He illustrated many popular books of the day. During World War II, he painted a series of murals entitled "*The Year of Peril*, which depicted the threats of fascism and Nazism to American democracy. He found time to paint commissioned works for popular entertainers.

He received numerous honors and awards, nationally and internationally, in the 1950s. In 1960, he began work on a commissioned mural for the main entrance to the Truman Library in Independence, Missouri, entitled *Independence and the Opening of the West*. It is an outstanding display of creative artistic expression. He continued to create murals around the Midwest, as well as personally commissioned works. In 1974, he began a commissioned work at the Country Music Hall of Fame in Nashville, Tennessee, entitled *The Sources of Country Music*. At the age of eighty-five, on January 19, 1975, Thomas died. His nearly completed mural remains today, unsigned.

His works continue to be seen by millions each year, and his unique artistic talent continues to be recognized. A tribute to Benton is summed up as follows:

> Benton's main contribution to the twentieth-century American art might be his thematic emphasis on images of ordinary people and common lore. His expressive realism stands out for its exaggerated curvilinear forms and shapes and bold use of key colors. By shifting attention away from New York and towards the Midwest, Benton expanded both the scope and of possible artistic subject matter and the potential public for American art.

Thomas Hart Benton was indeed a Missouri innovator. His legacy will be on public display for many years to come.

Chuck Berry
St. Louis
Musician

When one is called the "Father of Rock-and-Roll" and the inspiration for the Beatles and the Rolling Stones, he can be described as an innovator in the field of music. Such a person is Chuck Berry.

He was born as Charles Edward Anderson Berry in St. Louis, Missouri, on Goode Avenue on October 18, 1926. His parents were both grandchildren of slaves who migrated from the South to St. Louis in World War I. His mother was Martha Berry who, at the time, was one of the few black women to earn a college degree. His father was Henry Berry, who was a carpenter and deacon at the Antioch Baptist Church. Their home was in the area of St. Louis known as the Ville, a segregated neighborhood with a growing middle class of black property owners and business owners. Berry began a music entertainment career very early by singing in the Antioch Baptist Church when he was just six years old. He attended Sumner High School in St. Louis, singing bass in the glee club. It was a very prestigious private institution that was "the first all-black high school west of the Mississippi River." He expanded his musical interest to playing a guitar. He was able to perform in the school's talent shows. He had black idols, such as Nat King Cole, and studied with the local jazz legend, Ira Harris.

He soon lost interest in his other studies and dropped out of school in 1944. With two friends, they set out for a joy ride to California. In Kansas City, they found an abandoned gun in a park and decided to go on a robbing spree. After several armed robberies, they stole a car and were arrested by highway patrolmen. The teens were sentenced to ten years in the Reformatory for Young Men outside of Jefferson City, Missouri. Berry served only three years and was released on good behavior on October 18, 1947, his 21st birthday.

He returned to St. Louis and worked in a number of odd jobs. He worked for his father's construction company, as a photographer, and as a janitor in an auto assembly plant and trained as a hairdresser. In 1948, he married Themetta "Toddy" Suggs. In 1951, he began to return to his musical ambitions and joined with former high school classmate Tommy Stevens' band. They performed in local black nightclubs. Berry created a unique stage presence. In 1952, Berry met a local jazz pianist, Jonnie Johnson, and drummer Ebby Hading and joined with their band, the "Sir John's Trio." He revitalized the band and introduced new forms of popular music genres—country, jazz, and pop. They played at the Cosmopolitan Club in East St. Louis, which was integrated with nearly 40% white audiences. Their popularity grew, and in 1955, they went on a road trip/vacation to Chicago, Illinois. They, by chance, met legendary blues artist Muddy Waters, who recommended them to local record producer Leonard Chess. At Chess Records they auditioned two songs, "Maybelline" and "Wee, Wee Hours." He was offered an immediate contract. The song "Maybelline" was an instant hit. Described as the first "rock and roll song," the song was the first to win a triple crown on the Billboard charts: number one in rhythm and blues, number one in country and western, and number one in pop.

He capitalized on his success with additional songs, such as "Roll Over, Beethoven," "Too Much Monkey Business," and "Brown-Eyed Handsome Man." In the late 1950s, he continued his Billboard chart rankings with "Johnny B. Goode" (named after Jonnie Johnson), "Sweet Sixteen," and "Carol." He was described as "the most influential figure in the development of rock-and-roll." Other groups growing in national and international popularity imitated his style of music. In 1958, Berry opened the Club Bandstand in the white downtown section of St. Louis. A year later, while traveling in Mexico, he returned with a fourteen-year-old waitress to work in his nightclub. Whether or not Berry knew is unknown, but the young girl also worked as a prostitute. He fired her after four weeks' work, but they were both arrested in 1961 and were convicted under the Mann Act for illegally transporting a woman across state lines for "immoral purposes." Berry served twenty months and was released in 1963.

Berry was a changed man in personal behavior but continued to write and record a number of popular songs, such as "Nadine," "You Can Never Tell," "Promised Land," and "Dear Dad." He produced several very successful albums of his greatest hits. He also developed Berry Park, an amusement and country club complex in Wentzville, Missouri. In 1973, he joined other rock groups on the Rock and Roll Festival tour. He later did a tour of London, receiving high praise. He continued to perform on stage even into his eighties. In 1985, he received the Grammy Lifetime Achievement Award. In 1986, he was the first person to be inducted into the Rock and Roll Hall of Fame. He retired back to Berry Park and at age ninety announced plans to release an album dedicated to his wife of sixty-eight years, Toddy. He died on March 18, 2017.

He recorded more than thirty Top Ten hits. In 2000, President Bill Clinton called him "one of the 20th Century's most influential musicians." The famed Beatle John Lennon once said, "If you had tried to give rock 'n roll another name, you might call it 'Chuck Berry.'" As an innovator, Chuck Berry left a lasting legacy and influence in the field of music.

Carl and Robert Boller
St. Joseph
Architects

The role of the ornate movie palace in society today is far less significant than it was over a century ago. With in-home movies available at our fingertips through internet and television, the movie theater lost its prominent position. The designers of those historic movie palaces have also lost their prominent place in history. Carl and Robert Boller were recognized as innovative designers of the country's most acclaimed movie palaces.

Their parents, Charles William Boller and Pauline W. A. Grutzmacher, emigrated from Germany to the United States. They married on July 4, 1865. They established their home in St. Joseph, Missouri. They would bring into the world ten children, three boys and seven girls. Carl Heinrich Boller, born in 1868, was the second child, and nineteen years later, Robert Otto Boller, born in 1887, was the last of the ten children. Carl and Robert both finished eighth grade at Ernst School in St. Joseph. The oldest son, Will, had pursued a career in vaudeville as "Boller the Magician" and painted scenery. In 1898, thirty-year-old Carl joined Will in the touring vaudeville company as another scenery artist. While Carl and Robert had no training in architecture or geometry, Carl was keenly interested in the theaters where the vaudeville group performed, mostly in Missouri and Kansas. He began to develop ideas on the appearances and functionality of those theaters.

In 1903, Carl was working with the touring company in Pittsburgh, Kansas. He was asked to help design the town's new theater. The La-Belle theater was a three-story brick building designed for attractiveness on the outside and practicality for the audience and entertainers on the inside. In 1904, the St. Louis World's Fair featured several European pavilions designed from the continent. These buildings served as inspirations for the American public and designers.

In 1905, Carl moved his office from St. Joseph to Kansas City, Missouri. At the age of nineteen, Robert joined Carl's architectural firm as an apprentice draftsman. A gold rush in Nevada caused towns to spring up overnight and the need for places of entertainment was immediate. Carl and Robert were asked to design several nickelodeon (charging a nickel to see moving pictures) theaters in several Nevada towns. Robert went on to the West Coast to supervise other architectural projects. After four years, he returned to the Kansas City office and became a business partner in Carl Boller and Brother.

In 1917, with the outbreak of World War I, Robert joined the United States Army Corps of Engineers. Carl, now fifty years old, remained in Kansas City to oversee the company's business. After the war, Robert rejoined the firm, now called Boller Brothers. By 1919, the brothers had designed over sixty-five theaters, mostly on the West Coast and in the Midwest. A "movie madness" swept the country in the 1920s. Robert helped to establish a temporary office in Oklahoma. A year later, Carl left for the West Coast, where he opened a branch office in Los Angeles, California. He designed three more theaters before retiring there.

In 1927, they worked with Thomas W. Lamb, an architect from New York City, to design the elaborate Midland Theater on the corner of Main and Thirteenth Streets in Kansas City. Other projects were completed in St. Joseph and Columbia, Missouri. They also built a historic theater in Albuquerque, New Mexico. The firm experienced continued growth with a staff of thirty-five employees. They had now designed eighty-eight theaters. The Great Depression of 1929 ended their period of growth. The financial crisis caused the company to cease operations after trying to recover from cancelled contracts and keeping all the employees on payroll. Robert left Kansas City for several years, retiring to a cabin in the Ozarks.

In 1936, Robert returned to Kansas City and built a home studio to house the office. With a smaller staff, their primary concerns were remodeling their theaters. Only a few more modern theaters were designed in that period. Their work was further limited during the World War II years of 1942–1944. The War Productions Board stopped the construction of new movie theaters and severely limited the use of materials for remodeling. Robert and his wife, Dorothy, moved to a new home in Hermitage, Missouri

On October 30, 1946, Carl Boller died of a heart attack in Los Angeles. He was buried in Forest Lawn Cemetery in Glendale, California. Robert tried to develop the firm with a new partner but was not successful. He designed a few drive-in movie theaters. In 1957, he closed the firm and moved to Texas.

On November 24, 1962, Robert Boller died of a heart attack.

The legacy of the Boller Brothers is significant. They designed or consulted on the design and construction of more than three hundred theaters. Among these are in the following states: Arkansas, 3; California, 10; Colorado, 2; Illinois, 4; Kansas, 33; Missouri, 37; Mississippi, 1; Nebraska, 1; New Mexico, 4, Oklahoma, 12; Pennsylvania, 1; Texas, 2; Wyoming, 2. Most of these are no longer standing, but at least fourteen are listed on the National Registry of Historic Buildings. Others are being restored as reminders of the great age of movie theaters. These two brothers may not be as well known as entertainers or others in the fine arts, but the Bollers are certainly among the great innovators from Missouri.

Grace Bumbry
St. Louis
Opera singer

The idea of an internationally known black opera singer as a Missouri innovator may seem foreign to some. The reality was found in a beautiful young lady from St. Louis, Missouri. Her name is Grace Ann Bumbry. She was born on January 4, 1937 and grew up at 1703 Goode Avenue in St. Louis. Her mother was Melzia Walker Bumbry, a school teacher from Mississippi. Her father was Benjamin James Bumbry, a freight handler for the Cotton Bell Route Railroad. She was raised with two brothers in a very religious, middle class household. The home was filled with music, and the Bumbrys were often found rehearsing with neighborhood kids after school.

Church was also a fertile ground for music education and performance. On Thursday nights, her parents left home for choir practice at the Union Memorial Methodist Church. Her brothers also attended the church's youth choir. Too young to stay at home alone, Grace was permitted to join her brothers at their choir practice. By age eleven, she was an active singer in the youth choir and featured as an admired soloist.

Bumbry attended Sumner High School and joined the a capella choir when she was thirteen. She devoted herself to constantly rehearsing and learning performance techniques. One of her greatest mentors was the voice teacher, Kenneth Billups. She was encouraged to enter local talent competitions, and she was very successful. She was also able to attend local concerts by the popular contralto Marion Anderson with her mother. Anderson took time to listen to Bumbry's performance of the aria "O Don Fatale" from *Don Carlos*. She marveled at Bumbry's talent and made a note to her agent, Sol Hurok, to keep his eye on this young performer.

In 1954, Bumbry's senior year in high school, local radio station KMOX held a teenage talent contest. She won and received a $1,000 war bond, a free trip to New York City, and a $1,000 scholarship to the St. Louis Institute of Music. Excited about the possibility of local advanced training, Bumbry discovered the reality of racial prejudice when the St. Louis Institute of Music denied her acceptance because she was black. Bumbry and her mother were indignant at the offensive action.

Also indignant were the executives at KMOX, who helped Bumbry get an opportunity to sing for the nationally televised Arthur Godfrey Talent Scouts program. Arthur Godfrey was reportedly moved to tears by Bumbry's performance of the aria "O Don Fatale" from *Don Carlos*. She won the show's first prize, along with national recognition. Afterward, scholarship offers came to her from across the nation.

She began her training at Boston University but became dissatisfied. She transferred to Northwestern University in Chicago. It was there that she met her most influential mentor, Lotte Lehmann, a retired opera immortal who desired to train upcoming students of opera. Bumbry received an invitation and a partial scholarship from Lotte Lemann to attend her Musical Academy of the West in Santa Barbara, California. She stayed there for three-and-a-half years. Besides advanced voice training, Bumbry also received training in dramatic interpretation. Her growing reputation enabled her to win the Marian Anderson Scholarship and a John Hay Whitney Award, both in 1957. In 1958, she was a semifinalist in the Metropolitan Opera Auditions of the Air and received a $1,000 prize. With other performance income, Bumbry was able to study in France one summer.

In 1960, she made her debut at the Paris Opera and signed a two-year contract with the Opera House of Basel, Switzerland. While in

Cologne, Germany, she caught the eye of conductor Wolfgang Sawallisch of Bavaria's Bayreuth Festival. She was recommended to Wieland Wagner, grandson of famed composer, Richard Wagner, and was offered the leading role in an opera. Controversy came quickly as the role had never been performed by a black woman. Wanting to overcome the racist history of the German culture's past, no consideration was given to anyone other than Bumbry for the role. In 1961, opening night proved the wisdom of Wagner's decision. Bumbry's performance was called unforgettable, and it was reported that "when the curtain came down, thunderous applause rocked the theater for a full 30 minutes and brought the cast back 42 curtain calls." Her acclaim came to the attention of Marian Anderson's agent, Sol Hurok. He brought her to London, where she signed "a five-year, $250,000 contract for recordings, television appearances, and opera and concert arrangements." She began an American tour in November 1962, which included a performance at the White House for President and Mrs. Kennedy. Mrs. Kennedy had requested Bumbry specifically through suggestions of French friends. The nine-week tour consisted of "a Carnegie Hall concert debut as well as 25 performances in 21 other cities, including St. Louis." She found time to spend Christmas with her family and renew friendships with high school and community friends.

Her success allowed her to spend on luxury items. She bought a villa in Lugano, Switzerland (near Basel), and numerous brightly colored sports cars. In 1963, she married Andreas Jaeckel, a Polish-born tenor she met in Basel. He managed her career until their divorce in 1972. That year, Bumbry received a Grammy Award. Her career continued to expand to new roles and challenges. In 1981, she sang at the inauguration of President Ronald Reagan. Her performance in *Salome* with the "Dance of the Seven Veils" thrilled the audiences. She switched from a mezzo-soprano voice to a higher range, and it seemed to fit for performances in *Ariane* and *Bluebeard*. In the 1985 Metropolitan Opera's production of *Porgy and Bess*, the performance on opening night ended with ten curtain calls.

In the 1990s, Bumbry seemed to mature as a performer with continued leading operatic roles. She gave her final opera performance in 1997 in Lyon, France. In December 2009 Bumbry received her most prestigious recognition, The Kennedy Centers Honors from President Barack Obama, America's first African American president. That same year, she founded the Grace Bumbry Vocal and Opera Academy in Berlin. She continued occasional opera performances in Europe. With her wealth, she was able to buy several residences in various European locations.

This internationally acclaimed opera star, with all of her awards and recognitions, had her start as a student in Missouri. Influenced by her local church and high school, she also received encouragement from a changing community. Grace Bumbry is, indeed, a Missouri innovator.

Walter Cronkite
St. Joseph
News broadcaster

A 1972 national poll determined that he was "the most trusted man in America." Surpassing the president and vice president, it was more astounding when it was considered that the man cited was a news reporter. It was quite a tribute given to Walter Cronkite. His innovative style of dependable news reporting steadied a country in the midst of nationally traumatic events. From assassinations to Vietnam to Watergate, he provided accurate information to a nation with questions. It is all the more amazing with today's skepticism about the news media and reporting. He began his journey in Missouri.

Walter Leland Cronkite, Jr. was born in St. Joseph, Missouri, on November 4, 1916, the only child of his dentist father, Dr. Walter Leland Cronkite, and mother, Helen Fritsche Cronkite. His family made two moves in his childhood—first to Kansas City, Missouri, and then to Houston, Texas. Cronkite found great encouragement from high school teachers at San Jacinto High School in Houston. He worked on the school newspaper, the *Campus Club*. While in high school, he took jobs selling newspapers and working part time for the *Houston Post*.

In 1933, he enrolled at the University of Texas. He stayed only a few years and decided that the offer of a general assignment reporter was far more attractive than a college degree. In 1936, while visiting his grandparents in Kansas City, he was offered a position with KCMO radio as a news and sports editor. The next year, he accepted a job in Oklahoma City for radio station WKV as a football announcer. He returned to Kansas City to take a job with Braniff Airways and returned to journalism as a United Press correspondent in 1939. On March 30, 1940, he married an advertising writer for the *Kansas City Journal,* Mary Elizabeth Maxwell, "Betsy." They would remain a devoted couple for the next six decades.

World War II found Cronkite among the first journalist with the American forces, covering the major battles in the Pacific Ocean and the European continent. His impressive war reporting record earned him respect in the news broadcasting industry. At the war's end, Cronkite stayed in Europe to help reestablish the United Press bureaus in Belgium, the Netherlands, and Luxembourg. He was the chief UPI correspondent at the war crimes trials in Nuremberg. During this time, he was offered a job with CBS by Edward R. Murrow but declined the offer. Upon return to the United States in 1948, he was assigned to Washington, D. C., as a reporter for a group of Midwestern radio stations. A second offer was made to join CBS in 1950, and Cronkite accepted for what would be a long, valuable, and historic tenure.

Television news reporting was viewed as acting and as less honorable than radio or print. Cronkite began to appear regularly on a variety of nationally broadcast public affairs programs, such as *Man of the Week, It's News To Me, Pick the Winner, You Are There,* and finally, with short-term success, *The Morning Show.* He also provided coverage for the 1952 and 1956 national political conventions. On April 16, 1962, Cronkite was named managing editor and anchored the first broadcast of the *CBS Evening News,* following Douglas Edwards. It was clearly behind NBC rivals Huntley and Brinkley. In 1963, the CBS Evening News expanded from fifteen minutes to thirty minutes. This gave more airtime for Cronkite to report the news. The most dramatic event of that year was on November 22, 1963, when CBS interrupted the soap opera *As the World Turns* and showed a poised Walter Cronkite reporting on the shooting of President John F. Kennedy in Dallas, Texas. A few minutes later, Cronkite would announce that President Kennedy had been killed. Two months earlier Cronkite had had the honor of an extended interview with President Kennedy. Cronkite gave the world a defining moment of grief, composure, and emotional control in his reporting of the assassination events. In 1967, CBS overtook NBC in ratings and remained on top until Cronkite's retirement in 1981.

Cronkite kept the audiences' attention with regular interviews of world leaders and firsthand coverage of major national events. He reported on the Civil Rights Movement, the Vietnam War, and the space program's advancements. In 1968, he returned from his reporting in Vietnam to announce on the *CBS Evening News*, "It seems now more than ever that the bloody experience of Vietnam is a stalemate. . . . It is increasingly clear to this reporter that the only rational way out then will be to negotiate, not as victors, but as honorable people who lived up to their pledge to defend democracy as best they could." President Lyndon Johnson said, following Cronkite's statement, "If I've lost Cronkite, I've lost America." President Johnson would later announce his intention not to run for re-election.

Cronkite was again called on to calm the nation after the assassinations of Martin Luther King, Jr. and Robert F. Kennedy. He was also there to share in America's great success in space. In 1969, Cronkite stayed on the air broadcasting for twenty-seven of the thirty hours of the Apollo XI mission. His excitement over the moon landing was contagious for the nation.

In the 1970s, Cronkite steadied the nation through the turmoil of the Watergate scandal. His objective and neutral reporting served to provide accurate information to a nation growing skeptical of its government. He was referred to as "America's security blanket." On March 6, 1981, Cronkite concluded his final regular evening broadcast as anchorman by saying, "Old anchormen, you see, don't fade away, they just keep coming back for more. And that's the way it is." The nation seemed to mourn the loss. One commentator said it was "like George Washington leaving the dollar bill."

Cronkite would try his hand at other public activities with still popular success. In 1995, he was voted the "Most Trusted Man in Television News," nearly fifteen years after his official retirement. Spending time at his summer home in Martha's Vineyard in 1996, he wrote his autobiography, *A Reporter's Life*. Cronkite wrote, "In seeking truth you have to get both sides of a story," and "Objective journalism and an opinion column are about as similar as the Bible and *Playboy* magazine."

In 2005, his wife Betsy died after a battle with cancer. Cronkite died July 17, 2009, in New York, surrounded by his family. He was ninety-two years old. The family said, "Errol Flynn died on a 70-foot boat with a 17-year-old girl. Walter has always wanted to go that way, but he's going to have to settle for a 17-footer with a 70-year-old."

Missouri is honored to have the claim of this innovator with such high respect from not only his peers but also from all categories of Americans. May we look forward to future innovators with such character?

Scott Joplin
Sedalia
Musician

Almost forgotten by American society for nearly fifty years, the acknowledged "King of Ragtime" was brought to the nation's attention in the 1970s. He found national success in his all-too-brief life while suffering from great personal loss. After his death, Scott Joplin's life story and accomplishments were quickly lost to history.

There are many questions about the actual date of his birth and the early family beginnings. One source indicates that Joplin was born on November 24, 1868, near Linden, in northeast Texas. His mother was Florence Givins, a freeborn African American from Kentucky. His father was Giles Joplin, an ex-slave from North Carolina. The family of six children lived on the farm of William Caves. In 1870, the family moved to Texarkana, Texas. His father worked as a laborer, and his mother was a house cleaner and laundress. Music was an important part of the Joplin family. Florence was a singer and played the banjo. Giles was a violinist. Joplin accompanied his mother to an employer's homes and learned to play their piano. He was also learning to play the guitar. As an elementary student, Joplin became obsessed with the piano. He was fortunate to catch the attention of Julius Weiss, a German Jew who migrated from Germany to the United States. He was a very kind man who tutored Joplin in maturing as a pianist, exposing him to different musical styles, including the classics. He helped Joplin's mother to buy a used piano from a former student.

In the 1880s, Joplin left Texarkana and worked as a traveling musician across the South and Midwest. He did spend some time in Sedalia, Missouri, attending Lincoln High School. Joplin enjoyed the small town and the opportunities for education and performance. Joplin also traveled to St. Louis, Missouri, and met Tom Turpin, another popular ragtime player. In 1893, Joplin traveled to Chicago during the World's Fair. He played cornet in a band that entertained outside of the fair grounds. He met Otis Sanders, who strongly encouraged him to write down his unique compositions and try to publish his audience-favored songs.

In 1894, Joplin took his message seriously and returned to Sedalia. He joined the Queen City Cornet Band and played in local clubs, one of which was called the Maple Leaf Club. In 1896, he enrolled at the George R. Smith College, for African Americans in Missouri. While there he concentrated on writing music that he created. In 1899, having completed several songs to sheet music, Joplin took the copies to a local music store owner and music publisher, John Stark. One of the songs was entitled "The Maple Leaf Rag." It became immediately popular and expanded quickly to a national audience. Joplin received one-cent royalty for each copy sold. It would become the first sheet music to sell over a million copies. With limited income, Joplin devoted his time to writing other ragtime songs. In 1901, Joplin moved with his new bride, Belle, to St. Louis. John Stark and other ragtime performers were drawn there and joined together to perform in the local clubs. Joplin also supplemented his income by teaching music lessons. He received the praise and attention of Alfred Ernst, conductor of the St. Louis Choral Symphony Society. Joplin's works were highly praised by the local press. Ongoing prejudice in the St. Louis area prevented Joplin and his family from being accepted in the white society. This prevented him from raising funds to finance his longer and more difficult works. He also faced very troubling personal crises. An infant was lost in childbirth. He left his first wife. In 1904, he married Freddie Alexander, who died shortly after they were married.

In 1907, he settled in New York City in an area known as Tin Pan Alley. He continued to write music and perform his tunes for income. He became discouraged when unable to find financial sponsorship for his new works. In 1911, Irving Berlin published "Alexander's Ragtime Band." If not stolen from Scott Joplin, it was greatly influenced by him. In 1913, he married a third wife, Lottie Stokes, who encouraged him and helped to him to form his own publishing company. He had worked five years on an opera named *Treemonisha*. He failed to find any interest in the work. Deeply discouraged, Joplin was also suffering from a prolonged battle with syphilis. The disease prevented his ability to continue his writing. He was admitted to Manhattan State Hospital, where he died on April 1, 1917.

A noted jazz historian wrote, "those few who realized his greatness bowed their heads in sorrow. This was the passing of the king of all ragtime writers, the man who gave America a genuine native music." In 1973, some fifty-six years after he died, Scott Joplin's work would become very popular with a new generation through the movie *The Sting*. The Academy Awards presented the film with an Oscar for the best musical score. In 1976, his opera *Treemonisha* was finally produced and performed. The Pulitzer Committee posthumously awarded Joplin a special Bicentennial Pulitzer Prize for his contribution to American music.

Sedalia, Missouri, still honors their famous resident with an annual Scott Joplin Ragtime Music Festival. Fans from around the world gather to give honor to this great musician and Missouri innovator.

Bill Mauldin
St. Louis
Cartoonist

It is very likely that someone whose name became known by millions of people because of his creative artistry, which would win him two Pulitzer Prizes, would be an innovator. But for that reputation to be earned by someone drawing cartoons is unusual. Such a person was Bill Mauldin. As the distance from World War II grows, the name of Bill Mauldin grows less meaningful.

William Henry Mauldin was born on October 29, 1921, on a family farm near Mountain Park, New Mexico. Living close by grandparents, Bill and his brother Sidney enjoyed a happy childhood. As with many people at that time, finances were tight. His parents moved the family around the Southwest, trying to find satisfactory work. They would often return to the family farm. During his later childhood, their parents divorced, and the brothers lived in Phoenix where they finished high school.

Mauldin had an early interest in drawing pictures. In a *Popular Mechanics* magazine, he discovered ads for several cartoonists' correspondence schools. He signed up for instructions with the Landon School in Cleveland, Ohio. While in high school, Mauldin was encouraged by several teachers who recognized his unique talent. He was directed to the Chicago Academy of Fine Arts.

After a year at the academy, in 1940, Mauldin joined the Arizona National Guard. As a part of the 45th Infantry Division, he was initially assigned as a rifleman. After discovering his art talent, Mauldin was reassigned to the staff headquarters at the *Division News*, the newspaper for the division. Here he developed his popular cartoon characters, Willie and Joe, two riflemen in World War II. The 45th Division became the first guard division to be federalized and made part of the regular army. Mauldin was shipped overseas with his division.

He soon caught the attention of the *Stars and Stripes* newspaper that published some of his cartoons. Although Mauldin never fought on the front lines, he did spend much of his time with some frontline fellow soldiers. His cartoons reflected the army life from the soldier's point of view and grew in popularity with the troops. It was said that "he gave the soldiers hope and an occasional laugh on the battlefield." His characters began as clean-shaven recruits, and after their years of battle experience, they developed into much rougher-looking men.

Although the troops enjoyed his cartoon portrayals, one person in high command was not as amused. General George Patton called Mauldin for a meeting and strongly criticized his portrayal of the soldiers as untidy and undisciplined men. Mauldin listened respectfully but continued his drawing with the approval of General Dwight Eisenhower. In 1943, Mauldin did receive the Purple Heart for injuries received from a German mortar fragment. In 1945, at the age of twenty-three (youngest age ever to receive the award), Mauldin received the first of his two Pulitzer Prizes for his editorial cartoons. He also appeared on the cover of *Time* magazine and published a best-selling book, *Up Front*.

After the war, Mauldin continued to draw the soldiers as they tried to fit back into civilian society after military service. He freelanced for a while with United Press Syndicate. His cartoons also dealt with the social issues of the day and the growing Red Scare hysteria, including the McCarthy-era paranoia. He wrote a few other books, one about a close-up tour of Korea. Mauldin had married Norma Jean Humphries in 1942, but the marriage lasted only four years. In 1947, he married Natalie Sarah Evans, and they had four sons. He would later divorce and marry for a third time.

In 1958, he joined the staff of the *St. Louis Post-Dispatch* as an editorial cartoonist. In 1959, he won his second Pulitzer Prize. His time as a Missourian was brief. In 1962, he joined the staff of the *Chicago Sun-Times*, where he stayed until retirement in 1991. His most memorable cartoon of that time was after the assassination of President John Kennedy in 1963. He showed the Lincoln Memorial statue of Abraham Lincoln bowed, with his head in hands in grief. Mauldin continued his cartoons, supporting civil rights, the environment, and a strong stand against the war in Vietnam. He visited the troops in the Persian Gulf War in 1991.

News came that Mauldin was in bad health and facing death. At his nursing home in Newport Beach, California, he received thousands of letters from veterans who had enjoyed his cartoons. His family cared for him until his death on January 22, 2003. He died from complications of Alzheimer's disease at the age of eighty-one.

Mauldin wrote and illustrated sixteen books and acted in two movies in his colorful life. He is remembered by those who he loved the most—the infantrymen. Although his experiences in Missouri were limited in time, they were important and influential in his career. It is with pride that he is remembered as a Missouri innovator.

Charlie "Bird" Parker
Kansas City
Jazz musician

The acknowledged great talent of an innovator is too often cut short by personal tragedy. Such was the case with the man regarded "as the most influential figure in modern jazz." He invented "bebop," a creative music style. He was Charlie "Bird" Parker.

Charles Christopher Parker, Jr. was born on August 29, 1920, in Kansas City, Kansas. His father, Charles Parker, was an African American stage entertainer. His mother, Addie Parker, was a maid-charwoman of Native American heritage. Charlie was the only child born to the couple. In 1927, the family moved across the state line to Kansas City, Missouri, which was becoming the center for a variety of African American music styles. Parker's father abandoned the family when Parker was twelve years old. In the public schools, Parker played the baritone horn in the school band. He switched to the alto saxophone and started playing with local bands. In 1935, he decided to quit school and devote himself to his music.

At this time, Parker also began his lifelong struggle with drugs, trying heroin for the first time. He became hooked, adding other drugs to the dangerous mix. In 1936, he married Rebecca Ruffin. After two children, they divorced in 1939. For the next four years, Parker worked with several blues bands. He encountered popular musicians, notably Jay McShann. He traveled with them on tours to various American cities. He was most impressed with the New York City area where he later moved. In 1939, he returned to Kansas City for the funeral of his father. He returned several months later to New York City. In 1940, he made his first recording with the McShann band. He toured with the band for four years. Legend has it that while they were traveling in Lincoln, Nebraska, their tour bus hit and killed a chicken. Charlie yelled at the bus driver to "go back there and pick up that yardbird." Afterward, his nickname was the shortened to "Bird." He settled again in New York City, encountering and touring briefly with nationally recognized musicians, such as pianist Art Tatum, jazz great Earl "Fatha" Hines, and Billy Eskstine and band. All of these influenced his musical style. His most significant meeting was with the great trumpet player, Dizzy Gillespie. In 1942, Parker married Geraldine Scott, whom he quickly divorced after financial disagreements. In 1945, Parker and Gillespie began a six-week nightclub tour of Hollywood, California, introducing their style of "bebop" music. Afterward, Parker stayed in Hollywood for additional performances. His habitual drug habit landed him in custody after a city-wide narcotic crackdown. Parker suffered from what was called a "psychotic breakdown" and was hospitalized in Camarillo State Hospital for six months. He continued to write jazz compositions. After his release in 1947, Parker returned to New York City. He led a quintet that included Miles Davis, Duke Jordan, Tommy Porter, and Max Roach.

In 1948, Parker married Doris Snyder, and within a year, their marriage failed due to Charlie's return to drug use. In spite of the drug influence, Parker's best performances and recording came from the period of 1947–1951. Some attributed his musical talent to the influence of drugs and tried to find that same musical genius with their own use of drugs. It is reported that Parker was so hooked on his drugs that he signed over half of his royalties from one of his popular songs to his drug dealer to keep his drug supplies steady. He was able to make a visit to the Paris International Jazz Festival in Europe and continued on to perform in Scandinavia.

In 1950, he found companionship with a live-in girlfriend, Chan Richardson. They had two children. His New York City club was renamed the Birdland Club in his honor. In 1951, Charlie was arrested for heroin possession and had his cabaret card revoked, no longer allowing him to perform in New York City nightclubs. His reputation for emotional outbursts, showing up late, and displays of irresponsibility greatly damaged his reputation. Many club owners refused to allow him to play. In 1954, affected by the death of his daughter from congenital heart failure, he tried twice to commit suicide by drinking iodine and was briefly admitted to Bellevue Hospital. In 1955, while staying with his friend, Baroness Pannoncia "Nica" de Koenigswarter, he suffered an ulcer attack and refused to get any medical care. On March 12, 1955, Parker, just thirty-four years old, died. The coroner estimated his age to be sixty because of the devastating effects of his longtime drug use. His body was interred in Kansas City's segregated Lincoln Cemetery.

His genius was an influence in jazz during his brief life and remains the standard today. His style was often copied and as one writer stated, "If Charlie Parker was a gunslinger, there would be a whole lot of dead copycats." Missouri had a great influence in the early life of this musical genius and innovator.

Joseph Pulitzer
St. Louis
Newspaper publisher

Rarely is a single name universally associated with the highest achievement awards in the fields of journalism, literature, music, and art. Not often is that name associated with a literal "rags to riches" life story. Even more unusual is the fact that the name would be associated with an immigrant from Europe to Missouri. But that man is Joseph Pulitzer.

Joseph Pulitzer, III was born on April 30, 1847 in Mako, Hungary. Joseph's father was Philip Pulitzer, a grain merchant. His mother was Louise Berger. He came from a large family with only one sibling surviving into adulthood. His family moved to Budapest in 1853. The family provided for education for the children in private schools and with tutors. They were multilingual. Joseph's father died in 1858 when he was eleven. His mother married Max Blau when Joseph was seventeen. He decided then to strike out on his own.

He first attempted to join for military service but was denied due to age and poor eyesight. In Hamburg, Germany, he was recruited to fight for the Union forces in the American Civil War in 1864. Although he could not speak English, he set sail for Boston, Massachusetts. After landing, Pulitzer left for New York to join up with a German unit, the Lincoln Cavalry. After the war ended in 1865, Pulitzer made his way from New York across the country to St. Louis, Missouri. He arrived in East St. Louis on October 10, 1865. Still poor, Pulitzer worked many local jobs, including deckhand, hack driver, grave digger, and waiter. He worked hard to learn basic English and was eventually hired to record land rights for the Atlantic and Pacific Railroad. He traveled throughout Missouri on horseback, and that gave him time to study law. He spent much time at the Mercantile Library in St. Louis to improve his English skills. He became a naturalized citizen on March 6, 1867, and was admitted to the bar in 1868.

At the library, Pulitzer met Carl Schurz, who was coeditor and part-owner of the local German newspaper, the *Westliche Post*. Pulitzer was hired as a reporter in 1868. He was aggressive in exposing local corruption practices. While covering the 1869 Republican state convention, Pulitzer was nominated to run in a special election against a prominent Democrat for the Fifth District in St. Louis. Much to his surprise and that of many others, he won the election and took his seat on January 5, 1870. Pulitzer continued to aggressively try to eliminate corruption in political circles, which eventually cost him local support. In the next year's election, he lost and changed political party affiliation.

Pulitzer returned to his first love, journalism, and the newspaper. He became part owner and managing editor of the German newspaper in 1872. In 1876, he sold his interest in the newspaper and took time to travel to Europe. He worked as a special correspondent for the *New York Sun*. He visited his home in Hungary.

In 1878, he returned to St. Louis and bought the *St. Louis Dispatch* at a public auction for $2,500. A few months later, John A. Dillon, owner of the *St. Louis Post*, agreed to merge his paper with Pulitzer. The *St. Louis Post-Dispatch* was born on December 12, 1878. The newspaper doubled from four pages to eight, and the name was shortened to the *Post-Dispatch*.

Pulitzer continued in his aggressive campaign to expose and eliminate local corruption. Although he continued to make enemies, he also found a huge increase in circulation and reputation. He had been courting Kate Davis, and they married on June 19, 1878. They would eventually have seven children. Pulitzer enjoyed mixing with the high society of St. Louis at festivities but did not let that interfere with the long hours he spent at the newspaper. His health and eyesight were failing from his strenuous lifestyle. By the 1880s, he needed to get away from it all.

He had an opportunity to purchase the *New York World* magazine from Jay Gould on May 10, 1883. The family moved to New York City, and Pulitzer threw himself into managing the *New York World* with the same intensity as he had the *Post-Dispatch*. He kept an active eye on his St. Louis newspaper while devoting his time to the New York newspaper. He also found time for politics. In 1884, he became a U.S. congressman from New York and divided his time between New York and Washington, D.C. He gave up the strenuous lifestyle and resigned his seat on April 10, 1886. He led his readers in a campaign to raise needed funds for the pedestal of the Statue of Liberty in New York harbor.

He found a conflict with William Randolph Hearst and the rival *New York Journal*. In 1895, Pulitzer allowed himself to compete with Hearst in publishing what was known as "yellow journalism," sensationalism of stories. After a while, Pulitzer regained his sense of ethical responsibility in journalism. He was now nearly blind, and his failing health required physical assistance just to get through each day. Joseph Pulitzer died aboard his yacht on October 29, 1911. He was sixty-four years old. He was buried at Woodlawn Cemetery in the Bronx.

Joseph Pulitzer had been a very generous man and looked after his employees. He died a very wealthy man with plans for the distribution of his estate. In 1903, he had given two million dollars to help create the Columbia University School of Journalism. After his death, an additional million dollar gift was made to the Columbia University Graduate School of Journalism. The school oversees the awarding of funds for the Pulitzer Prizes for "outstanding accomplishments in the fields of journalism, literature, music and art." The first prizes were awarded in 1917. Pulitzer also left equal gifts of $500,000 to the New York Philharmonic Society and the Metropolitan Museum of Art.

Joseph Pulitzer was a unique innovator with a love for truth and justice. He was gifted in journalism publication and management and a generous benefactor with a legacy lasting for beyond a grave. Missouri is proud to claim an important role in the development of this great man.

Other Missouri Innovators in the Fine Arts

Burt Bacharach • *Kansas City* • composer/producer

Harry Caray • *St. Louis* • sports announcer

Sheryl Crow • *Kennett* • musician

Jane Froman • *Clinton* • musician

Dave Garroway • *St. Louis* • television announcer

Ferlin Husky • *Flat River* • musician

Johnny Mullins • *Springfield* • musician

Stone Phillips • *Ellisville* • news reporter

Virgil Thomson • *Kansas City* • composer

Porter Wagoner • *West Plains* • musician

Chapter Three

Education and Literature

Maya Angelou
St. Louis
Poet

When a person shares a platform at a presidential inauguration, wins national literature awards, and is friends with civil rights leaders and television stars, that person likely is noted as an innovator. All these experiences are even more meaningful for an African American woman from St. Louis, Maya Angelou.

She was born Marguerite Ann Johnson on April 4, 1928, in St. Louis, Missouri. Her father was Bailey Johnson, and her mother was Vivian Baxter Johnson. Her brother, Bailey, Jr., gave her the nickname "Maya." When Angelou was three, her parents divorced. She and Bailey, Jr., were sent to live with her grandfather in Stamps, Arkansas. As a young child, she experienced the harsh reality of racial prejudice and segregation in south Arkansas. In 1935, the children were returned to St. Louis to live with their mother and her boyfriend, Mr. Freeman.

Soon after returning to St. Louis, as a seven year old, Angelou experienced a life-changing tragedy. She was raped by her mother's boyfriend and told no one for several days, except her brother. Bailey, Jr., finally told his mother, and soon after the boyfriend was killed, allegedly by other family members. Angelou felt her words had caused the murder and refused to talk again for several years. The children were again sent to live with the grandparents in Arkansas.

In 1941, the children joined their mother, who had moved to San Francisco, California. Angelou attended George Washington High School, where she studied dance and drama. She was helped by a teacher, Bertha Flowers, who encouraged Angelou's interest in literature and was able to get Angelou to talk again. Angelou, dropping out of school, found work as San Francisco's first female and first African American cable car conductor. She returned to high school and found a love interest, who left her pregnant. In 1943, she graduated a few weeks before giving birth to her son, Guy B. Johnson.

Angelou was devoted to raising her son as a single mother in her own home. She worked as a waitress and a cook. In 1950, she met and married a Greek sailor named Anastasios Angelopulos. The marriage lasted only for a few days. Angelou used her high school studies in dance and drama to begin a career as a local nightclub singer. She created her stage name as Maya Angelou. She landed an important role in the touring production of *Porgy and Bess*. She performed in twenty-two countries. She was able to perform in several other notable play productions. During this time, Angelou began to develop her love for writing, especially poetry, and settled in New York City. She became a member of the Harlem Writers Guild. She also became involved in the growing Civil Rights Movement, working with Dr. Martin Luther King, Jr. and Malcolm X.

In 1960, Angelou met a South African civil rights activist and moved to Cairo, Egypt. She worked there as an editor of an English-speaking weekly newspaper. She later moved to Ghana, teaching at a university for several years. In 1967, she returned to the United States and began to work with the Southern Christian Leadership Conference. She faced the tragedy of the assassination of Dr. Martin Luther King, Jr., on April 4, 1968, on her 40th birthday. Angelou never celebrated her own birthday for over thirty years because of the King assassination.

Angelou had been encouraged by her writer friend James Baldwin to write about her life experiences. In 1970, Angelou published her most famous and first of six volumes of autobiographical works, *I Know Why the Caged Bird Sings*. It was very successful and provided a unique avenue for memoirists. It was the first nonfiction bestseller by an African American woman.

Angelou was very productive in her acting and writing in the 1970s. She received nominations for Tony and Grammy awards. In 1973, she married Paul du Feu, and the family moved to Sonoma, California, where she continued her work. They would remain together until they divorced in 1981. She became a lifelong friend of Oprah Winfrey. In 1986, Angelou received the Fulbright Program 40th Anniversary Distinguished Lecturer award. In 1991, she received the Langston Hughes Medal. In January 1993, Angelou wrote and recited her most famous poem, "On the Pulse of Morning," for the inauguration of President Bill Clinton in Washington, D. C. Later that year, she received a Grammy Award for "Best Spoken Word Album" for her poem.

Throughout the 1990s, she hosted radio talk shows and made special guest appearances on radio and television. In 1995, Angelou had the distinction of being on the New York Times paperback bestseller list for two years—the longest-running record in the chart's history. In 1996, she received the Martin Luther King, Jr. Legacy Association National Award. She also made directorial productions. With a growing interest in healthy eating, Angelou published several popular cookbooks. In 2006, she received the Mother Theresa Award, and in 2008, Angelou was the first recipient of the Hope for Peace and Justice Voice of Peace award. The Presidential Medal of Freedom Award was presented to her by President Barack Obama in 2011.

Angelou began to experience health issues and died in her home in Winston-Salem, North Carolina, on May 28, 2014. Accolades poured in from around the nation. President Obama called her a "brilliant writer, a fierce friend and a truly phenomenal woman who had the ability to remind us that we are all God's children; that we all have something to offer." Oprah Winfrey called her "one of the greatest influences in her life." Sidone Ann Smith from the *Southern Humanities Review* summed up her talent: "Her genius as a writer was to recapture the texture of the way of life in the texture of idioms, its idiosyncratic vocabulary and especially in its process of image-making." Angelou acknowledged, "I've learned that people will forget what you said, people will forget what you did, but people will never forget how you made them feel." She also recorded her own legacy in her work, "Still I Rise:"

You may write me down in history
With your bitter, twisted lies,
You may trod me in the very dirt
But still, like dust, I'll rise.

This woman of Missouri origin is indeed an innovator in the field of education and literature.

Susan Blow
St. Louis
Education

A few people make significant contributions and changes to the American lifestyle with such little name recognition. Such is the case with Susan Blow. She was the innovator who changed the landscape of American early childhood education by creating the first public school kindergarten program in St. Louis, Missouri.

Blow was born on June 7, 1843, in St. Louis, Missouri. She was the oldest of six children. She had the great fortune to have been born into a very wealthy family. Her father, Henry Taylor Blow, was a rich industrialist who made his fortune in the lead mining business. He became a very influential political force in Missouri. Tragedies confronted the Blows in 1855, when fire destroyed much of the riverfront area, including their home. They moved downriver about five miles. That same year a deadly cholera epidemic also struck the city, leaving about seven thousand dead and causing the resettlement of many families.

Blow was immersed in education through the tutoring of governesses and briefly attending a private school in New Orleans. Her father recognized her great intellectual abilities and encouraged her advanced education. In 1859, she was sent to a private school in New York City. Study there was interrupted by the outbreak of the Civil

War. She returned to St. Louis to the family home, where her father had a large library. There she continued her education by reading many of the books. She also joined a local thinkers' discussion group.

In 1869, her father was appointed the U.S. ambassador to Brazil. She accompanied him and for fifteen months worked as his secretary. Blow expanded her education by traveling with her family to Germany. There she was able to meet and see the work of famed Swiss educator Friederich Froebel. He has established early childhood classrooms in what was called kindergarten (children's garden). Blow was amazed at the abilities developed by these young students in creatively designed classrooms.

Upon her return to the United States, Blow became obsessed with implementing kindergarten into the St. Louis education system. Her father was very willing to help her start a private school. Fortunately, Blow felt strongly that the program was needed for all children in the area, not just the wealthy. The city had grown in population from 30,000 in 1840 to over 300,000 in 1870. New schools were created to meet the growing needs for public education.

She found a very compatible ally in the St. Louis superintendent of schools and U.S. Commissioner of Education William Torrey Harris. Blow's father consulted with Harris and agreed with the concept. Blow insisted that the school district should provide her with a classroom and a paid assistant teacher that she could train. In 1873, with the school board approval, Blow directed the very first public school kindergarten program. The class met in the Des Peres School with sixty-eight students. The classroom was unusual for that day with bright-colored walls and pictures, educational toys, and low tables and chairs. The children were also taught the importance of cleanliness and good health practices. In 1885, the school board attempted to cut operating costs by eliminating the program. Over 1,500 people signed a petition in opposition, saving the program. In 1876, Blow was honored with recognition by the United States Centennial Commission in Philadelphia for "the excellence of kindergarten within the public school system." Blow oversaw classroom teaching in the mornings and trained future kindergarten teachers in the afternoons. After eleven years of growing the program, there were over 9,000 students enrolled in program throughout the city schools. By 1883, every public school in St. Louis had a kindergarten program.

Blow was in demand around the nation to help cities establish their own kindergarten programs.

Poor health, due to overwork, caused Blow to retire in 1884. She traveled to New York City and Boston. She continued writing books, providing limited teaching opportunities. She spent some time teaching at the Columbia University Teachers College. She did make several tours in the country when physically able. She suffered from Graves' disease and died on March 26, 1916, and was buried in her family's plot at Bellefontaine Cemetery in St. Louis.

Although she never completed high school, Susan Blow was dedicated to the improvement of early childhood education. While she never married, she found the school children and her trained teachers to be a large and supportive family. Even though the nation is very familiar with the important kindergarten program, very few could recall the name of the person responsible for its implementation. Even fewer would know that Missouri was the state that began this innovative program.

Dale Carnegie
Maryville
Writer

He was the most internationally known and requested public speaker in the 1930s and 1940s. He grew up in a struggling farm family in northern Missouri. He found his fortune in his writing and speaking. He established schools around the world in public speaking and interpersonal relationships. His schools would instruct over 450,000 men and women in personal and business responsibilities.

He was born as Dale Breckenridge Carnagey on November 24, 1888, in Maryville, Missouri. His father, John William Carnagey, was a poor farmer. His mother, Amanda Elizabeth Harbison, worked with her husband on their farm. Because of pressing financial difficulties, as a young boy, Carnagey would get up every morning at 4:00 a.m. to milk the cows and tend to other farm chores. After that he would go to school. He was unable to participate in sports but found social acceptance with his ability to learn from public speakers and imitate their speaking styles in the classroom. He was able to earn a place on his high school's debate team and received honors and the respect of his fellow students. He graduated from high school in 1906.

When he was sixteen years old, his family moved to a farm outside of Warrensburg, Missouri, so he could attend the Missouri Sate Normal School (now the University of Central Missouri). Unable to afford the $1 a day room and board, Carnagey lived at home and rode his horse to school. He used this time to practice and improve his speaking skills.

He was able to attend the popular traveling Chautauqua programs in Warrensburg. He learned many lessons from the speakers, which added to his own abilities. He was initially shunned by his fellow students because of his "shabby, ill-fitting clothes." His initial effort at joining the debate team was not promising. Over time, as students looked beyond his physical appearance, they discovered a very accomplished public speaker. He did join the debate team and even had several students pay him to give them personal tutoring in public speaking.

In 1908, he graduated from college and went to work as a traveling salesman for the International Correspondence Schools, located in Alliance, Nebraska. He took on another job as a salesman for the meatpacking business of Armour and Company. He sold their meats, soap, lard, and other byproducts. He became their best salesman in Omaha.

Taking the advice of others, he considered exploring a career in professional acting. By 1911, he had saved $500, which enabled him to move to New York City. He began attending the American Academy of Dramatic Arts. He tried acting with a touring group but found the experience not to his liking. He ended his interest in pursuing that dream. Carnagey enlisted in the United States Army and served stateside at Camp Union on Long Island. After his military service, he found an opportunity to work with writer and broadcaster Lowell Thomas as business manager for Thomas' traveling lecture tour.

In 1912, he was living at the local Young Men's Christian Association (YMCA) hostel in New York City. He persuaded the hostel manager to allow him to teach a night class on public speaking for 80% of the net fees collected. The class was immediately successful. He was asked to teach the class in other YMCAs with equal success. In 1913, he and J. Berg Esenwein wrote *The Art of Public Speaking; Influencing Men of Business*. It was used as a textbook for the class and also became a national bestseller. The income allowed him to move from the YMCA facilities to create his own Dale Carnegie Institute, a five-story brownstone building on West Fifty-Fifth Street. In 1915, he was able to rent out Carnegie Hall in New York where he spoke to a sold-out crowd. It was then that he changed the spelling of his name to "Carnegie," capitalizing on the association with the famed Carnegie family. It was a prudent move for him.

Many of the top national organizations, such as General Motors and IBM, began sending their employees to attend his classes. Carnegie expanded his Institute to locations around the country and even in Europe to meet the growing demand for this kind of professional instruction.

In the early 1920s, while in Europe, he met and married Lolita Baucaire. The marriage was very unhappy and produced no children. The couple divorced in 1931.

He added to his wealth in 1926 with the publication of another book, *Public Speaking: A Practical Course for Business Men*. Like many other successful businessmen, in 1929 Carnegie lost all of his savings in the stock market crash. Drawing on his own experiences in business, he rebounded in 1936, with the publication of his most famous book, *How to Win Friends and Influence People*. The first printing was for only 5,000 copies. It would require sixteen other printings to meet the public demands for the book. The best-selling book would sell over five million copies during his lifetime and be translated into every major language. It would eventually continue on the national best-seller list for months. Publisher Simon and Schuster reports that the book has had seventy-one printings in hardback and fifty-two printings in paperback. It is also printed in twenty-nine languages and thought to be second only to the Bible in nonfiction sales.

The book was for the common person and provided from his personal experiences "simple sound, practical common sense." In 1932, Carnegie wrote *Lincoln the Unknown*. He also wrote several books of biographical sketches. In 1934, he wrote *Little Known Facts about Well Known People*. In 1937, he wrote *Five Minute Biographies*. In 1945, he wrote *Biographical Roundup*. The next year, he wrote a very successful instruction book, *How to Stop Worrying and Start Living*.

On November 5, 1944, Carnegie met and married Dorothy Vanderpool, his former secretary. Their only child, Donna Dale, was born in 1951. His wife helped her husband to create special courses for women. In 1955, Carnegie was awarded an honorary doctorate degree from Central Missouri State College in Warrensburg, Missouri. Later that year, on November 1, 1955, in Forest Hills, New York, Carnegie died of Hodgkin's disease and kidney failure. He was buried in Belton Cemetery in Belton, Missouri.

His influence continued through his writings and teachings. In the late 1950s, Soviet leader Nikita Khrushev visited America with top Soviet experts to learn successful business techniques to be used in the Soviet government. Carnegie's books were allowed to be printed in Russian for public use. A Carnegie spokesman reported that at the time of Carnegie's death, over 450,000 persons had taken his courses that were conducted in 750 cities in this country and fifteen foreign countries with issued licenses.

Dale Carnegie's teachings are said to be summed up in two very simple maxims: "Forget yourself; do things for others" and "Cooperate with the inevitable." He said, "Success is getting what you want. Happiness is wanting what you get." He offered a challenging piece of personal advice: "Try leaving a friendly trail of little sparks of gratitude on your daily trips. You will be surprised how they will set flames of friendship that will be rose beacons on your next visit."

His simplistic teachings and advice found universal acceptance in private and professional lives. It can be traced back to his strong Missouri beginnings and education experiences. He remains an authority, even today, for students and professionals in interpersonal relationships.

Samuel Clemens (Mark Twain)
Florida
Writer/humorist

There are those few persons whose names and innovative contributions are very familiar internationally. One such person was Samuel Clemens, better known as Mark Twain. He is called "the father of American literature." Much has been written by and about him that provides a detailed accounting of his life. He developed a uniquely Midwest style of writing and a keen sense of humor. He said, "The source of all humor is not laughter, but sorrow." He would know his share of both.

Samuel Langhorne Clemens was born on November 30, 1835, in the small community of Florida, Monroe County, Missouri. He was born on the day that Halley's Comet appeared. He was the sixth of seven children. His father, John Marshall Clemens, was struggling a businessman who rarely smiled. His mother, Jane Lampton Clemens, was a homemaker with a tender heart and an ability to provide family entertainment with her storytelling. When Clemens was four years old, the family moved to nearby Hannibal, Missouri. It was hoped that the active Mississippi River town of about 1,000 people would provide his father with better business opportunities. Trying a variety of business and political jobs, his father could not find the desired success. The family continued to struggle financially, leaving a lasting impression on Clemens. The town also provided much experience for a young boy to gain in observing riverboat traffic and other activities. The nearby wooded area, which included caves, also gave Clemens memorable adventures he would later recall. Much of his writing would recall childhood memories of growing up in Missouri.

When Clemens was twelve, his father died, leaving the family in a more destitute situation. Clemens quit school in the fifth grade and sought work to help support the family. He found limited work as a store clerk and delivery boy. He also worked as an apprentice typesetter at the *Hannibal Courier* newspaper. In 1851, went to work for his brother, Orion, as a printer and occasional writer at the *Hannibal Western Union* newspaper. In 1853, Clemens used his new talent as an experienced typesetter and printer to freelance at newspapers throughout major cities in the Midwest. He then traveled to the East Coast. In 1854, he returned to the Midwest and freelanced for newspapers in St. Louis; Keokuk, Iowa; and Cincinnati, Ohio. His brother, Orion, had settled in Keokuk, working at the *Keokuk Journal*. Samuel Clemens' short humorous articles earned him recognition, and he was offered a commission to write accounts of a trip to the Amazon River in South America. Boarding a steamboat, the *Paul Jones*, Clemens' dreams became realized. Forgetting his South American trip, he was offered training as a steamboat pilot by Horace Bixby. The pilot apprenticed young Clemens for two years. He became a licensed pilot in 1859 and began to learn to navigate the boats on the challenging Mississippi River. His dream job was cut short in 1861, with the outbreak of the Civil War and Union control of the Mississippi River.

After two weeks as a volunteer with the Confederate forces, Clemens wanted to find new adventure. His brother, Orion, was a Union sympathizer and was appointed by President Abraham Lincoln as the territorial secretary in Nevada. Word of a silver rush attracted many adventurers. Clemens traveled by stagecoach from Missouri to Nevada. He met up with Orion in Carson City, Nevada. Clemens' dream of striking it rich in ore mining ended in failure, as was the case with many others. In 1862, he was able to fall back on his newspaper experience with his brother, Orion. He became a reporter for the *Virginia City Territorial Enterprise* in Virginia City, Nevada. He was given a generous salary to produce weekly reports on local mining activities and also submitted some humorous articles. He now began to use the famous two-word pen name, Mark Twain. It was taken from a term from his steamboat days, indicating a river depth of two fathoms, sixteen feet—a safe boating depth.

In 1864, Clemens needed a change and desired more adventure. He moved to San Francisco, California, and wrote for several newspapers under his new pen name. There he received tutoring from famed writer, Bret Harte. He hit the national spotlight when, in 1865, he published his short story, "Jim Smiley and His Jumping Frog." Readers around the nation loved it, and he became a recognized, requested writer. From that story, he began performing popular lectures in 1866. He toured in the Western states and gained wealth and grew his reputation with his natural talent for humorous storytelling.

In 1867, Clemens, on assignment by the *San Francisco Alto California*, left for a five-month tour of Europe and the Mideast. He was to write reports of his travels and combined his usual vivid descriptions, as well as his quick wit and sarcastic observations. The audience appeal was overwhelmingly favorable. In 1869, he used his letters and notes as the basis for his best-selling book, *The Innocents Abroad*. On the trip Clemens met Charles Langdon, his future brother-in-law. After being shown a photo of Langdon's sister, Clemens fell in love. Clemens was now, at the age of thirty-four, one of the most popular and recognized writers in America.

After his return to the United States, Clemens settled in New York. While continuing his work, he courted twenty-four-year-old Olivia (Livy) Louise Langdon of Elmira, New York. They married in February 1870. They settled in Buffalo, New York, where Clemens became a partner, editor, and writer for the daily newspaper, the *Buffalo Express*. Their first child, a son named Langdon, was born and tragically died two years later from diphtheria. In 1871, the family moved to Hartford, Connecticut, where Clemens had found a community of fellow writers, publishers, and journalists. In 1872, Clemens drew on the experiences of his earlier travels in the Wild West to write his widely-read book *Roughing It*. The family welcomed the birth of the first daughter, Susy, after the death of their son. In 1874, the family moved from their rented home into a luxurious twenty-five-room house on Farmington Avenue in Hartford. They were also blessed with the birth of two other daughters.

Clemens now turned his primary attention to writing books. Like his father, it seemed that all of Clemens' attempts to invest in new business investment ventures failed and produced debts. His book sales and lectures would create a pattern of the means of paying for those debts. During the period in Hartford, Clemens produced some of his most famous works. In 1876, he published *The Adventures of Tom Sawyer*. In 1881, he published *The Prince and the Pauper*. In 1884, he published *The Adventures of Huckleberry Finn*. In 1885, he contracted for his printing company to publish the two-volume set of memoirs of former President Ulysses S. Grant. In 1889, he published *A Connecticut Yankee in King Arthur's Court*. A combination of bad business investments left Clemens in bankruptcy.

In 1891, in the hopes of improving his wife's heath and to cut their living expenses, the family moved to Europe. In 1894, he began a European tour to raise funds for his family. But within a few years, Clemens would experience the first of several family tragedies. In 1896, while on tour in England, he received word of the death of his favorite daughter, twenty-four-year-old Susy, who died from spinal meningitis. His youngest daughter, Jean, was diagnosed with severe epilepsy. He was unable to return for Susy's funeral and never returned to Hartford again. He continued his tours throughout Europe until 1900, when the family returned to the United States, financially sound. Living now in New York City, the family tragedies continued. In June 1904, Livy died following a long illness. Their thirty-four years of marriage, the only real security that Clemens could rely on, was gone. He had grown estranged from his middle daughter, Clara. In 1906, Clemens worked writing his autobiography with Albert B. Paine. The book's proceeds enabled him to purchase a large house in Redding, Connecticut, which he called Stormfield. In 1909, twenty-nine-year-old Jean died of a heart attack. Their thirty-four years of marriage, the only real security that Clemens could rely on, was gone.

For the past decade, his life had begun to drift into periods of darkness in his personality, private relationships, and writing. He was still very personable in public activities, but his private life was described as "living in hell." Four months after Jean's death, Clemens died on April 21, 1910, at the age of seventy-four. He used to joke that he was born when Halley's Comet appeared in the sky, and he would die when it came back. The forecast was eerily accurate with Halley's return in April 1910. Clemens was buried at Woodlawn Cemetery in Elmira, New York, next to his wife and children.

He wrote over sixty books, but his most acclaimed book was *The Adventures of Huckleberry Finn*. Ernest Hemingway said that all American literature begins with this book. His wit and witticisms have been quoted by many. Clemens once stated, "I didn't attend the funeral, but I sent a nice letter saying I approved of it." He was known and respected internationally. But like so many performers who brought laughter and joy to the public, Clemens had personal experiences with pain and sorrow.

His legacy continues with his name on schools, books in libraries, tourist facilities, and annual events honoring his life. He is likely the most famous internationally known Missourian. His major works were reflections of his life as a Missourian, and his innovative style of literature was a reflection of Midwest language.

T. S. Eliot
St. Louis
Writer

One of the most significant poets in the twentieth century was also a publisher, editor, and playwright. He held dual citizenship as an American and an Englishman. He had his roots and early education in Missouri. He was the only Missouri-born citizen to win a Nobel Prize. He was T. S. Eliot.

Thomas Stearns Eliot was born in St. Louis, Missouri, on September 26, 1888. He was born into a wealthy family with deep ties to academia and the Unitarian faith. His cousin was the 24th president of Harvard University, serving a forty-year tenure. His paternal grandfather had founded the Unitarian Church in St. Louis. His father, Henry Ware Eliot, was a very successful businessman and carried on the many charities and social activities started by Henry's father. His mother, Charlotte Champ, moved from New England to St. Louis. She raised six children and became involved with education and rights for the young. She also was a school teacher, a writer, and an accomplished poet.

Eliot was the youngest of the six children. He suffered early in childhood from congenital double inguinal hernia. This limited his activities and exposure to childhood friends. He was able to experience the world of literature by reading books. He was able to enjoy some of the local natural beauty in the rivers, songbirds, and vegetation. He received early private tutoring and attended Smith Academy, founded by his grandfather. There he studied languages—Latin, Ancient Greek, French, and German. He began to write his first poems at the age of fourteen. He spent most of his summers in New England with his relatives. He was able to attend the 1904 World's Fair in St. Louis.

At the age of sixteen, he left St. Louis to attend Milton Academy in Massachusetts. It was a prep school for those who planned to go to Harvard University. During the year, Eliot grew in his writing, and his poetry began to appear in print. In 1906, he enrolled in Harvard University. His cousin was still president. He majored in philosophy and wrote poetry for the *Harvard Advocate.* He completed his four-year degree in just three years. After graduation, he worked at Harvard as a philosophy assistant. In 1910, he left America for Paris, France, to attend the Sorbonne University. He spent time with other experienced and budding writers. He was able to develop his own unique style of writing. A year later, he returned to Harvard to work on his advanced degree. In 1914, he won a scholarship to study at Merton College in Oxford. He again left America to study in England. On a side trip to Marburg, Germany, his plans for study were halted by the outbreak of World War I. He settled in Oxford and spent much time in London. There he met his greatest mentor, friend, and supporter, the famed poet Ezra Pound. Pound would be his guide into the world of literary society in London. Pound was impressed with Eliot's writings and encouraged him. Eliot was tiring of academic life and sought to make changes in his life. He taught languages in London's Highgate Junior School. In 1915, he wrote his first major work, "The Love Song of J. Alfred Prufrock." The poem created a stir with its unique use of poetry. He was introduced to a friend's sister, Vivienne Haigh-Wood. She was a local dancer. Eliot was smitten, and they married in June 1915. This allowed Eliot to gain British citizenship. Eliot's family was very disappointed by the marriage. The marriage was a disaster. Vivienne had mental disabilities, and she accused Eliot of closeted homosexuality. There were rumors of affairs by Vivienne, and they separated.

In 1916, Eliot completed his work for his doctorate degree from Harvard. Although the degree was approved, the war prevented Eliot from returning to the United States as required to defend his degree. He never officially received his degree. Becoming very disappointed in the world of academia, Eliot made an abrupt professional change by working for the foreign section of Lloyd's Bank. His knowledge of languages was needed by the bank. This position allowed him to earn a living during the day and enabled time for his writing at night. In 1917, Pound was instrumental in getting Eliot's first book published, *Prufrock and Other Observations*. In 1919, Eliot's father died without reconciliation over the estrangement caused by Eliot's marriage. His wife's deteriorating health and mental stability required her institutionalization. In 1921, life's pressures caused Eliot to suffer his own mental breakdown. On his physician's advice, Eliot left for a three-month stay at a sanitarium in Switzerland. He used his time to complete a major work he had started two years earlier, *The Waste Land*. It was a literary masterpiece and explored Eliot's dark world of his life experiences and observations.

The pressures of work at the bank, the demands of his writing success, and his own personal struggles nearly led him to a second nervous breakdown. Another change in his lifestyle brought him some relief. In 1925, he left the bank and became literary editor for the new publishing firm of Faber and Faber. He also grew dissatisfied with his family's long devotion to the Unitarian faith. Eliot began to enjoy the greater stability of the Anglican Church. In 1927, Eliot was baptized into the Anglican Church and found a more meaningful religious faith.

Eliot continued to find liberation and success in his poetry. Many major works were created by 1930. One work dealing with his personal struggle of faith was *Ash Wednesday*. In 1935, he found success with his play *Murder in the Cathedral*. It was performed at the Canterbury Cathedral. Many of his past works found their way into print in *Poems 1909-1935*. To the more contemporary audiences, his wrote his famous *Old Possum's Book of Practical Cats* in 1939.

Eliot received requests for lectures, writing essays, and continuing his own poetry. In 1947, Vivienne died. In 1948, Eliot was awarded the Nobel Prize and the British Order of Merit. In 1957, he married Esme Valerie Fletcher, thirty-eight years younger and his secretary at Faber and Faber. They would continue together until Eliot's death. In 1964, Eliot had been awarded the Presidential Medal of Freedom. On January 4, 1965, he died of emphysema at his home in London. At his request, he was cremated in London and his ashes buried at Michael and All Angels Church in East Coker. A large stone was placed later in the Poets' Corner in Westminster Abbey.

Eliot received four Tony Awards for his plays. Two while living and two posthumously in 1983 for the musical version of *Cats*.

Eliot's often dark expressions were captured in his quote, "So far as we are human, what we do must be either evil or good; so far as we do evil or good, we are human; and it is better, in a paradoxical way, to do evil than to do nothing; at least we exist." But he also wrote, "Mankind cannot bear very much reality." His belief was that "Poetry should aim at a representation of the complexities of modern civilization in language and that such representation necessarily leads to difficult poetry."

He was called "one of the most daring innovators of twentieth-century poetry." In a speech delivered at Washington University, Eliot said, "St. Louis affected me more deeply than any other environment." He was very conscious of the Missouri influence early in his life.

Langston Hughes
Joplin
Writer/activist

He was an American poet, social activist, playwright, and columnist. He was also one of the earliest innovators of a new literary art form, jazz poetry. He was an African American who continually fought racism and discrimination. He was Langston Hughes.

James Mercer Langston Hughes was born on February 1, 1902, in Joplin, Missouri. He was the second child of Caroline Mercer Langston and James Nathaniel Hughes. His parents separated soon after his birth. His father wanted to establish a law practice in Oklahoma but was refused permission to even take the bar examination because he was black. Angrily, his father ran away to Cuba and then to Mexico, trying to find escape from the growing racism in the United States one generation after the Civil War. He became a successful rancher and businessman. Hughes' mother was a schoolteacher, and Hughes was left to be raised by his grandmother and a neighbor couple in Lawrence, Kansas. He attended public schools in Kansas and Illinois. He found relief by watching movies in the theater house. He earned admission through janitorial work. He was denied admission one day when the owner put up a sign, "No Colored Admitted."

His mother had made a continued effort to teach Hughes about racial pride. His childhood was an unhappy one with the loss of his father and grief after his grandmother's death. In elementary school, he was known as the poet, although he had not written an actual poem. His mother had remarried, and the family moved to Cleveland, Ohio. Hughes attended high school in Cleveland. In 1918, the family home was sold in foreclosure, and his mother and stepfather moved to Chicago. Hughes stayed in Cleveland to finish high school. He was greatly influenced by the writings of Walt Whitman and Carl Sandburg. He wrote his first of the new-style poetry while in high school, and it was published in the *Central High Monthly*, the school newspaper. Hughes eventually joined the newspaper staff and became a regular contributor. During high school, Hughes was invited one summer to live with his father in Toluca, Mexico. He had harsh conflicts with his father, who discouraged his continued education and hopes for writing. Hughes returned to Cleveland to finish high school. He also began to write short stories and dramatic plays. His submissions to various magazines were all rejected.

After high school graduation, Hughes returned to Mexico to try and convince his father of the need for a college education. Hughes' poem, "The Negro Speaks of River" was submitted to and printed in *Crisis* magazine in 1921. His father was satisfied of his son's talent and agreed to pay for a year of study at Columbia University in New York City. Hughes dropped out of Columbia after one year because of his personal dissatisfaction with the school and the community. He discovered a new cultural community in what was called the Harlem Renaissance. He worked at local odd jobs until 1923, when he signed on as a steward on a freighter, the S. S. *Malone*. He was able to travel to Africa and Spain. His experience in Africa was very frustrating. He found he was considered too white to the Africans. In 1924, he left the ship to live in Paris, France. He stayed there for six months and in a happy environment produced works that were published in *Vanity Fair* magazine. Now he was gaining attention from middle and upper-class American families beyond the African American community.

Later that year, Hughes returned to America and went to live with his mother in Washington, D.C. He found work as a hotel busboy and wanted to raise funds for additional education. His earnings were inadequate, and the racial tensions in the city were equally unsatisfactory. But he continued to write and caught the attention of several influential writers. They encouraged him and introduced him to writing contests that offered cash prizes. In 1925, Hughes' poem, "The Weary

Blues" won first prize in a contest that awarded him a scholarship to Lincoln University in Pennsylvania. He began attending the university and again caught the attention of influential writers who enabled him to get his first book of poetry, *The Weary Blues*, published in 1926. A second book was published in 1927. Hughes graduated from Lincoln University in 1929. That year he published his first novel, *Not Without Laughter*. His popularity as a writer was nationally recognized, and he began a series of annual lecture tours throughout the United States. He also had gained recognition abroad and toured in the Soviet Union, Japan, and Haiti. His writing was now influenced by his interest in socialism. His exposure to socialism in his travels made a big impact in his personal life.

In 1940, Hughes worked as a columnist for the *Chicago Defender*, an African American newspaper. He created a fictional character, Jesse B. Simple, that he used to illustrate misconceptions and problems of the African American in society. That year Hughes wrote the lyrics for a successful Broadway musical, *Street Scene*. He was now able to have funds to purchase his own house in Harlem. He began a teaching career at Atlanta University and was in demand as a guest lecturer around the country. He continued his prolific writing with consistent acclaim. He was awarded numerous honors and honorary degrees. He wrote his autobiography and revealed his homosexuality.

In the 1950s and 1960s, Hughes' writings caught the attention of many young black activists in the national Civil Rights Movement. They read and revered his writings that provided them with a source of racial pride.

At his home on May 22, 1967, Hughes died from complications after abdominal surgery and prostate cancer. His ashes are interred in the floor of the Arthur Schomburg Center for Research in Black Culture in Harlem. His home place was added on the list of National Registry of Places in 1982.

Hughes accomplishments are numerous. He wrote forty-seven volumes that bear his name. He authored collections of poetry, novels, short stories, nonfiction books, works for children, and major plays. He challenged his readers and listeners with the words, "Hold fast to dreams, for if dreams die, life is a broken bird that cannot fly." Although his time in Missouri was limited, this innovative writer of jazz poetry was a product of this state.

Reinhold Niebuhr
Wright City
Theologian

He is described as the "most influential theologian of the twentieth century." He had significant influence on the national leaders of his day and on three of the last seven U.S. presidents (Jimmy Carter, Bill Clinton, and Barack Obama) and at least two other presidential candidates (John McCain and Hillary Clinton). He allowed himself to evolve and mature in his religious beliefs. He was a social activist who found enemies and friends along the path of his maturing faith and practice. He is said to have written the familiar "Serenity Prayer."

Rienhold Niebuhr was born in Wright City, Missouri, on June 21, 1892. His parents were Gustav and Lydia Niebuhr. They were part of the great immigrant settlements in the United States. Gustav Niebuhr was a German Evangelical pastor with liberal views. One brother, H. Richard, was born, and the two sons developed a close relationship all their lives. The family later moved to St. Charles, Missouri. Little is written about his childhood and early education.

Wanting to follow in his father's profession, he attended Elmhurst College in Illinois, graduating in 1910. He went on to begin theological studies at Eden Seminary in St. Louis and continued his studies at Yale University. He received his Bachelor of Arts degree in Divinity in 1914 and Masters of Arts degree in 1915. The environment at Yale provided a more liberal base for theological interpretation and application. The popular trend in theology at that time was the "Social Gospel."

Niebuhr was ordained in 1915 as a German Evangelical minister. The denominational board assigned him to the Bethel Evangelical Church in Detroit, Michigan. His arrival coincided with the auto industry boom. His original congregation of sixty-five members blossomed into nearly seven hundred during his ministry in Detroit. The growth pains of the rapid rise in worker/management conflicts affected Niebuhr and his church, with membership including wealthy management and laborers. He also faced the anti-German discrimination during and after World War I. His church began changes from using German to English in 1919. He sided with the workers and the growth of the union movement. He traveled to Europe in 1923 and saw the deplorable situation in the aftermath of World War I. He had discussions with clergy and academic leaders. He became disappointed in what he called the "social incompetence of Protestant liberalism." He wrote his first book, *Does Civilization Need Religion?*, in 1927. He was critical of pastors who simply taught religious ideals "without any clue to their relation to the controversial issues of their day." He believed that one's religious faith required participation in solving pressing societal problems. He strongly denounced the religious prejudice being practiced against Catholics and Jews. He also worked as an observer for *The Christian Century* magazine. His teaching and views gained national attention and brought notoriety to Niebuhr.

He gained the attention of Henry Sloane Coffin, the president of Union Theological Seminary in New York City. Even without a doctoral degree, Coffin offered Niebuhr a teaching position at the seminary in "Applied Christianity." Niebuhr accepted the position in 1928 and moved to New York City.

In 1931, Niebuhr married Ursala Keppel-Compton, a visiting English fellow at Union Seminary. They had two children. In the early 1930s, Niebuhr became a militant leader in the growing Socialist Party of America. He also leant early support to the Communist Party USA. His purpose was to support the rights of workers. By 1934, he had seen the hypocrisy of Marxism and its ideal society. He would become an active anti-communist. The Great Depression had challenged Niebuhr's thinking about the welfare of workers in the United States.

He found much sympathy and support in President Franklin Roosevelt's New Deal programs.

His theological odyssey found challenges at Union by debating visiting fellow Dietrich Bonhoeffer. His brother, Richard, who had also entered the ministry profession, was studying the theology of Karl Barth. Reinhold's original dismay with Barthian theology evolved into eventual acceptance. It would have great influence on his writing at the end of that decade. In 1939, he was asked to deliver the Gifford lectures at the University of Edinburgh. The resulting lectures were published in a two-volume book, *The Nature and Destiny of Man*. The publication in 1941–43 was his best and most popular writing. It had profound influence among national and internal ecumenical organizations.

In World War II, Niebuhr became a strong proponent of U.S. military actions. He challenged the pacifism of some clergy and even supported the development of nuclear weapons to challenge the aggression of Communism. In 1952, he wrote a confessional account of his theological development in the book, *The Irony of American History*. He continued to be a controversial figure throughout the 1950s and 1960s. He supported the anti-communist purpose of McCarthyism but was critical of its ineffectiveness. He criticized the popular evangelist, Billy Graham, for being passive in applying his theology to the social needs of the day. He saw hypocrisy in holding religious crusades in mostly segregated areas of the country. He argued that "religion is so frequently a source of confusion in political life, and so frequently dangerous to democracy, precisely because it introduces absolutes into the realm of relative values."

Niebuhr retired from Union Seminary in 1960. He continued his writing and speaking, often sharing his theological journey. He had admirers and avid opponents. Some thought he was "too secular for many of the religious and too religious for the secular." He died in 1971. His writings had great influence on future leaders in America. There are and will be revivals of his teachings as our country continues the struggle for national and international identity. Former President Jimmy Carter quoted Niebuhr: "The sad duty of politics is to establish justice in a sinful world."

Niebuhr's daughter, Elisabeth Sifton, credited her father with writing the familiar "Serenity Prayer." Her assertion is questioned by some, but it does illustrate Niebuhr's struggle with the relationship between faith and works: "God grant me the serenity to accept the things I cannot change, courage to change the things I can, and the wisdom to know the difference." A modern historian said, "You really can't understand Niebuhr's political theology unless you appreciate the fact that his life was bracketed by war."

Marlin Perkins
Carthage
Zoologist

He became the best-known zoologist in the world. He was director of the top zoos in the country and host of a very popular television show emphasizing animal rights and environmental concerns. He never completed his college education but was awarded numerous honorary academic degrees. He had an appealing Midwestern voice and patient demeanor. He would become a household name to millions of Americans, as well as those in many other countries.

Richard Marlin Perkins was born March 28, 1905, in Carthage, Missouri. His parents were Joseph Dudley Perkins and Mynta Mae Miller. He was the youngest of three sons. As a young child, he became interested in animals. When he was seven, his mother died, and he was sent to live with his aunt in nearby Pittsburg, Kansas. The family owned a farm, and Perkins found great pleasure in the animals, even creating his own miniature zoo. After nine years, Perkins returned to live with his father in Carthage. Joseph Perkins was now a prominent judge in Jasper County, Missouri.

Perkins attended public school through the eighth grade. He then entered Wentworth Military Academy. He graduated from high school and enrolled at the University of Missouri in Columbia, Missouri. He began with a major in agriculture and quickly changed to zoology. He lost interest in academic study and wanted more firsthand experience with animals. He was accepted as a maintenance worker at the St. Louis Zoo at the age of twenty-one. His past experience and confidence in working with reptiles provided the opportunity to oversee the small reptile exhibit of just five snakes. He was able to increase the exhibit numbers and physical facilities. Surprisingly to the zoo staff, public interest grew in the exhibit. In 1928, Perkins was named the curator of reptiles. Within ten years, the exhibit grew dramatically from the original five animals to over 500. During this time, Perkins married Elsie More, and they had one daughter.

His success in St. Louis caught the attention of other zoos in the country. In 1938, Perkins accepted a position as the director of the New York Zoo in Buffalo, New York. His experience in St. Louis was a benefit as he gave special attention to developing the reptile exhibits. The zoo prospered as its reputation developed nationally and public response was positive. His work led him to one of the greatest opportunities in his life.

In 1944, he became the director of the famed Lincoln Park Zoo in Chicago, Illinois. It was here that his zoological activities would expand far beyond the borders of an enclosed zoo. The new medium of television gave the occasion for Perkins to expand his zoological teaching locally and nationally. Local Chicago station WBKB allowed Perkins to feature news segments that became popular. In 1945, those were expanded into a program entitled *Zoo Parade*. In 1950, NBC, noting the program's local popularity, broadcast it as part of their national programming. Perkins filmed the programs at Lincoln Park Zoo and traveled to other zoos for broadcasts. He also made international trips to the Nairobi National Park, Mount Kilimanjaro, and the Amazon Forest. The program was cancelled by NBC in 1957.

Perkins' personal life suffered after a divorce from his wife in 1953. He continued international expeditions and, in 1960, traveled with Sir Edmund Hillary, famed conqueror of Mount Everest, to explore the possibility of the existence of the Abominable Snowman. In 1960, he married Carol Morse Cotworth. They would remain together until his death in 1986.

In 1962, Perkins and family returned to St. Louis where he accepted the position of director of the St. Louis Zoo. Almost immediately,

Perkins explored the idea of another nationally-televised program. On January 5, 1963, NBC aired Mutual of Omaha's *Wild Kingdom*, hosted by Marlin Perkins and fellow zoologist, Jim Fowler. The program focused on endangered species and conservation. He was one of the earliest leaders in the environmental movement. The program lasted for twenty-seven years and earned five Emmy Awards. It was aired on two hundred stations in North America and in forty countries around the world. It was the first television series to receive the Parent Teacher Association's "Recommended for Family Viewing" designation.

Perkins' work at the St. Louis Zoo was not distracted by the television shows. He set out to make improvements at the zoo by starting a zoo nursery, a children's zoo, and the Zoo Line Railroad. His emphasis was always on education and animal care. His workers always remembered his absolute insistence of treating the animals with loving care. Perkins realized his time limitations and resigned as zoo director in 1970, staying in St. Louis. He kept interest and involvement in the zoo, continued his *Wild Kingdom* program, and founded the Endangered Wolf Center in nearby Eureka, Missouri. In 1982, Perkins wrote his autobiography, *My Wild Kingdom*. His last hosting of *Wild Kingdom* was in 1985. A year later, in declining health, he died at his home in Clayton, Missouri, on June 14, 1986. He was buried in Park Cemetery in Carthage, Missouri.

Marlin Perkins was an innovator in zoology, environmental concerns, and educational television. He desired to educate the public about animals and their significance to the world. He faced personal dangers while dispelling myths about unfounded animal dangers. Missouri is honored to be associated with his life and accomplishments.

Laura Ingalls Wilder
Mansfield
Writer

She is a world-famous author introducing a national and international audience to life on the American frontier through her books and later through a popular, long-running television series. She came from very humble beginnings with a family often on the move. After she married, the new couple moved to Missouri to spend most of their lives as successful farmers and proud Missourians.

Laura Elizabeth Ingalls was born in a log cabin on February 7, 1867, near Pepin, Wisconsin. She was the second of four daughters born to Charles Philip Ingalls and Caroline Lake Quiner. Her father was described as a jolly but reckless provider. Her mother was an educated and gentle encourager. A younger brother, Charles, Jr. (Freddie) died nine months after his birth. During Ingalls' childhood, the family moved often by covered wagon to Minnesota, Kansas, Missouri, and the Indian and Dakota Territories. In 1879, the family finally settled in De Smet, South Dakota. Since being on the move meant no regular school attendance, the daughters taught themselves and each other the basics of education. The oldest daughter, Mary, loved to read and always desired more educational opportunities. She wanted to become a schoolteacher. Ingalls was not as educationally inclined and preferred the outdoors and observing nature. The two became very close friends. Ingalls did keep a journal of the family's travels that became an invaluable source in her later writing. She also wrote of her experiences during the second extremely difficult winter with blizzards and the resulting challenge of limited food and fuel supplies.

When Mary was fourteen, she became very ill. Over the following weeks, Mary began to lose her eyesight until she became totally blind. Ingalls, twelve years old, became obsessed with helping her sister. Her father encouraged her to become Mary's eyes, to "see out loud for Mary." As Ingalls used her descriptive observations, she developed a talent for the effective use of language. Although Laura disliked studying, she was dedicated to helping Mary with her studies. She read lessons aloud to Mary. Ingalls knew of Mary's desire to attend college. A minister told Mary's father about a special college for the blind in Iowa. Her father worked an extra job and offered Ingalls a job sewing shirts for a local dry goods store. As much as she disliked the town, being around people, and the work, she wanted to help Mary afford school. With all of their extra efforts, Mary was able to begin school in the fall. Ingalls continued to help Mary with her studies and learned in the process.

Ingalls's experience in the academic world, although motivated by assisting Mary, enabled her to pass the test for a teacher's certificate by the age of fifteen in 1882. She was not excited about teaching, but the income would help Mary and the family. She agreed to teach at Bouchie School, a one-room school located about twelve miles from her home. She boarded during the week with a nearby family. On Fridays, Ingalls' family had a neighbor friend, Almanzo Manly Wilder, to bring her home for the weekend and return her to school by Monday. Almanzo was ten years her senior, but the two became good friends, courted, and eventually married on August 25, 1885. Ingalls quit teaching to help on their farm and a year later, December 5, 1886, gave birth to their daughter, Rose. Almanzo was a gifted woodworker and built furniture for their house. Farm life was difficult on the prairie, and the Wilders experienced additional hardships in the following years. In 1889, a son was born and died a month later. Almanzo came down with diphtheria, resulting in partial paralysis. In 1890, their house burned down. With much debt, they lived temporarily with Almanzo's family in Florida. They returned to De Smet in 1892 where Laura worked again at sewing to save money for a new home.

They had heard about opportunities in the Missouri Ozarks, a land described by railroad advertising as the "Land of the Big Red Apple." With a sizeable amount of savings, they left by covered wagon on July 17, 1894, for Missouri. They brought Ingall's portable writing desk that Almanzo had made for her. She kept a journal of their travels across the frontier. They arrived in Mansfield, Missouri, and bought an eighty-acre farm they named Rocky Ridge. Ingalls begin to do some writing for several publications, receiving some success and notoriety. Rose, who had become a reporter for the *San Francisco Bulletin*, joined them in Missouri. Rose encouraged her mother to write a book from her travel journals. After purchasing stacks of orange-covered school tablets of lined paper from Springfield, Ingalls began writing in pencil, filling both sides of each page. Her first attempts at publication, at the age of sixty-five, were rejected, largely because of more autobiographical, first person perspective. Rose helped her mother to edit the writing to the third person point-of-view, a common theme and tone and a new title, *Little House in the Big Woods*. In 1932, the book became an instant success and readers clamored for more. Laura published seven more books in a series. The books were translated into many languages and became popular around the world. She was seventy-six when she finished her last book. The couple retired to a peaceful life on the farm. Almanzo died in 1949, at the age of ninety-two. About a half mile from Rocky Ridge, Rose had a smaller house built for her mother to escape the growing number of visitors. The house, called the Stone House, was used for Ingalls to read and personally respond to the many letters from fans around the world. On February 10, 1957, Laura Ingalls Wilder died at her home from complications of diabetes, three days after her ninetieth birthday.

But her story was not yet complete. Although her books would be a lasting legacy for her, there was a new adventure ahead. Rose Wilder Lane began to edit her mother's travel journals. The book *On the way Home: The Diary of a Trip from South Dakota to Mansfield, Missouri, in 1894* was published in 1962. A decade later, the book caught the attention of screenwriters who developed a television series based on the book *Little House on the Prairie*. It debuted in 1974 and ran until 1982. The successful series increased interest in new readers about the adventures of Laura and Mary and their pioneer family.

The Wilders' farmhouse has a National Historic Landmark designation today. The museum and houses are visited annually by more than 45,000 during their eight-and-a-half months of operation to the public. Wilders' style of writing and picturesque descriptions came from early talents at "seeing out loud" for people years beyond the frontier experiences.

Tennessee Williams
St. Louis
Playwright

His experiences in Missouri were usually negative but impressionable. His family experience was even more negative and consequential. His tragic experiences in life caused him to focus inward and find release and relief in writing about those experiences through other characters. He would receive national recognition and awards as the most successful American playwright of the twentieth century.

Thomas Lanier Williams, III was born on March 26, 1911 in Columbus, Mississippi. He was the second of three children born to Cornelius Coffin Williams and Edwina Dakin Williams. He had an older sister, Rose and a younger brother, Walter Dakin. His father was a traveling shoe salesman for the International Shoe Company. His father was a violent person with characteristic traveling salesman vices and thought by some to even be homosexual. His mother was the daughter of Reverend Walter and Rose Otte Dakin, who lived later in Clarksdale, Mississippi. She was an emotionally unstable person who saw herself as a Southern Belle and desired that lifestyle. Williams' family would serve as models for his future plays. His early childhood in Columbus was happy and content, living most of the time with his mother's parents. From the ages of five to seven, Williams was afflicted with paralysis and spent time writing.

In 1918, Williams' father accepted a managerial position with the shoe company in St. Louis, Missouri. With fear and caution, the family was persuaded to move to St. Louis. Williams, at age seven, did not like the move to the city environment or the idea of living with his toxic family. In the local school, the other children made fun of his thick Southern accent and ridiculed him and also his sister, who had some mental problems. They both began to skip classes, and Williams used the time to find relief in reading available classic literature. The family would often wait in fear for their father's return home, usually late at night.

Williams attended Soldan and the University City High School in the St. Louis area. His mother encouraged his writing and gave him a typewriter. When he was sixteen years old, Williams won a five dollar third prize in an essay contest. A short story of his was published in *Weird Tales* magazine in 1928.

In 1929, he enrolled at the University of Missouri in Columbia, where he majored in journalism. His fraternity brothers made fun of his thick Southern accent and nicknamed him "Tennessee." During the Great Depression years, limited funds caused him to drop out after two years. He returned to St. Louis and reluctantly agreed to work in his father's shoe store. He took evening classes at Washington University in St. Louis. He was able to find students with similar interest in writing, which further encouraged his talent. After suffering from the first of several nervous breakdowns, he enrolled at the University of Iowa in Iowa City in 1937. He found success in having his plays performed on campus, where they were warmly received. He won the Group Theater Award for one of his one-act plays. He received his Bachelor of Arts degree in 1938.

In 1939, he moved to New Orleans, Louisiana. There he changed his name to Tennessee Williams and worked for the Works Progress Administration in their writers program. He won another Group writer's award and received a one hundred dollar prize. He attracted the attention of an agent, Audrey Wood, who helped him learn the playwriting business. He continued to write and rewrite his plays. He used his experiences in St. Louis and New Orleans and his family members as background for his most successful plays. On March 31, 1945, his play *The Glass Menagerie* opened on Broadway. The response was praise by critics and audiences. It finally offered Williams financial rewards and encouragement. Two years later, his play *A Streetcar Named Desire* opened to even greater acclaim. It even was given a Drama Critics' Award and his first Pulitzer Prize.

Although Williams was receiving public acclaim, he suffered from one of his most tragic family events. In 1944, his parents agreed for Rose to undergo a too common but tragic procedure, a prefrontal lobotomy. It was not successful and resulted in Rose's institutionalization for the rest of her life. Williams never forgave his parents for their decision and carried guilt for not having prevented it.

Williams' works reached a much larger, worldwide audience when, in the early 1950s, the two successful plays were brought to the motion picture screen with popular actors of the day. It was challenging for Williams to continue his monumental success, but he produced many other plays in the 1950s. His plays included *The Rose Tattoo* (1951), *Camino Real* (1953), *Something Unspoken* (1958), and *Suddenly Last Summer* (1958). *The Rose Tattoo* won two Tony Awards for Williams—Best Author (Dramatic) and author of the Best Play. His most outstanding work in this period was *Cat on a Hot Tin Roof* (1955), which earned him his second Pulitzer Prize.

As successful as the 1950s were for Williams, the 1960s proved to be the opposite. His plays received little praise, and performances had short runs on the stage. He found some solace in his live-in companion, Frank Merlo, who he had met in 1948 and who served as his personal manager and secretary. In 1963, Frank died of cancer. With the loss of his companion, lack of successful plays, and growing dependence on alcohol and pain medication, Williams suffered from a severe nervous breakdown. His brother, Dakin, had him institutionalized in 1969. It was a horrible experience for Williams, and he never recovered from his dependence on prescription drugs.

After his release in the 1970s, Williams made attempts at writing other plays, without success. In 1975, he wrote *Memoirs*, describing his life story. He wrote about his life experiences and his homosexuality. He made other attempts at writing plays but again without much success. On February 25, 1983, Williams died in a New York City hotel room. His death was attributed to choking on a bottle cap. His room was described as being filled with half-empty bottles of wine and pills. He was seventy-one years old.

Williams described his life in 1982: "I don't understand my life, past or present, nor do I understand life itself. Death seems more comprehensible to me." When asked earlier about his motive for writing, he replied, "Why do I write? Because I find life unsatisfactory." The demons Williams experienced early and throughout his life were reflected in his plays. They often created controversy because of their sexual darkness and depressing portrayals. But they found receptive audiences and continue to attract interest today. His experience in Missouri was not pleasant, but it did provide the background for his most successful work.

Walter Williams
Booneville
Educator

He dropped out of school at the age of fourteen. He had no college education, but he became the popular president of the University of Missouri. He was from rural Missouri but was respected worldwide for his innovative approach to journalism as a profession. He is known as the Father of Journalism Education.

Marcus Walter Williams was born on July 2, 1864, in Boonville, Missouri. He was the youngest of eight children born to Marcus and Mary Jane Littlepage Williams. He was born eleven years after the second-youngest child was born, which gave him much of the attention of the family. His mother and oldest sister, Susan Ann, taught him to read at a very early age. Williams had little athletic or active outdoor interests. He enjoyed reading, observing the plants in his parents' garden, and creating his own chemistry lab. Williams was pushed to spend one summer on a farm to improve his physical growth and develop more useful skills. He hated farming and gladly returned to his more academic pursuits.

At the age of fourteen, Williams' parents died, leaving the family in need of economic support to stay together. Williams quit school and found work at the local newspaper, the *Boonville Topic*, as an apprentice. The meager salary of seventy-five cents a week provided some help for the family. But the greatest opportunity for Williams was his learning the various aspects of the newspaper business. He did clerical work, set and cleaned type, and brought in new business through subscriptions and advertising orders. He also began to write a few articles for the newspaper. He matured quickly in his skills and began writing more articles. In 1884, when the *Boonville Topic* merged with the *Boonville Advertiser*, Williams was hired to be the editor. In 1886, he became part-owner of the newspaper. His growing reputation among his fellow newspapermen around the state resulted in his election as president of the Missouri Press Association in 1889. At the age of twenty-five, he was the youngest person to hold the distinguished office.

Williams was offered a position as editor of the *Columbia Herald* newspaper. The owner and publisher, E. W. Stephens, was impressed with Williams' talent and philosophy of a trained, professional journalist. Williams accepted the position and moved to Columbia, Missouri. He truly enjoyed the city and the contacts with the University of Missouri. He also enjoyed the limited social activities he attended. He met Hulda Harned and began to court her. On June 30, 1892, they were married and eventually had two sons and a daughter. He taught a very popular Sunday School class at the First Presbyterian Church. He helped to found the State Historical Society of Missouri in 1898, housed on the campus of the University of Missouri.

In addition to improving the quality and status of the *Herald,* Williams also expanded other publications around the state in St. Louis and Jefferson City and the *Country Editor,* a trade magazine. He continued his push for a school of journalism at the university. He was dismayed with his experiences with untrained journalists in the state. He met much opposition from the university faculty who considered journalism a trade, not a profession. Their argument hinged on the traditional apprenticeships and training on the job.

In 1904, Williams was invited to World's Fair Commission, held in St. Louis, to serve as publicity director for the fair and to promote it on an international scale. He made a nine-month world tour promoting the fair, logging twenty-five thousand miles, and visiting twenty-seven countries. After his return, Williams continued his campaign to have the university seriously consider a school of journalism. The Missouri Press Association, responding to Williams' annual request for support of the idea, jokingly approved the idea to Williams' surprise. While they were still not convinced, Williams found a chance to advance his idea when he was appointed by Governor Lon V. Stephens to the university board of curators.

In 1905, Williams became president and a major shareholder of the *Columbia Herald*. The next year, his campaigning efforts finally produced the desired result. The board of curators and the state legislature gave approval for the establishment of a school of journalism at the University of Missouri in Columbia. It would take several years of work to put the organization in place on campus and promote it in the state. Williams was selected to serve as the first dean of the University of Missouri School of Journalism. This was the first such academic program in the world.

On September 14, 1908, the school welcomed its first class of students. There were only three faculty members and ninety-seven students. Williams taught the History and Principles of Journalism class. He emphasized, "There are five I's necessary to success in newspaper work: Independence, Industry, Information, Ideas and Instinct." He immediately created an actual community newspaper on campus, the *University Missourian* (eventually changed to the *Columbia Missourian*). The students could immediately apply their classroom instruction to real-life newspaper production. The concept became known as the "Missouri Method." In spite of opposition around the state for a state-sponsored, competitive newspaper, the program continued and began to be recognized and copied by other universities in the country. He helped to establish the Yenching University School of Journalism.

Williams worked hard to grow the school's prominence nationally and internationally. He established "Journalism Week" and hosted conferences that attracted national, well-known journalists. He was able to host a World Press Congress at the university. These were all well attended. He traveled around the world promoting the school, resulting in many international students attending the university.

Williams also recognized the need for a professional journalists' organization within the state. In 1915, he helped to organize the Missouri Writer's Guild. It encouraged professional, amateur, and would-be writers to meet and share writing skills. It is still actively in existence today. Each year, the Missouri Writer's Guild holds an annual meeting for workshops and to present writing awards. The most prestigious is the Walter Williams Major Work Award. [The author has been honored to receive two of these awards in the last five years—2013 for *Robert S. Kerr; Oklahoma's Pioneer King* and 2017 for *The History of Fort Leonard Wood.*]

In 1918 Hulda Williams died from an unknown illness. Nine years later, on October 22, 1927, he married Sara Lockwood, a 1913 graduate of the University of Missouri School of Journalism.

Wanting to make sure that the new programs around the country maintained similar strong standards; in the 1920s, Williams created the "Journalists' Creed." It would serve as the standard in journalism and continues to the present day.

In 1930, the University of Missouri President Stratton Brooks was fired. Walter Williams was named as his successor. The honor for Williams, who never was able to attend college, was tested by the difficult years of the Great Depression. Like many schools around the country, the university was fortunate to have someone like Williams to guide them through the rough financial times. Through limited cutbacks in faculty, staff, and operations, the university survived the crisis. At the same time Williams fought for increases in faculty salaries while cutting his own.

In 1934, Williams was diagnosed with prostate cancer. He delayed any treatment to continue his duties. His last public appearance was addressing the graduating class of 1934. He encouraged them, "Do public service. Remember you have taken out of the wealth of the state to obtain that which is yours today. Give back to the state to enrich its common wealth from that which you have obtained at its hand." On July 2, 1935, Williams resigned as president of the university. He died at home weeks later on July 29, 1935.

His innovative style allowed "top editors, reporters and other executives to say that Missouri graduates are among the best prepared to work and contribute to the organization from their first day on the job." His legacy continues today with a new journalism building on campus named in his honor. His hometown of Boonville honored him with a bronze bust dedicated in 2003. It stands just outside of city hall. The University of Missouri School of Journalism is still regarded as one of the best programs for professional journalism majors today. He still brings great acclaim to the state he loved.

Other Missouri Innovators in Education/Literature

Eugene Field • *St. Louis* • writer

Mary Paxton Keely • *Independence* • writer

William Least Heat-Moon • *Kansas City* • writer

Phoebe Apperson Hearst • *St. Francis County* • philanthropist

Barclay Moon Newman, Jr. • *Springfield* • Bible translator

Sara Teasdale • *St. Louis* • writer

Chapter Four

Business

Henry and Richard Bloch
Kansas City
Tax preparation

Two brothers, educated in business administration, began with the lofty goal of helping businesses. They adapted their goals to meet the needs of small businesses, as well as the business needs of individuals. They took advantage of the changing times and policies to expand their business. Their company became nationally recognized and continues to meet business needs today.

Henry Bloch was born on July 30, 1922, in Kansas City, Missouri. He was the second son of Leon and Hortense Bloch. He had an older brother, Leon, and a younger brother, Richard. His father was a successful lawyer in Kansas City. Motivation for their interest in business was probably prompted by their father. Henry attended Southwest High School in Kansas City. He started his college education attending classes at the University of Missouri in Kansas City. He transferred to the University of Michigan, graduating in 1944. His older brother, Leon, attended the University of Missouri in Columbia, graduating with a law degree. His younger brother, Richard, had graduated from the Wharton School of Finance at the University of Pennsylvania.

As with many other Americans, Henry put his career plans on hold to enlist in the military during World War II. He joined the Army Air Corps (forerunner of the Air Force) and served in the Eighth Air Force as a navigator on B-17 bombers. He distinguished himself in service flying in thirty-one missions over Germany, three of them being combat missions over Berlin. He received the Air Medal and three Oak Leaf Clusters.

After the war, Henry took advantage of the GI Bill and enrolled at the Harvard Business School for graduate training in statistical control. While at Harvard, Henry was greatly influenced by Professor Sumner Schlicter, who was a noted authority on economics and labor relations. Schlicter explained that big businesses had the resources and abilities to handle their business needs. But he was quick to point out that the small business, a majority in America, did not have access to the growing demands to support their business needs and interests. Henry was impressed with the unfulfilled need and saw a good opportunity for a new career to help small businesses. He shared his idea with his brothers. Leon responded favorably, and in 1946, the two brothers started United Business Company, which would provide bookkeeping and other services to small businesses. Part of their other services included free tax preparations. Success was not immediate, and after a few months, Leon left the business to return to law school. Henry had confidence in his business plan and carried on. With eventual growth, Henry was in need of administrative help. His brother, Richard, was hired as a business partner.

In the mid-1950s, business was doing well, and the tax preparations were not a great source of income for the company. The brothers decided to discontinue the service. However, several things happened that fortunately changed their minds. First, a client and friend suggested they advertise the tax preparation service in the *Kansas City Star*. They agreed and ran ads in late January 1955. Coincidentally, at that time, the local Internal Revenue Service (IRS) office in Kansas City quit offering free tax assistance services. The Bloch's business immediately boomed due to the need of tax preparation.

In July 1956, the Blochs replaced the United Business Company with a new venture, H&R Block, Inc. The family name was changed because of the common misspellings and easier pronunciation. Their rapid success motivated their desire to expand their business to another major city. They discovered that the next city where local IRS would discontinue the free tax assistance services was New York City. They coincided advertising with the local IRS announcement and saw business rapidly expand. Wanting to move back to Kansas City, the brothers offered the business for sale. When an interested buyer could not raise needed funds, the brothers agreed to franchise the business for a fee and percentage of income. With that success, they opened offices in Columbia, Missouri; Topeka, Kansas; Des Moines, Iowa; Oklahoma City, Oklahoma; and Little Rock, Arkansas.

By 1962, the company had 206 offices and became a public company with "a $300,000 offering of 75,000 shares." By the 1970s, H&R Block numbered 8,600 offices. They had a national reach and began an advertising campaign on television, with Henry appearing in his own ads. By 1978, one out of every nine Americans had their annual tax preparation done by H&R Block.

That year, Richard was diagnosed with terminal lung cancer. He was determined to beat the odds and was successful in defeating the disease. He would dedicate the rest of his life to cancer awareness.

Struggling to find capable trained tax preparers, the brothers founded H&R Block Income Tax Schools around the country. By 2003, more than 250,000 took the training classes. In 1986, always looking for innovative ways to improve their operations, the brothers initiated a system of electronic filing of the tax preparations. The practice provided their clients with faster tax refunds and fewer tax preparation errors. Their company expanded into eleven other countries

Henry became chairman of the company in 1989. He retired as chairman in 2000. Richard died of heart failure July 21, 2004, at the age of seventy-eight. Richard left a wife and three daughters. Henry stated, "I've always wanted to do something different, something more than a job, something to contribute to society." Following that desire, Henry devoted much of his time to community interests and philanthropy. He helped establish the Henry W. Bloch School of Management at the University of Missouri in Kansas City. He contributed to the Nelson-Atkins Museum of Art and Saint Luke's Hospital. In 2011, prior to her death, Henry and his wife, Marion, established the Marion and Henry Bloch Family Foundation for bettering the quality of life in the Kansas City area. Marion died in 2013. Henry lives in Kansas City and has four children, twelve grandchildren and seven great-grandchildren. He has received numerous honorary doctorate degrees, and many local, state and national awards.

Henry and Richard Bloch had strong ties to and love for Missouri. They were also creative individuals and worked as a team to meet small business and personal economic needs in innovative ways. They have a legacy that will continue for many years.

Aldolphus Busch
St. Louis
Beer production

He was not born in Missouri; he was not even born in the United States. But he came to this country and chose to become a Missourian. He began by working as a laborer doing menial tasks. He became one the wealthiest persons in the country, heading one of the biggest industries. He brought innovative ideas to his production processes. As a genius in marketing and advertising, he created a universal household name for his products that continues today.

Adolphus Busch was born in Kastel, Germany, on July 10, 1839. He was the youngest of twenty-one children born to Ulrich and Barbara Pfeifer Busch. His father was a very wealthy businessman in Mainz, Germany. The family was able to provide the best education for their children. Young Busch attended the gymnasium in Mainz, the academy in Darmstadt, and the College Institute of Brussels. He worked for a while in his father's lumberyard before finding enjoyable work in a shipping house on the Rhine River port town of Cologne. He grew in his knowledge of river trade. He had heard of great business opportunities for immigrants in America. In 1857, the social and political conditions in Germany and the desire for adventure and business success caused the eighteen-year-old Busch to travel by boat to the United States and settle in another river port town, St. Louis, Missouri.

His past work experience helped him to find a job as a clerk in a shipping house. Busch arrived in St. Louis at a time when the influx of German immigrants was rapidly growing. He started as a simple laborer doing basic maintenance work. The German tradition of beer drinking found few resources in St. Louis, and small breweries were started to meet the growing demand. Busch became very familiar with the brewery supplies needed that were brought in by the riverboats. He became a very knowledgeable judge of good brewery supplies, such as hops, malt, and barley. He was noticed by his employers for his hard work and helpful business knowledge. He became well known to the local German clients needing the brewery supplies.

In 1859, his father died and left him a sizeable inheritance. He used that to buy a partnership in a new company, Wattenburg, Busch & Company. Among the other German immigrants arriving in St. Louis at that time was a wealthy soap manufacturer, Eberhard Anheuser. He set up his soap manufacturing business and bought the Bavarian Brewery. The brewery was not financially stable. As Anheuser bought the needed supplies for his brewery, he met Busch and the two became friends. Anheuser amassed a large debt for the brewery supplies and offered Busch an interest in the brewery as payment. Busch readily agreed. Busch was introduced to Anheuser's daughter, Lilly. Busch's older brother, Ulrich, having also arrived in St. Louis, had been seeing Anheuser's other daughter, Anna. The two couples were married in a double wedding ceremony on March 7, 1861.

Business and family life was interrupted one month later with the start of the American Civil War. Busch joined the Union army for a three-month tour of duty. He did fight a few skirmishes in northern Missouri but saw no major battles. Busch was honorably discharged with the rank of corporal. Returning to home, Busch found business opportunities expanding. Anheuser was very involved with his successful soap manufacturing and was losing interest in the brewery. The two men established a complementary business relationship. Anheuser knew how to make beer, and Busch knew how to sell it. In 1865, Busch invested more funds into the brewery and became the manager.

Business at the brewery grew rapidly under Busch's management. He concentrated on salesmanship and hiring skilled employees. The growth attracted the attention of the financial community, and loans became available for expansion. The company became a stock-selling corporation. Busch and his wife were the major stockholders. By 1879, the corporation's name was changed to Anheuser-Busch Brewing Association.

Busch also succeeded in his family life. Between 1863 and 1884, Busch and Lilly had thirteen children—five boys and eight girls. His son would eventually carry on the family business. They lived on a country estate called "Grant's Farm."

In 1880, Eberhard Anheuser died, and Busch was left in charge of the business as president. Busch began some of his innovative ideas to improve sales. He concentrated on local sales first by buying saloons and planting patrons in other saloons to promote his brands. He caught saloon owners and operators' attention by giving expensive gifts for them and their families on special holiday occasions. With the advent of newly developed bottled beer, Busch saw the opportunity for short-term shipping of his beer by rail.

The competition for beer was challenging. The competition for a good, cheap beer was even more of a challenge. A friend of Busch's returned from a trip to Bavaria and discovered a very good beer in a monastery. He bought the recipe from them and gave it to Busch. They produced the beer in their brewery and found a good reception. The beer was named "Budweiser" after the location of the Bavarian town of Budweis, where the monastery was located. By 1885, Anheuser-Busch became the leading beer in St. Louis.

A new process of pasteurization allowed the beer to remain unspoiled much longer. Busch found this process not only an advantage locally but also allowed his beer to be shipped safely all over the country. By 1890, Anheuser-Busch became the highest selling beer in the country. Busch bought several railroads and used refrigerated railcars to ship his merchandise nationwide. Budweiser became a nationally known brand of quality beer. Busch would buy other houses around the country to help with his business promotions.

The business operations greatly expanded, covering a large area of St. Louis. It covered 142 acres of ground with 110 individual buildings. It also employed 7,500 workers. The payroll exceeded $10,000,000 a year. Busch went to great effort to improve the lives and conditions for his workers. The "average wages of the workers was increased and the hours per week declined" in the following years. In 1910, Busch established a "happiness fund" that provided entertainment, pensions, and family aid to his workers. He also became a philanthropist, making donations to Washington University in St. Louis and to Harvard University. He also gave significant amounts to community charities. He became an important political figure locally and nationally.

Busch began to expand the business to a growing European market. He bought a castle on the Rhine. He became friends with European royalty and political leaders.

There were mixed reactions locally to the influence of Busch. He was never allowed to join the local country club because of their resentment of the German immigrant population. He was named "First Citizen of St. Louis" by local religious leaders because of his large donations to local charities. Busch also served as director and a major promoter of the 1904 World's Fair in St. Louis. On the occasion of his fiftieth wedding anniversary, in 1911, a large celebration was held in Pasadena, California. It was noted that "his wife was seated on a large throne and given a crown worth $200,000." Another celebration was held in St. Louis for the workers where "an estimated 50,000 bottles of beer, 10,000 cigars, and 30,000 sandwiches were provided."

In 1906, Busch developed pneumonia and struggled from its effects for many years. He had allowed his sons to take over some of his business workload. He and his wife traveled. He was at his castle on the Rhine, named Villa Lilly after his wife, when he died of a heart attack on October 10, 1913. His estate was estimated to be worth 60 million dollars. The funeral in St. Louis was on a massive scale. Six thousand employees marched in line and there were twenty-five trucks needed to transport the floral tributes. Foreign representatives and national figures attended the funeral observances. There were also services held around the country in all thirty-six cities where there were branches of Anheuser-Busch.

Adolphus Busch II was named the new president of the company. That line of family ownership continues until 2008. The company has survived, overcoming several national obstacles. The Prohibition movement and two world wars brought attacks on the beer business and strong anti-German sentiment. In 2008, Anheuser-Busch was purchased by the Brazilian-Belgian brewer, InBev. This resulted in the new company becoming the largest brewing association in the world.

Adolphus Busch was an example of a great innovator, promoter, philanthropist, family man, and Missourian. It was said, "Beer made St. Louis and Busch made beer." Busch himself stated, "For every man of responsibility there must be ready another to succeed him. . . ." Busch will be forever known as the man who made "The King of Beers."

James Buchanan Eads
St. Louis
Architecture

He had very little in the way of any formal education, yet he became a leading, innovative engineer in his day. Early in his life, he traveled with his family and lived in several large Midwestern cities until they settled in Missouri. He found fortune and fame in Missouri but would lose his fortune several times.

James Buchanan Eads was born on May 23, 1820, in Lawrenceburg, Indiana. He was named after his mother's cousin, a Pennsylvania Congressman named James Buchanan, future fifteenth president of the United States. He was the son of Thomas C. and Ann Buchanan Eads. His father was a struggling merchant with many business failures. This prompted moves to Louisville, Kentucky, and Cincinnati, Ohio, in search of success. In 1833, when young Buchanan was thirteen years old, the family traveled to St. Louis by steamboat, the *Belle West*, with their possessions on board. They had planned to use their possessions to start a new business venture in the city. As they arrived in St. Louis, the boat caught fire, and all of their possessions were lost.

Young Eads went to work immediately in the city to help his family's finances. He sold apples and worked at other odd jobs, but with the approaching winter, he would not be able to continue. He found a steadier job running errands for Barrett Williams, who owned a dry goods store. Williams learned of Eads' intellectual abilities and interests. He knew that Eads had little schooling but desired a more formal education. Williams allowed Eads to use Williams' personal library. Eads was especially interested in the books dealing with engineering.

The dry goods store was very close to the Mississippi River. During the time Eads worked there, he became aware of the river and its dangers. At the age of eighteen, Eads became a purser on a riverboat. He heard the stories of boats that were wrecked because of the dangerous obstacles in the river and the vast amount of lost cargo. He used his self-taught knowledge of engineering and observations of the river to develop an innovative concept of wreckage recovery. In 1842, at the age of twenty-two, Eads created a salvage boat that used an attached diving bell he called a "submarine." It would allow him to walk on the bottom of the river and discover the lost cargo from the sunken ships. He began to create a great fortune over the next few years. He tried to retire and start a family. In 1845, he married Martha Dillon. They would have three children before she died in 1852. Eads invested in a glass factory in the West that was ruined by the Mexican War. He once again went back to his salvage business in 1848. He built additional improved submarines and eventually had a fleet of ten boats. He married a widow, Eunice Hagerman, in 1854. He made another fortune and retired in 1857.

The Civil War saw the prosperous river trade close to businesses. Eads was a sympathizer with the Union cause and wanted to help. He was aware of the significance of military control of the Mississippi River. He proposed to the U.S. Attorney General, Edward Bates, that Eads would construct steam-powered, ironclad boats to help the Union ground forces to secure ports and land south of St. Louis. The idea seemed far-fetched at the time. But Bates was from Missouri and knew of Eads' reputation and successes. Eads was summoned to Washington, D.C., to present his case. The idea was accepted, and Eads won the bid for construction. The first of the gunboats, the *St. Louis*, was constructed in a record time of just five weeks. Six other gunboats would be constructed rapidly with 4,000 men working day and night shifts seven days a week. The gunboats proved to be decisive in major battles on the Mississippi River. The Union forces, with the gunboats' assistance, won battles at Fort Henry, Donelson, Memphis Island, Vicksburg, and Mobile Bay.

After the war, Eads developed another innovative idea to build a bridge spanning the Mississippi River. The expanding railroad business helped to make Chicago a major trade center. Because the railroad ended at the river, St. Louis was losing significant business. Such a bridge able to carry train traffic would also open up the West for additional business. Anticipating the danger of a successful project, the Illinois legislature approved Lucius Boomer, a bridge builder, the right to build the bridge. Boomer had no intention of building the bridge. He only wanted to prevent it from being built. Despite the politics involved, Eads continued with his project plans. Knowing of the demands for continuous river traffic during such a project, Eads presented innovative material and construction concepts. He proposed using a new material for construction, steel as the major component. A bill had been passed to set a minimum span of five hundred feet for the continuous river traffic. Eads' plan had a steel bridge with three spans, each over 500 feet. After the public became aware of Boomer's nefarious scheme, Eads was awarded the design plans in January 1868.

Eads' plan was to have each of the three connecting spans supported by very sturdy piers. The piers would have to be driven into the river's bedrock, some one hundred feet below the river bottom. Having studied similar challenging projects in other countries, Eads used a "cantilever system" to support the unjoined arches of the spans. The chrome steel had to meet Eads' standards of strength and quality. The steel from Andrew Carnegie's company, the Keystone Bridge Company in Pittsburgh, Pennsylvania, was often returned because it lacked the required standard and, therefore, needed to be redone. The bridge contained over thirteen million pounds of steel, iron, and wood. The construction process was also costly in the loss of lives and being a cause of sickness. The bridge was completed with General William Tecumseh Sherman driving in the last spike. With a 100-gun salute (fifty on each side of the river), the Eads Bridge officially opened on July 4, 1874. Eads wanted to show its strength by parading a pack of elephants across the bridge and sending fourteen loaded locomotives across the spans. Fifteen thousand onlookers cheered at the success. The Eads Bridge was the largest of any kind built in that day and was regarded throughout the world as a "landmark engineering achievement."

The success for Eads was short lived as the railroads boycotted the use of the bridge. They owned a large part of the Wiggins Ferry

Company, which would later lose much money. As a result, Eads was forced into bankruptcy four years after the bridge opened. Eads would find other works of success on the river with the construction of a permanent navigational channel in New Orleans. He was also involved in other major works of construction in Mexico, Panama, England, and Canada.

In 1884, Eads was presented the Albert Medal by Queen Victoria. This was the first time that the honor was bestowed on a foreigner. While in Nassau, Bahamas, hoping to regain his failing health, Eads died suddenly on March 8, 1887, at the age of sixty-six. He would not live to see the true success of the Eads Bridge that finally occurred in the 1890s with the full use of the railroad association. The bridge still stands today as a marvel of architectural and engineering ability.

In 1927, the deans of the American engineering colleges were asked to select the five greatest engineers. They chose Leonardo da Vinci, James Watt, Ferdinand de Lesseps, Thomas Edison, and James Buchanan Eads. This was high praise for a self-taught engineer, who overcame obstacles in life and business to achieve such a great honor. His innovations prompted even greater construction projects in the years ahead. He is acknowledged as a great Missouri innovator.

Joyce Hall
Kansas City
Greeting cards

He rose from abject poverty to lead a multibillion dollar company. He started at the age of eight, selling products door to door, and his life ended as a successful land developer. His company would be identified by millions around the world with the phrase, "When you care enough to send the very best."

Joyce Clyde Hall was born on August 29, 1891, in David City, Nebraska. He was the youngest of three sons born to Reverend George Nelson Hall and Nancy Dudley Hall. Young Hall was named after a visiting Methodist bishop, Isaac W. Joyce. The name "Joyce" was strongly disliked by Hall. He was usually referred to as "J. C." Hall's father was an itinerant preacher and his mother was a semi invalid. The family lived in poverty. At the age of seven, Hall's father is reported to have abandoned the family (some sources indicate that Hall's father died.). The three sons were responsible for providing income for the family. Hall worked briefly as a farmhand and at the age of eight began selling cosmetics door to door for the California Perfume Company (later to become Avon). His two older brothers moved to Norfolk, Nebraska, as part-owners of a book and stationery store. At the age of ten, Hall and his mother joined the brothers in Norfolk. They found moderate success with the store and decided to expand their inventory with imported postcards from Europe. When Hall was sixteen, the three brothers invested in the store and established the Norfolk Post Card Company. The company struggled to keep sales up, and Hall considered how to expand their sales market. Dropping out of high school in 1910, Hall left Norfolk and traveled by train to Kansas City, Missouri. With him, he brought two shoeboxes of postcards. He found housing in the local YMCA and began to distribute samples of the postcards to local dealers. About one-third sent orders and checks to Hall, which enabled him to make a small profit. This prompted Hall to invite his two brothers to join him in Kansas City. They set up their business in the downtown area. Hall expanded the imported postcards to include more seasonal cards with envelopes for Christmas and Valentine's Day. He decided to call their new business Hallmark. Not only was that a play on their name, but it also represented a historic reference from the 1300s to the highest quality of precious metals stamped with the marker, "Hall mark."

By 1912, the company expanded into a larger facility. In 1915, a fire destroyed the offices and all of their card supplies. They were now $17,000 in debt. They quickly borrowed money and purchased a local engraving company near the old shop. With the engraving press, they could print their own cards. They expanded their lines with other specialty cards, such as birthday, sympathy, best wishes, anniversary, get well, and inspirational cards. They were able to produce their first cards just before Christmas 1915. The uniquely designed cards immediately became very successful. They moved their emphasis from imported cards to a brand of what they called "everyday occasion" cards. Their hope was that these more inexpensive cards would catch on as a social custom. In 1919, they produced their first everyday card. It featured a line from American poet Edgar Guest, "I'd like to be the kind of friend you've been to me." It became a bestseller. Business increased, and the company now operated in four separate buildings with 120 employees. In 1922, Hall married a family friend, Elizabeth Ann Didlay. They had three children.

In 1923, the company moved into a new six-story building. Hall continued to add innovative marketing operations to the business. He established self-service display racks, an automatic recorder system, and a functional inventory. Business rapidly increased, and additional employees were hired. The 1930s, with the Great Depression, was a challenging time for all businesses in the nation. Hallmark went to great efforts to insure employees of their job security. He developed the Joyce Hall Prosperity Plan and worked nationally through local Rotary Clubs to promote an optimistic business operation. The plan was credited with helping many businesses survive the economic crisis.

In 1944, Hallmark executive C. E. Goodman coined the famous phrase, "When you care enough to send the very best." Hall called on the works of popular current and historic master artists, using their designs on his cards. World War II added a market for cards to be sent to American soldiers.

After the war, Hall became concerned and involved in peace-keeping activities. In 1956, President Eisenhower invited Hall and other businessmen to the White House to help establish an organization to promote world peace. Discussions resulted in the establishment of the People-to-People organization. Hall not only served on the group's board of directors but also served as chairman of the executive committee. In 1959, Hall expanded their business market, selling cards through retail chain stores. In 1959, he began Ambassador Cards, specifically for those retail stores.

In the 1960s, Hall became more involved with local philanthropic activities. He founded the Hallmark Corporate Foundation. He also helped establish the Hallmark Hall of Fame television specials, resulting in numerous Emmy awards. Hall continued to oversee quality control of every card produced. By 1966, he stepped down as chief executive. He turned administrative control over to his son, Donald. By then Hallmark was the country's largest greeting card operation.

Concerned with the urban decay around Kansas City, Hall initiated a redevelopment campaign. He constructed an eighty-five-acre, $400 million Crown Center development on the southern edge of the city. It contained a residential, office, hotel, and entertainment district. In 1976, his wife died. Hall continued daily work at his office when he wasn't traveling or on vacation. He never allowed his company to go public. It is the largest privately owned company in the world with 17,000 employees, and 20,000 card shops; it is valued at $1.5 billion, and 10 million Hallmark cards are sold every year. The family held 75% of the company, and the employees were able to invest in the remaining 25%.

Hall died in his sleep on October 29, 1982, in Kansas City. He was ninety-one years old. His father had told him, "The Lord will provide." Hall's response was, "It's a good idea to give the Lord a little help." Hall once commented, "If a man goes into business with only the idea of making money, chances are he won't. But if he puts service and quality first, the money will take care of itself. Producing a first-class product that is a real need is a much stronger motivation for success than getting rich." The measure of Joyce Hall's success is surely found beyond the accumulation of monetary wealth. In summing up his life, Hall stated, "All I was trying to do was make a living. In those days, if you didn't work, you didn't eat. And I like to eat."

Hall would be honored with numerous awards for his life's service. Among these are the Commander of the Order of the British Empire, the French Legion of Honor, the Horatio Alger Award, Emmy awards, and honorary degrees. His innovative ideas and marketing concepts continue to benefit the Kansas City area and the State of Missouri.

Ewing Kauffman
Kansas City
Entrepreneur

He was born on a poor family farm in rural Missouri and remained in Missouri to become one of the wealthiest men of his time. He left his limited education to pursue successful business ventures and happily shared his wealth and talents with others. Over three hundred of his employees would become millionaires investing in his businesses. He left an ongoing foundation to improve the lives of children and young people. He also left an innovative foundation to promote the creative discussion of ways to improve the lives of ordinary citizens.

Ewing Marion Kauffman was born near Garden City, Missouri, on September 21, 1916. He was the son of John S. Kauffman and Effie May Winders. He had a sister, Irma Ruth Kauffman. John, being unable to adequately provide for his growing family, moved with the family to Kansas City, Missouri, when Ewing was two years old. Young Kauffman very early developed his trademark salesmanship skills by peddling eggs and magazines door to door. He also spent time "noodling," diving into the Grand River and catching and selling big catfish. When he was eleven years old, he was forced into bed rest to deal with a heart problem. Kauffman used that time to indulge in the reading of books—many of them, often up to forty books a month.

When Kauffman was seventeen years old, he graduated from Westport High School in Kansas City. After a year hitchhiking to Colorado and returning, he began attending Kansas City Junior College. He received his Associate of Arts degree in business. With the approach of World War II, Kauffman joined the United States Navy. He served as a sailor of ships, spending long tours of duty on board. He used his skills in playing poker to amass a large amount of savings (some sources say as much as $90,000) that would be useful later in his life.

Returning to Kansas City after military service, Kauffman found work as a salesman for the Lincoln Laboratories, a local pharmaceutical company. He did not receive a salary, only a commission of twenty percent of his sales. He was very successful, and by the end of his second year, he was earning more than the president of the company. His percentage and his sales territory were cut.

In June 1950, very dissatisfied with the new arrangement, Kauffman quit the company and, with a $5,000 investment, started his own pharmaceutical company, Marion Laboratories, in his basement. He had no research division, only contacts and skills at sales. He convinced three local doctors to stay with him, and he would provide equal or better-quality drugs. In the pharmaceutical business, "He knew how to sell drugs and he was confident he could learn the rest." His first year was challenging. He made only $36,000 in sales, with only $1,000 in profit. He was already familiar to other buyers, and over time his business grew. He was able to get in on the ground floor of a new drug on the market, Os-Cal. The drug was very popular and much in demand. Along with other new drugs becoming available, Kauffman saw his business and profits rise dramatically. In 1959, Marion Laboratories reached sales of one million dollars. In the 1960s, his company went public.

In 1962, he married Muriel Irene McBrien. Kauffman knew, from his former, personal negative experiences in business, how to treat his growing number of employees. He offered them a profit-sharing plan, stock options, and education benefits. By 1968, "twenty of his employees were millionaires (Including a widow in the accounting department)."

Kauffman also began to develop interest in the city he loved. In 1969, he brought the Kansas City Royals to the then baseball poor area. He used his innovative ideas to help create a new baseball stadium that was decades ahead of the other franchises. Royals Stadium (later renamed Kauffman Stadium in 1993) was completed and opened on April 10, 1973, as part of the Truman Sports Complex (next to Arrowhead Stadium). It was completed just in time for the 1973 baseball season. It was uniquely designed with all seats facing second base and the largest, privately funded water fountain (322-feet) behind the center field wall.

He was able to see his Kansas City Royals win six division championships, two American League pennants, and the 1985 World Series Championship over the St. Louis Cardinals. He championed the cause of the local fan base, insisting on lower prices and some proceeds going to local charities. He once limited the sales of season tickets to fifteen thousand in favor of the other twenty-five thousand tickets being available to non season ticket holders. It was said that to Kauffman, the Kansas City Royals was not "a part of his financial portfolio. It was part of his civic philanthropy."

Kauffman and his wife, Muriel, were becoming increasingly concerned with the negative impact of dangerous drug use on the community, families, and lives. They established the Kauffman Foundation to help address the growing problem. In 1988, Kauffman went back to Westport High School and presented Project Choice to the freshman class. He offered to fund their postsecondary education if they would "stay off drugs, avoid teenage parenthood, commit to being good students and graduate on time." He also had strict requirements for parental involvement in the education process. The program later expanded to five other area high schools.

In 1989, Marion Laboratory merged with Merrill Dow Pharmaceuticals. Marion now had annual sales over one billion dollars with hundreds of investing employees becoming millionaires. In 1995, the merger was bought by Marion Roussel Hoechst for 7.1 billion dollars.

In 1990, he established the Ewing Marion Kaffman Foundation. The purpose of this foundation was to promote an opportunity to dialogue about innovative ways to improve the lives of ordinary people. Originating from this was the creation of the Center for Entrepreneurial Leadership to "train entrepreneurs, form networks, develop curricula and foster research." This would become the country's largest foundation having a value of over two billion dollars. Kauffman summed up his philosophy in his foundations, "I think that the greatest satisfaction I have had, personally, is helping others, doing something that either inspires them or aids them to develop themselves in their future lives so they'll not only be a better person but be a better productive citizen of the United States."

Ewing Marion Kauffman died August 2, 1993, at his Kansas City home. He died of bone cancer and was buried at the Ewing and Muriel Kauffman Memorial Garden. His wife, Muriel, died in 1995 and was laid to rest beside her husband. Besides the foundations, funding was also provided for the nationally recognized Kauffman Foundation Conference Center. It has attracted 65,000 participants annually for the past five years with many other visitors and guests. He was indeed an innovative Missourian. He found his fortune in Missouri and unselfishly gave back generously to Missourians.

Johnny Morris
Springfield
Retailer

He turned the simple pleasure of fishing into a national retail business. He brought his love of the outdoors to an indoor kingdom of needed fishing and hunting supplies. He provided an opportunity for individuals and families to enjoy the beauties and bounty of the outdoors. He continues to expand a growing company to the present day. He prefers to wear worn blue jeans and a customary green shirt to the usual expensive wardrobe of a man with his riches.

Johnny Morris was born in 1948 in Springfield, Missouri, to John A. and Ginny Morris. The family loved the outdoors and spent many hours fishing on the Missouri Ozark lakes around their home in Willard, Missouri. After serving honorably as a decorated veteran of World War II, his father opened a Brown Derby Liquor store in Springfield, Missouri. Growing up in Springfield offered young Morris the chance to receive a good education and experience the requirements for a successful business. Morris helped his father with regular clerking duties, such as stocking shelves, greeting customers, and pricing items for good sales. He graduated from Glendale High School in Springfield. He attended the local Drury College.

His real interest was in fishing. He participated in a bass tournament on nearby Table Rock Lake. He did well and qualified as a member for five years. In 1969, hearing complaints from the other participants about the difficulty in finding good fishing equipment, Morris got permission from his father to set up an eight-by-eight foot display case of desired fishing equipment in the back of the liquor store. Fisherman would stop by the store on the way to the lake and buy their needed equipment. Morris' display was very successful. In 1971, with the help and encouragement of his father, Morris filled up a U-Haul with the hard-to-find quality supplies and took it to the lake. His innovative style allowed him to meet the needs of his fellow fisherman and also continue to enjoy the sport himself. That was the beginning of Bass Pro Shop. His reputation and business grew.

The store and U-Haul continued to house the display for the next thirteen years. Morris had no intention of anything beyond the simple store display and U-Haul inventory. When fisherman returned home after the tournaments, they needed to restock their fishing and tackle box supplies. They would call or write to Morris requesting those supplies. In 1974, Morris produced an extensive Bass Pro Shop catalog. He took his father's advice and did a mass mailing to outdoor enthusiasts in twenty states.

In 1978, to meet the discovered needs of fishermen, Morris offered for sale the Bass Tracker. It was described as a "fish-ready package-the first professionally-rigged boat, motor and trailer." In 1981, with his business demands accelerating and income rapidly increasing, Morris opened the first Bass Pro Shop Outdoor World Headquarters Showroom in Springfield. It was one of the largest retail stores in the world. It housed a "four-story waterfall, live animals, acres of outdoor items and an upscale restaurant" (Hemingways). Almost immediately, it began to attract four million visitors a year. The expanded catalog was now sent to over 34 million homes around the world. In 1982, he met his wife, Jeanie. They would have four children.

Morris was interested in providing a place for potential boat buyers to try out the Bass Tracker boats manufactured now by Tracker Marine. He and his wife selected property on Table Rock Lake. It was purchased in 1987 and became the Big Cedar Lodge. It was expanded to incorporate family vacations and became recognized as one of the world's best family hotels. The 4,600-acre property has grown into rustic lodges, a spa, four restaurants, and five swimming pools. It also provides for many nature and water-related activities for the family. *Southern Living* magazine listed it as one of the top ten resorts in the country. Morris continued to invest in properties in south Missouri.

As an active conservationist, Morris created the Dogwood Canyon Nature Park. In Lampe, Missouri, near the Arkansas border, the park is a sanctuary for buffalo and elk and offers places for fishing and hiking. Morris' friend, Dr. M. Graham Clark, president of College of the Ozarks, was going to sell his palatial home and 243-acre property. The property on the highest point in Taney County offered a panoramic view of the Ozark countryside. In 1995, Morris and his wife bought the property and created a classy restaurant. In June 2005, a fire in the restaurant caused the property, known as the Top of the Rock, to close. It would be a decade later before the much-expanded operation was reopened. The new Top of the Rock was opened in June 2014. It now included four restaurants, a nature trail, a cave, a natural history museum, a chapel, and golf courses designed by Jack Nicklaus, Arnold Palmer, and Missourian Tom Watson. One of the golf courses hosts an annual PGA tournament, attracting many famous professional golfers and their families.

Morris was the recipient of numerous important awards, including the Teddy Roosevelt Conservationist Award in 1990, the 1992 Fisherman of the Year, and the International Association of Fish and Agencies Prize in 1996. While all of the creative ventures were being realized, the home base of Bass Pro Shops began expanding to other cities. Today there are over ninety retail stores, hosting an estimated 116 million visitors each year. The Springfield store is Missouri's largest tourist attraction.

Scheduled to open in late 2017, the Wonders of Wildlife Museum, adjoining the first store, will only increase visitor interest nationally and internationally. Morris' personal wealth is estimated at over $4.3 billion. But he still drives a well-worn, Toyota pickup truck and prefers to rent his golf clubs rather than purchase his own. A person of such wealth could choose to live anywhere. Morris said, "I've been blessed to travel a lot of places, but I think we're lucky to live right here [Springfield, Missouri]. This is one of the most special places around."

Morris began his business career with a simple goal, to meet the needs of common people with quality fishing supplies. He used innovative concepts in establishing an internationally known company. He formed creative vacation facilities that provided thrilling family activities while enjoying nature. He has remained faithful to his Missouri upbringing.

James Cash Penney
Hamilton
Department stores

He came from rural Missouri and created a company well known throughout the country. He lived by the Golden Rule and ran his business by that standard. He had limited education, but his innovative business techniques were the model for other businesses. He traveled around the nation establishing new stores but never forgot his strong Missouri roots.

James Cash Penney was born on September 16, 1875, on a farm near Hamilton, Missouri. He was the seventh of twelve children born to James Cash Penney and Mary Frances Paxton Penney. His father was a college-educated, Primitive Baptist minister who preached at a local church without pay. To provide for his family, he farmed and raised stock. His mother had attended a convent school for Southern young ladies. His mother and father were cousins. The family eventually moved into Hamilton while they continued farming. That provided the ability for the children to finish high school. The family maintained a strong religious atmosphere in the home, constantly emphasizing the Golden Rule: "do unto others as you would others do unto you." Eventually, Penney's father was dismissed from the small church because he wanted to start a Sunday School class. The anti-education feeling of the church members soured Penney on the organized church for many years.

Penney was small for his age and wore the well-used, hand-me-downs from his older siblings. When Penney was eight years old, he was confronted with a harsh dose of reality from his father. He was told that if he wanted new shoes and clothes, he would have to buy his own. Penney helped his father on the farm to earn money. He helped with haying and caring for the livestock. He finally had enough money to buy his shoes and a pig. He developed salesmanship talent very early in his life. He bought additional animal stock and fed them by collecting neighbor's garbage. The neighbors complained about the smell and the noise, and Penney had to sell his stock.

In 1893, Penney graduated from Hamilton High School. He had dreams of becoming a lawyer. He continued to help on the farm to earn money and help his father whose health was failing. He did not like farm work but felt the obligation to help his family. His father was diagnosed with tuberculosis and facing death. Six weeks before he died, Penney's father made arrangements for Penney to take a clerk job at J.M. Hale and Brothers Dry Goods Store. The owners did not need another clerk but wanted to help the minister and his family. It was agreed that Penney would learn the business and earn $25 a month. He began work February 4, 1895, just before his father's death.

Penney found the need to learn much about sales in the dry goods store. He learned about different materials and the importance of being attentive to the customer's needs. He learned to rise above the bullying of other salesmen. The store owners became impressed with his drive and honesty in ethical sales practices. By the end of his second year, his salary was two hundred dollars a month. Penney's health began to fail. Concerned that he, too, would succumb to tuberculosis, he took the doctor's recommendation to seek a drier climate. In 1897, Penney moved to Denver, Colorado, and worked in a dry goods store. He used his savings to buy a butcher shop. Business failed because Penney refused to cater to powerful customers, accustomed to special favors. The next year, he went to work for Thomas Callahan and Guy Johnson in their Golden Rule Dry Goods Store. The three worked together well, and Penney was offered a chance to work in a new store in Evanston, Wyoming. They were testing him for a potential business partnership. While in Evanston, Penney met and married Berta Alva Hess. Penney was offered a partnership, and the offer to open his own Golden Rule store in Kemmerer, Wyoming. He traveled to Kemmerer with his wife and infant son. The store was opened on April 14, 1902. He set high standards for the merchandise he sold and the hired salesmen he employed. He operated a "cash only" business, allowing no credit. This was an unusual and risky business practice. He was immediately successful and respected by the local residents. Callahan and Johnson sold their shares of the businesses to Penney. He explored opening new stores in the West. Another innovative business approach was calling his employees "associates." They would become business partners and share in the profits. All were expected to adhere to the Golden Rule in their treatment of the customers and each other. In 1909, the stores were incorporated as the J.C. Penney Company with headquarters in Salt Lake City, Utah.

In 1910, Penney faced a family tragedy. His wife, Berta, died of pneumonia, leaving him to care for two sons. He overcame a long period of grief. He continued to renew his interest in his business, and stores were expanded around the country. By 1912, there were thirty-four stores, and sales surpassed $2 million. In 1914, the company headquarters moved to New York City, closer to the merchandise source. The company motto, "Honor, Confidence, Service and Cooperation," along with effective advertising, provided for a growing reputation of good customer service and quality products at affordable prices. In 1917, Penney retired and became chairman of the board. He was just forty-one years old. There were now 127 J.C. Penney stores with annual sales of more than eight million dollars. In 1918, Penney opened his first store in Missouri at Moberly.

In 1919, Penney married Mary Hortense Kimball. Sadly, she died four years later, leaving him with another son. In 1924, Penney opened his 500th store in his hometown of Hamilton, Missouri in the same store where he began his sales career. In 1926, he married Caroline B. Autenreith. They had two daughters. In 1929, his personal worth was about $40 million. The tragedy of the stock market crash brought great personal financial loss for Penney. For a brief period in 1932, he found the need for institutionalization in a sanitarium in Battle Creek, Michigan. He had to begin his sales career again at the age of fifty-six. He did recover well, and his businesses continued to prosper. He attributed his success to his faith in God. He would eventually expand to over two thousand stores in all fifty states, Puerto Rico, and Belgium, with about 180,000 employees.

Penney began a philanthropic career in memory of his past experiences. To honor his parents, he established the Memorial Home Community in Penney Farms, Florida. It is a sanctuary for retired men and women in ministry. In 1937, he founded the Foremost Guernsey Association, Inc., in New York. The large operation was turned over to the University of Missouri in 1953. In 1954, he purchased his father's farm near Hamilton, Missouri, and established a purebred Aberdeen Angus herd. That same year, he established the J.C. Penney Foundation, which assisted in programs that support community renewal, the environment, and world peace.

Penney spent his final years active as a guest speaker. He received many honors and honorary degrees. He lived to see his humble first store grow into the second-largest, national, non-food merchandiser, just behind Sears, Roebuck and Company. He died on February 12, 1971, at the age of ninety-five. He was buried at Woodlawn Cemetery in the Bronx, New York.

James Cash Penney was proof that a person with moral motivation can succeed in business. He said, "I have found that unselfishness pays because it tends to engender unselfishness." He overcame personal and financial tragedies with his personal trust in God. He was quick to share his wealth with fellow workers and put a high priority on treating customers fairly. He used innovative business practices to expand his stores and give a positive trademark to the name J.C. Penney.

Footnote: Internet sales and the loss of large mall business sales have challenged the Penney's brand and future status in retail sales.

Sam Walton
Shelbina
Department stores

Although he has been more associated with his Arkansas-based company, he had his beginning as a Missourian. He had business failures and was criticized by others, but his confidence in himself and his innovative ideas made him an international success. He may have learned some valuable business lessons from another Missouri-born businessman, James Cash Penney. He came from a poor, unsettled family and, in the mid-1980s, became the richest man in America.

Samuel Moore Walton was born on March 29, 1918, in Kingfisher, Oklahoma. He was the oldest of three sons born to Thomas Walton and Nancy Lee Walton. Although his father worked as a banker and a farmer, there was not adequate income to settle his family anywhere permanently. When young Walton was five years old, the family moved to Missouri and found a suitable location in the northeast town of Shelbina. Walton was a good student. He found early on a life pattern of multitasking. He did well in school and helped the family during the Depression years by selling magazine subscriptions, delivering newspapers, milking cows, and selling the bottled milk door to door. He was also active in community activities and as an eighth grader became the youngest Eagle Scout in Missouri.

Wanting to find better work in a larger city, the family moved to Columbia, Missouri, where Walton attended Hickman High School. Walton quarterbacked his high school football team to a state championship in 1935. He was elected president of his senior class. He also continued with his family chores and odd jobs to help with the family income. After high school he enrolled as an ROTC cadet at the local University of Missouri in Columbia. He majored in economics and maintained an active college lifestyle, becoming president of his senior class. He graduated in 1940, after his twenty-second birthday.

After graduation, Walton wanted to put his economics degree to good use. He took a job in Des Moines, Iowa, at a J.C. Penney store. There, he learned valuable lessons about treating customers and effective sales techniques. His starting salary was seventy-five dollars a month. His boss's frustration with Walton's poor required paperwork was offset by Walton's growing skills in salesmanship.

With the beginning of World War II, Walton started working in a munitions plant in Tulsa, Oklahoma. There, he met and married Helen Robson. They had three sons. He joined the U.S. Army Intelligence Corps and worked for three years in airport security at a prisoner-of-war camp. He achieved the rank of captain.

In 1945, after the war, Walton began his search for retail business ownership. With $500 saved and $25,000 borrowed from his father-in-law, he opened a Ben Franklin store in Newport, Arkansas. His store prospered, and eventually fifteen other stores were opened. He changed the name of the stores he owned to Walton Five and Ten. He hit a snag five years later when the leases on the buildings were not renewed. The Ben Franklin executives disagreed with Walton's concept of attracting rural customers with discounted prices and quality goods. Frustrated, Walton and his brother James searched and found an opportunity for growth in the northwest area of Arkansas in Bentonville. On July 2, 1962, he opened his first store in nearby Rogers, Arkansas, with the name, Walmart.

Walton brought several innovative business practices to his stores. He wanted "smiling sales people selling only quality, brand-name products at low prices." While that was not a new concept, he added what at that time were risky business practices. He targeted rural areas instead of major cities. He banked on the idea that people were willing to drive a short distance for savings. He built a huge warehouse in Bentonville, allowing him to buy products in bulk at lower prices than his competitors. The process worked, and over the next few years, other stores opened in Arkansas and Missouri. By 1967, the Walton family owned twenty-four stores with annual sales of $12.7 million. A few years later, the company was officially incorporated and went public in 1970. By 1970, there were forty-one stores with annual sales of $72 million and over 3,000 employees. In 1972, the company was listed on the New York Stock Exchange.

Walton always remembered his employees in the growth of the company. He set up a college scholarship fund for his employee's children. He created a disaster relief fund to rebuild homes lost in fires, floods, and tornados. His employees who had participated in the profit-sharing options were becoming millionaires. He traveled around the country in his red pickup truck, visiting his stores and listening to his store clerks for their suggestions and new ideas. His annual stockholders meetings were pep rallies in which he was the head cheerleader. In 1979, the Walmart Foundation was established to contribute to the underprivileged.

By 1977, there were 190 stores owned by the company. By 1980, the company had reached $1 billion in annual sales and were opening new stores at the rate of 100 per year. In 1983, he opened a warehouse outlet chain named Sam's Wholesale Club, catering to small businesses and individuals wanting to buy in bulk. In 1985, *Forbes* magazine named him the richest man in America, with a personal estimated worth of $2.8 billion. By 1987, Walmart was the third largest retailer in the country, behind Sears and Kmart. In 1988, the first of the new Walmart Supercenters (which included groceries) opened in Washington, Missouri. It was now a one-stop shopping experience. In 1988, Walton quit as the company's CEO but remained active in the company's operations.

By 1990, Walmart's stock worth was up to $45 billion. In 1991, the company surpassed Sears, Roebuck & Company to become the country's largest retailer. At a time when the country was experiencing a serious economic downturn, Walmart's sales increased by 40%! The company continued to use innovative techniques to improve its business operations. The new concept of "discounting" was coupled with tight inventory control. To help in accurate inventory needs, Walmart became the first retailer to use electronic scanners that were linked to a central inventory-control computer at cash registers. Today, Walmart's database is second to the Pentagon in capacity. The company is multinational with over 11,000 stores in twenty-eight countries under sixty-five banners.

While Walton's company grew, his day-to-day life remained unchanged. He lived in his original house in Bentonville, continued to drive his red pickup truck, and wore farmer's work attire. He was known as "Mr. Sam" to friends and employees. He remained faithful in his Presbyterian Church as a teacher and elder. He made charitable contributions to his church and community.

As his health began to fail, he traveled less. In 1992, President George H. W. Bush awarded him the Presidential Medal of Freedom, the nation's highest honor, in a White House ceremony. He was acknowledged as "an American original who embodies the entrepreneurial spirit and epitomizes the American dream." Soon after the ceremony Walton was admitted to the University of Arkansas Medical Center in Little Rock. He was being treated for cancer. He died on April 5, 1992 at the age of seventy-four. In 1998, Walton was included in *Time* magazine's list of 100 most influential people of the 20th Century.

Samuel Moore Walton remained a down-to-earth person excelling in retail business by employing innovative ideas. He had a simple business philosophy: "There is only one boss. The customer. And he can fire everybody in the company from the chairman on down, simply by spending his money elsewhere." He said, "The key to success is get out and listen to what the associates have to say." He created what was called Sam Walton's 10 Commandments:

1. Commit to your business.
2. Share your profits with your associates and treat them like partners.
3. Energize your colleagues.
4. Communicate everything you possibly can to your partners.
5. Appreciate everything your associates do for the business.
6. Celebrate your success.
7. Listen to everyone in your company.
8. Exceed your customers' expectations.
9. Control your expenses better than your competition.
10. Blaze your own path.

After Walton's death, the company continued to grow. There were some difficult moments, usually when the leadership failed to follow Walton's business model. The company continues to adapt to new innovative sales practices with the customer in mind.

Samuel Moore Walton was a product of his Missouri upbringing during his formative years. He is still recognized as a significant innovator in the area of modern retail business.

Other Missouri Innovators in Business

John Danforth • *St. Louis* • feed production

Howard Hughes • *Lancaster* • tool production; oil tycoon

James Smith McDonnell • *St. Louis* • aircraft production

Danny Meyer • *St. Louis* • restaurateur

Paul Mueller • *Springfield* • manufacturer

Jack C. Taylor • *St. Louis* • Enterprise car rental

Chapter Five
Science and Technology

George Washington Carver
Diamond
Agriculturalist

He was an orphaned black child who became a respected scientist and the friend of U.S. presidents and international leaders. He was denied local education because of his color and became the leading educational authority on agriculture. He enjoyed the peaceful beauty of nature and lived in the midst of racial hostility.

George Washington Carver is an important and well-known figure in American history. His Missouri roots established his lifelong appreciation of the natural and spiritual world. There are several conflicting accounts about his early life. The most common and likely events will be presented.

He was born probably in July 1864 in the one-room farmhouse of Moses and Susan Carver near Diamond (Grove), Missouri. His mother was a slave owned by the Carvers. He had an older brother and, evidently, several sisters. His father was a slave named Giles who lived nearby and died in a farm accident before Carver was born. The Carver farm was located in the hotbed area of Civil War vigilante raiders. When Carver was just a few weeks old, raiders kidnapped him, his sister, and his mother and took them to sell in Arkansas. Susan hid Carver's brother in the woods. Moses hired a tracker to find them and buy them back with his most expensive workhorse. Carver was found and returned to the Carvers, but his mother and sister were never found.

The Carver infant was suffering from a severe case of whooping cough when found, and the Carvers' care kept him alive.

The Carvers had no children and raised Carver and his brother as their own. Carver's poor health did not allow him to help with the regular farm chores. He helped Mary in the house with cleaning and cooking. He spent many of his free hours exploring the wooded areas near the farmhouse. Carver would later recall:

> As a very small boy exploring the almost virgin woods of the old Carver place I had the impression someone had just been there ahead of me.... I was practically overwhelmed with the sense of some Great Presence.... I knew even then it was the Great Spirit of the universe.... Never since have I been without this consciousness of the Creator speaking to me through flowers, rocks, animals, plants and all other aspects of His creation.

The Carvers spent time helping the boys to read and write from an old copy of Webster's *Elementary Spelling Book*. Carver wanted to go to school, but the local school did not allow blacks to attend. After a few years, the Carvers allowed him to go to Lincoln School for Colored Children in Neosho, Missouri. It was an eight-mile walk. He found a childless black couple, Mariah and Andrew Watkins, who allowed him to sleep in their barn. The couple worked out an agreement with him go to school if he helped Mariah with her laundry work. After a while, Carver was dissatisfied with the mediocre quality of education and moved on to Fort Scott, Kansas. Soon after his arrival, he was witness to the mob beating and lynching a black man. That incident caused him to leave Fort Scott and move to Minneapolis, Kansas. There he was able to complete his high school education. Desiring further education, he applied and was accepted to the Highland Presbyterian College in Highland, Kansas. When he arrived for the first day of classes, he was denied entry because of his color. Discouraged, he tried homesteading a farm for several years and traveling around the country. He worked at various jobs and saved money, always looking for a college that might accept him.

He had tried entry to the Iowa State College of Agricultural and Mechanical Arts but was again turned down because of his race. In 1890, he found an acceptable college, Simpson College, in Indianola, Iowa.

To support his college expenses, Carver worked as a cook at a hotel in nearby Winterset, Iowa. He majored in art and was very talented, even winning awards in art contests. After several years, he was encouraged by friends to reapply at Iowa State College in the agriculture program. He was accepted as the first African American student to attend the school. He found immediate respect and acceptance by students and faculty for his scholarly abilities and gentle nature. After receiving his Bachelor of Arts Degree, he was invited to assist the faculty and work toward an advanced degree. In 1896, he earned his master's degree in Agriculture. He was also nationally recognized as an expert in his field.

That same year, Carver was contacted by Booker T. Washington, who had started a black college in Tuskegee, Alabama. Washington, as principal of the school, invited Carver to head up a new agricultural department. It was a major turning point in Carver's life. He strongly desired "to be the greatest good to greatest number of my people." The letter from Washington was a unique offer:

> I cannot offer you money, position or fame. The first two you have. The last from the position you now occupy you will no doubt achieve. These things I know I ask you to give up. I offer you in their place: work—hard work, the task of bringing people from degradation, poverty and waste to full manhood. Your department exists only on paper and your laboratory will have to be in your head.

He was offered a salary of $125 per month and two-room living quarters. In spite of the cut in salary and offer, it seemed to match Carver's life purpose. He accepted the offer. On October 8, 1896, Carver completed his 800-mile train trip from Iowa to Chehaw, Alabama. He began his service at the Tuskegee Normal and Industrial Institute that would continue until his death.

Carver faced two challenges from the beginning. First was to set up and create an agricultural laboratory from scratch. He accomplished this with creative use of materials found in trash piles. The second challenge was to provide assistance to local sharecroppers dealing with poor quality land and ignorance of effective farming techniques. The challenges of the latter were more significant for Carver. He realized the main problems were the longtime priority of farming cotton, which had depleted the soil and no reliable alternative crop to rotate. He experimented and came up with several innovative solutions.

He discovered that raising peanuts and sweet potatoes replaced the low levels of nitrogen in the soil. But the farmers were not encouraged by the glut of peanuts and sweet potatoes on the market and their limited use. In 1903, Carver experimented with both and discovered over 300 uses and products from the peanut and 118 products from the sweet potato. Once manufacturers discovered the profitability of these byproducts, the demand for peanuts and sweet potatoes was considered a feasible alternative to the traditional cotton crop.

Carver created innovative ways to communicate his new findings to local farmers. He had published over forty bulletins on suggested methods of better farming. He held numerous town hall meetings. For those unable to attend, he invented a horse-drawn wagon that served as a classroom and demonstration laboratory. It was called a "Jessup Wagon." It was named after a New York financier and Tuskegee donor, Morris Ketchum Jessup.

In 1908, Carver returned to Diamond, Missouri, to visit his ninety-six-year-old guardian, Moses Carver, and his brother's grave. After World War I, Carver officially added his middle name, Washington, in honor of Booker T. Washington.

In 1914, the cotton crop in the South was becoming devastated by the boll weevil. As many farmers turned to new crops of peanuts, sweet potatoes, and pecans, the Southern economy was able to continue. Carver was very instrumental in saving the agricultural economy of the rural South. He also consulted with and advised international leaders, such as Mohandas K. Ghandi. In 1916, Carver was elected to the prestigious British Society for the Encouragement of Arts, Manufacturers and Commerce. It was a rare honor for an American. In 1921, Carver was invited to appear before Congress to support a tariff on imported peanuts. His ten-minute testimony was extended several times by the committee because of their deep interest in Carver's knowledge. The tariff was passed in 1922. From 1923-1933, Carver worked with the Commission on Interracial Cooperation. He toured white colleges speaking about racial harmony and common agricultural challenges.

He traveled the country as a respected speaker and authority on agricultural and soil conservation. But even in his travels, he encountered instances of racism. Given a first-class rail ticket, he was forced to travel in the lower-class train cars. When provided housing in major hotels, he was forced to use the servants' entrance and eat with the workers. He demonstrated a calm demeanor through all of these experiences. He stayed outside of the growing political and civil rights activities. He felt strongly that educating African-American students was the path to freedom.

By 1938, peanuts had grown to be a $200-million-per-year crop in the United States, the chief agricultural product grown in the state of Alabama. In 1939, Carver received the Theodore Roosevelt Medal for distinguished achievement in science. He refused an offer of a $100,000 annual salary by Henry Ford. He refused to claim patents for his products. He felt like they were gifts from God for everyone.

George Washington Carver died on January 5, 1943, at the age of seventy-eight. He had fallen down stairs in his home. He was buried next to the grave of Booker T. Washington on the Tuskegee Institute grounds. His epitaph reads: "He could have added fortune to fame, but caring for neither, he found happiness and honor being helpful to the world." He had founded the George Washington Carver Foundation at Tuskegee, and after his death, the estate of over $60,000 was donated to the foundation. In 1942, Missouri Senator Harry S. Truman introduced a bill in Congress to establish a monument in Carver's honor in Diamond, Missouri. President Franklin Roosevelt signed the unanimously approved bill and dedicated $30,000 for its construction. It was the first national monument to be dedicated to an African American.

George Washington Carver provides one of the best examples of a true Missouri innovator. His rise from poverty, discrimination, and societal obstacles should challenge all Missourians to set their life's purpose to do the "greatest good to the greatest number for all people."

Thomas Anthony Dooley
St. Louis
MEDICO

Some people use their talents and abilities to create wealth and fame. Some people use their talents and abilities to invent new products that may or may not bring them personal gain. Then there are those few who use their talents and abilities to personally help individuals in need.

Thomas Anthony Dooley III was born on January 17, 1927, in St. Louis, Missouri, to Thomas A. Dooley, Jr. and Agnes Wise Dooley. His parents were active members of a prominent Irish Catholic family and community. Dooley attended St. Roch Catholic School, a private school in the city. In 1944, he graduated from St. Louis University High School. He enrolled at the University of Notre Dame in Indiana, but his studies faced several interruptions.

His freshman year, he quit school and enlisted in the U.S. Navy corpsman program. He served at a naval hospital in New York. In 1946, he returned to Notre Dame. He again quit his studies there and entered the St. Louis University School of Medicine in 1948. He was an undisciplined student and often skipped classes. He had to repeat his senior year before finally graduating with his college degree. He wanted to begin his residency in St. Louis, but his professors did not feel he was ready for that serious commitment of time and energy.

Dooley decided to reenlist in the U.S. Navy. He was allowed to complete his medical residency at Camp Pendleton, California. He was assigned to Yokosuka, Japan. In 1954, he was assigned to the USS *Montague*. It was participating in a program, Operation Passage to Freedom. This program assisted refugees from communist North Vietnam who were evacuating to South Vietnam. They helped over 600,000 refugees evacuate. Dooley was a key leader, serving as a French interpreter and helping to establish refugee camps. He wrote of his experiences in a book, *Deliver Us from Evil*. It became a bestseller and gave rise to Dooley's recognition as a strong anti-communist.

Dooley began a book publicity tour in the era of strong anti-communist fever in the United States. During his tour, rumors began circulating of his homosexual orientation. He was quietly forced to resign from his naval career. He became committed to providing continued help for the people of Southeast Asia. In 1956, he and three naval colleagues established a hospital in Luang Namtha, Laos. He found that there was only one medical doctor for the 3,000,000 people. He was able to begin a weekly radio program, *That Free Men May Live*, broadcasted on KMOX in St. Louis. He and his team established additional hospitals throughout the region. He wrote two other books, *The Edge of Tomorrow* and *The Night They Burned the Mountain*, about his medical experiences in Laos. He was active as a fundraiser and increasingly becoming recognized for his humanitarian work.

He organized an international medical organization called the Medical International Cooperation Organization (MEDICO). The organization served as a stockpile of medical supplies, equipment, and personnel who were interested in humanitarian service. The goal was to create hospitals that would eventually be turned over to the local countries for control.

In 1959, Dooley was listed in a Gallup Poll as the 7th most admired man in the world. That same year, Dooley returned to the United States and was diagnosed with aggressive cancer. He underwent surgery but died a year later on January 18, 1961. At his funeral service, U.S. Senator Stuart Symington described him as "One of those rare Americans who is truly a citizen of the world." He was buried in Calvary Cemetery in St. Louis.

He was posthumously awarded the Congressional Gold Medal on May 27, 1961. His work was cited by President John F. Kennedy when the Peace Corps was established in 1961. He had also received Legion of Merit Award, the National Order of Vietnam, and numerous others from Catholic and local organizations.

MEDICO was eventually operated under the direction of CARE. It would be very difficult to imagine the millions of people benefitting from Dooley's work and the thousands of medical personnel who have given their talents and abilities in service to others around the world. All of this was initiated by a Missourian who cared more for others than himself.

Charles Stark Draper
Windsor
Inventor

He was from a very small town in central Missouri and brought about major innovations in "inertia guidance systems." Those innovations would have a great impact in the navigation and delivery systems of airplanes, ships, submarines, missiles, rockets, and space flight vehicles. He developed guidance systems that helped the United States keep the competitive edge in World War II and the Korean War. He was honored by U.S. presidents, as well as national and international science communities.

Charles Stark Draper was born on October 2, 1901, in Windsor, Missouri. His father was the town dentist. Draper attended the local high school and then, at the age of fifteen, attended the University of Missouri campus at Rolla, Missouri. He studied the liberal arts curriculum considering a career as a physician. In 1919, he transferred to Stanford University in California. He graduated in 1922, with a Bachelor of Arts degree in Psychology. After graduation, he intended to enroll in Harvard University. On a trip to Harvard, he happened to stop by and explore the attractive campus of the Massachusetts Institute of Technology (MIT). He fell in love with the school and enrolled in September 1922. His interest was drawn to the new area of electrochemical engineering. He received his Master's in Science degree in that field in 1928. He was asked to stay at MIT as a research assistant teacher and doctoral student. He stayed in that position for ten years and received his Doctorate of Science in physics in 1938. The following year, Draper formed the MIT Instrumentation Laboratory with a dedicated following of interested students.

He was an aircraft owner and pilot, fascinated by flight navigational systems. The work in the new lab provided significant help for the country after its entry into World War II. They developed a spinning gyroscope that stabilized the gun sights for the U.S. Navy. It was first used on board for targeting systems and later for navigation. The system, called the Mark 14, could detect small degrees of drift and quickly correct them. It was put to use in the 1942 battle of Santa Cruz on board the *USS South Dakota*. Thirty-two Japanese planes were shot down. Its success resulted in standard use on all U.S. Navy antiaircraft guns. By the war's end, more than 85,000 Mark 14 sights had been installed on American and British warships.

In the Korean War, U.S. aircraft was able to gain supremacy over the Soviet-built jets with Draper's A-1 gun sight system built for aircraft. After the Korean War, Draper continued his research into improving navigational systems for ships and submarines. His new system was called Marine Stable Element (MAST) and later a program called Ship's Inertial Navigation System (SINS). These programs were advanced through the encouragement and support of influential Vice Admiral Hyman Rickover.

These advances led Draper to be asked to develop a navigation system for the new Polaris ballistic missiles that would interface with launchers from submarines. For his success in the task, Draper was presented a Distinguished Public Service Award.

Draper continued his research and work for government agencies. For the Air Force, he designed navigation systems for the Thor, Minuteman, and long-range Titan rockets. For the U.S. Navy he continued work developing guidance systems for the Poseidon and Trident missiles. He was an important figure in providing the country with greater security in the Cold War.

In 1961, Draper was asked to develop a guidance system for the Apollo space program. This was the kind of challenge for which Draper had prepared. With the country in a space race with the Soviet Union,

President Kennedy had set the goal of a moon landing by the end of the decade. James E. Webb, the space agency director, asked Draper just several weeks before the famous moon landing launch, "Stark, this is going to be a hell of a job. Can it be done?" Draper replied, "It'll be ready before you need it." After the moon landing, Draper would go on to develop systems for the space shuttle program.

In 1965, Draper was awarded the national Medal of Science from President Lyndon Johnson. Throughout his career, Draper earned more than seventy awards, including the Langley Medal of the Smithsonian Institution, the NASA Public Service Award, and the Dr. Robert H. Goddard Trophy of the National Space Club. There were also awards from several other nations.

Problems arose in the turbulent 1970s, with protesters demonstrating against universities doing military research on their campuses. The MIT lab moved from the campus and in 1973 became an independent facility named the Charles Stark Draper Laboratory. Regretfully, Draper was relieved of his directorship duties.

In 1978, MIT established the Charles Stark Draper Professorship of Aeronautics and Astronautics in Draper's honor. Charles Stark Draper died on July 25, 1987, at his home in Cambridge, Massachusetts. He was survived by his wife, Ivy Hurd Willard, and their four children. In 1988, the National Academy of Engineering established the Charles Stark Draper Prize to honor "innovative engineering achievement and its reduction to practice in ways that have contributed to human welfare and freedom."

It is with great pride that Draper is recognized as a Missouri innovator. That such a brilliant engineer could come from a small central Missouri town is evidence that it can be repeated over and over by other young people from this state. They, too, can accomplish significant things on a national and international scale.

James Fergason
Wakenda
Inventor

While his name may be unfamiliar, everyone all over the world sees his innovative creation every day. Digital watches and alarm clocks, medical imaging devices, computer displays, advertising signs, and other consumer electronics show his invention. He began his career in a one-room, country schoolhouse and helped create a billion-dollar electronics empire.

James Lee Fergason was born on January 12, 1934, on a farm about four miles from the small Missouri town of Wakenda. He was the youngest of four children. His family was very interested in the sciences. Some of Fergason's relatives were acclaimed scientists, and his older siblings entered into scientific fields of study. He attended a one-room schoolhouse for students in the first through eighth grade. When he was in the seventh grade, the family moved to nearby Carrollton, Missouri, to attend a larger school. He graduated from Carrollton High School in 1952.

The University of Missouri at Columbia was close by, and he enrolled right after high school graduation. He majored in physics. He said, "I look at things differently because of the role models that surround me." He graduated in 1956, with a Bachelor of Arts degree in physics.

Upon his college graduation, Fergason accepted a commission as second lieutenant in the U.S. Army. The following Sunday he married his wife, Dora. They would have four children. After his service in the Army, he was hired by Westinghouse Research Laboratories in Pennsylvania. He had developed an interest in the area of liquid crystals. The limited knowledge about liquid crystals did not allow for their practical use. Fergason's experimentation led to the formation of the first industrial research group in their study. His pioneer research produced exciting new possibilities of liquid crystal use in daily life. In December 1963, he received the first patent on the practical use of cholesteric liquid crystals.

Several years later, Fergason moved to Kent State University in Ohio. He joined the Liquid Crystal Institute in the late 1960s. He became the associate director of the institute. The practical use of liquid crystals faced challenges because of their short lifespan and instability. Fergason's experiments found solutions to those challenges by creating "the twisted field nematic effect of liquid crystals." This discovery allowed their use in long-term, flat panel display. Becoming aware of the commercial possibilities, in 1970, Fergason started his own company, International Liquid Crystal Company (Illixco). His first customer was the Gruen Watch Company of Switzerland. They used the new technology to make and market the first liquid crystal display (LCD) watches. Later, many other digital watch companies would use this technology.

In the 1980s and 1990s, Fergason continued to refine the ability and usage of liquid crystals in popular, personal computer screens. His self-funded research provided huge financial rewards for him and his associates. In 1998, he was inducted into the National Inventors Hall of Fame and received the Ron Brown Technology Award from the U.S. Department of Commerce.

To help in the processing of numerous licenses and patents, Fergason founded Fergason Patent Properties LLC in 2001. That year he also received an honorary doctorate degree from the University of Missouri. He has continued to expand on his initial success to other areas of practical use today, such as "surface mode LCDS, polymer dispersed liquid crystals (PDLC), head mounted displays (HMD) and eye protection technology." He is acknowledged for earning 130 U.S.

and 500 foreign patents. In 2006, he received a $500,000 award from MIT-Lemelson Program for his LCD research. In 2007, he received the Optical Service (OSA) David Richardson Medal for "outstanding contributions to the understanding of physics and optics of liquid crystals, and particularly for his pioneering contributions to liquid crystal display technology." In 2008, he received the IEEE Jun-Ichi Nishizawa Medal. He continued his interest in encouraging and supporting young scientists.

James Lee Fergason died on December 9, 2008, at the age of seventy-four in Menlo Park, California. His work continues on at MIT through a foundation named in his honor. The various companies he established and the many students he motivated continue to find improvements for his creations. This internationally-recognized innovator received his early education and foundational roots in Missouri.

Leonard Goodall
Warrensburg
Inventor

Anyone old enough to remember the challenge of pushing a reel-type, blade lawn mower is very grateful for this man's creation. Many people have spent long hours on hot summer days behind one of these machines invented in the very heart of Missouri.

Leonard Berton Goodall was born on November 17, 1895, near Delphos, Kansas. He was the youngest of seven children born to Walter and Catherine Ferguson Goodall. They were a farm family. Before he was five years old, the family had moved to Sheridan, Kansas. Goodall helped on the farm with family chores. He received a limited education, completing only the eighth grade.

As a teenager, Goodall assumed more of the farm responsibilities. He developed an interest in the operations of all things mechanical. This responsibility and curiosity led him to experience a major tragedy in his life. While working on repairing a tractor with the engine running and the drive exposed, the vibration caused the tractor to jump into gear. His left leg was caught in the gears with damage severe enough to require an amputation of the leg.

Goodall adjusted to his physical handicap and continued life, showing interest in mechanics, radios, and automobiles. In 1919, he moved to Salina, Kansas. There he met a young woman named Troy. She was working as a mechanic in a garage. They married and had one child, Viva. Their marriage ended in divorce a year later.

Goodall moved to find work in Kansas City, Missouri. In 1927, while reading the *Kansas City Star*, he noticed an ad for a radio repairman for a privately owned book and school materials store in Warrensburg, Missouri. He applied and was accepted. He moved to Warrensburg and rented a room in a boarding house on West Culton Street. The store's owner, Kenneth Robinson, became a lifelong friend and encourager.

Unable to prepare meals in his single room, Goodall ate most of his meals at the nearby Estes Hotel coffee shop. He developed a friendship with a waitress, Pansy Eula Johnson. With the help of a friend, he also accepted a new job as a mechanic at the local Ford dealership. The owner, Theodore Shock, was impressed with his abilities and made him shop foreman. The employment would help him survive through the difficult Great Depression years. It also allowed him to propose marriage to Pansy Johnson. They were married on May 11, 1929. He was thirty-four, and she was twenty-four.

Together, they built a small two-bedroom bungalow at 444 East Market Street. The basement of the house became Goodall's workshop. On most evenings, Goodall tinkered with ideas to help with family income and improve the difficult homeowner tasks he faced with one leg. Their first project was creating wooden jigsaw puzzles. She pasted pictures on the wood, and he cut unique pieces that allowed the completed puzzle to be picked up and displayed. He sold the puzzles and even rented them out for ten cents per puzzle. He also used his woodworking skills to create bases for lamps made of inlaid wood. He and Pansy sold the lamps around town.

The Estes Hotel coffee shop faced financial difficulties during the Depression. The couple took over the operation of the coffee shop. Pansy was the owner, manager, and waitress. Goodall would open the shop at 6:00 a.m., and when Pansy arrived, he would leave for his regular job by 8:00 a.m. He returned to help close the shop by 9:00 p.m. They would operate the shop every day except Christmas Day. Their only child, Leonard Edwin, was born in 1937.

Goodall kept working in his workshop with a new personal challenge. He could not mow his own lawn with the reel-type, blade lawn mower. He could not push off with having one leg. He began to experiment with creating a "power mower." After a number of failed attempts, Goodall settled on using a gas-powered motor to turn blades beneath the mower housing. He used the 7/8-horsepower, two-cycle engine from his wife's Maytag washing machine. He was able to create a powerful direct vertical drive, rotary power mower.

Goodall was confident enough in his creation that he explored the means of marketing and sales. Local businessmen Charles S. "Sam" Baston and Hardy Wray agreed to invest in the new company for minority shares of interest. On January 14, 1939, the Articles of Association provided the necessary incorporation of the company. On July 23, 1939, the U.S. Patent Office granted the patent for the "Rotary Grass Cutter." Goodall would receive three other patents on newer models over the next decade.

On June 1, 1939, the *Warrensburg Star Journal* reported on Goodall's work. It stated that he had spent eight years developing his new creation, and it would sell for $98.50. Although only the wealthy could afford the machines, they began to sell well. The first national publicity appeared in the October 1941 edition of the *Maytag News*. Maytag was the sole provider for the mower engines.

World War II put a halt to the growing business. Engines were in high demand, and metal was also scarce for non-war-related businesses. Goodall attempted to use a cheaper and inferior engine but found it below his standard, and he experienced many consumer complaints. He decided to wait out the war's end and resume his operation. The Goodalls sold their ownership of the coffee shop and waited for the end of the war.

It was a wise business decision. After the war, returning veterans began living their American dream with a house, car, family, and a yard that needed care. His power mower business boomed in late 1945 and for the next seven years. In a series of negotiations, Goodall changed from the Maytag engine to the Lauson engine that provided a unique lubrication system for the mowers. Advertising for the mowers resumed in 1946, in the "Lawn and Garden" section of the *Kansas City Times*. The seasonal ads appeared between February and May. An ad in March 1947 featured Goodall's daughter, Viva, pushing a mower. The ad listed four models priced from $110 to $174 each.

In 1949, Goodall began construction of three buildings on property he owned by his house. This allowed for greater production. Dealerships were created around the country. By 1950, Goodall was earning dividends of over $57,050. But the business growth, which had expanded through the early 1950s, experienced a drop in 1952. Competition was expanding, and challenges to the patents would prove to be too expensive to fight in court. Goodall began considering selling the company.

He began to experience health problems resulting from stress over his business concerns. That stress caused him to develop bleeding ulcers. In 1952, the company was sold to Foley Manufacturing Company of Minneapolis, Minnesota. It was sold for $317,520 with the agreement that they would have first rights on any other Goodall creations. Several later inventions were bought by the new company. In 1953, the Goodalls purchased a country home in the Missouri Ozarks near Stover, formerly known as Boyler's Mill.

In 1962, Foley moved the Warrensburg operation of the Goodall Manufacturing Corporation to Minneapolis. The Warrensburg community fought unsuccessfully to retain the company. The Goodalls traveled regularly from Warrensburg to Stover. In retirement, Goodall kept working on new projects. He built grandfather clocks for his family and sold some. Goodall's deteriorating health led to his death at the Johnson County Medical Center in July 1971 at the age of seventy-six. Pansy sold the Warrensburg home and lived in Stover until her death in 1983.

After the death of Goodall, the Kansas City Star referred to him as "the father of the rotary power mower." It is said "Goodall's legacy, which began in a basement on East Market Street in Warrensburg, can be seen today on every suburban home lawn, park or golf course cut by rotary mowers." Maybe because of, but certainly in spite of, his physical handicap, Goodall was an important innovator.

Edwin Hubble
Marshfield
Inventor

It is amazing to consider how relatively short a time in the totality of earth's history that humankind has gained observable knowledge of space. There were certainly speculations and theories about its structure and operations but only recently has humankind discovered factual knowledge of its mysteries. One person who helped the world to become more knowledgeable about space was from a central Missouri town.

Edwin Powell Hubble was born on November 20, 1889, in Marshfield, Missouri. He was the third of eight children born to Virginia Lee James and John Powell Hubble. His father was a well-to-do lawyer and insurance salesman. The family lived in a luxurious house and had a very comfortable lifestyle. The children were still required to perform various household chores. Hubble was fascinated by his grandfather's telescope and had his first glimpse of space at night before he was eight years old. Hubble was a good student and excelled in all academic areas. He was an avid reader but especially drawn to the stories of Jules Verne and H. Rider Haggard.

Before Hubble was ten, the family moved to Chicago, Illinois, because of his father's insurance business. There were also numerous business trips made to Louisville, Kentucky. Hubble was an outstanding student at Wheaton High School near Chicago. He not only excelled academically, but he was even more recognized for his athletic abilities in all sports. He was growing into a six-foot-two-inch, strongly built, and attractive young man. He graduated from high school in 1906 at the age of sixteen. He received a scholarship to the University of Chicago, and that fall began his course of study in physics and astronomy. He also continued in his pursuit of athletic interests. He graduated in 1910, with a Bachelor's of Science degree.

Hubble was faced with a dilemma about his career choice. While he was interested in pursuing his personal love of astronomy, he was also pulled toward his father's desire for him to follow in a law profession. He was selected among the first Rhodes Scholars to study at the University of Oxford. He left the United States to study in England at Oxford and studied jurisprudence to please his father, who was in failing health. As his father was facing certain death, Hubble desired to return home, but at his father's insistence, Hubble remained at Oxford. His father died in January 1912, and later that spring, Hubble was awarded his Bachelor of Arts degree. He spent a year traveling throughout Europe.

In 1913, Hubble returned to the United States and was accepted to a teaching position in New Albany High School in New Albany, Indiana. He taught Spanish, physics, and mathematics while also working as the basketball coach. Although he was a very popular teacher and coach, Hubble was not satisfied.

After his father's death and an unsatisfying teaching career, Hubble decided to pursue his long-delayed interest in astronomy. At the University of Chicago, at the age of twenty-four, Hubble began his real life's academic and career interest. In 1917, he graduated with a Ph.D. in astronomy. He did his doctoral thesis on the topic of "Photographic Investigations of a Faint Nebulae." Just before his doctoral work was completed, he was invited to accept a position with the Carnegie Institute's Mount Wilson Observatory in Pasadena, California. He quickly accepted but would again have to put his desired career choice on hold. The day after Hubble submitted his doctoral thesis and completed his oral exams, he volunteered for service in World War I. He did a tour of duty in France for one year and rose to the rank of major. He returned to the University of Chicago for a year to complete his research projects.

In 1919, at the age of thirty, Hubble was able to finally begin his career at the Mount Wilson Observatory. He came there at an opportune time. The 100-inch Hooker telescope had just been completed. At that time, it was the largest and most powerful telescope in the world. In February 1924, at the age of thirty-four, Hubble married Grace Burke Leib, a graduate student of Stanford University. They would have no children.

In the next thirty-four years, Hubble would make discoveries that would revolutionize the fields of astronomy and cosmography. Located on the high mountaintop, the thinner atmosphere offered a much clearer look at the universe. It also created a very cold and frigid working place. It was a very slow and patient process of comparing space photographs over long periods of time to discover changes in light positions and intensity. The prevailing cosmography at the time considered the Milky Way as the totality of the universe. Other groupings of lights and identifiable objects were assumed to be smaller objects on the far edges of the Milky Way. Hubble would dramatically change that assumption.

Hubble's first major astronomical breakthrough was the proof that there were many other galaxies besides the Milky Way. He was able to develop a system of measuring distances between space objects. He discovered that distances of some objects were millions of light years beyond the assumed limits of the Milky Way. He also found that some objects were clustered together in organization much as the Milky Way. Many new galaxies were discovered and located using their light densities. On November 23, 1924, the *New York Times* reported, "Finds spiral nebulae are stellar systems. Doctor Hubble confirms that they are 'island universes' similar to our own."

Hubble continued to make and record observations of these nebulae, especially noting their movements. He was able to develop a means of measuring their speed and direction of movement. In 1929, he made an even greater discovery. He announced, "all galaxies seemed to be receding from us with velocities that increased in proportion to their distance from us." This dramatic announcement, known as Hubble's Law ($v=Hr$), gave much credence to the speculative concept of the Big Bang theory of creation. The discovery also gave support to Albert Einstein's theory of General Relativity. In recognition of Hubble's great contribution to the study of space, Einstein made a personal visit to

California to see the telescope, meet with Hubble, and express thanks for his work.

In 1936, Hubble published *The Realm of the Nebulae*. His book recounted his history and research in the field of extragalactic astronomy. He was also becoming a popular society figure. He became friends with celebrities, such as Charlie Chaplin, Harpo Marx, Helen Hayes, Lillian Gish, and William Randolph Hurst. Hubble and his wife became very close friends with Aldous Huxley and his wife.

Even with Hubble's fame, he continued to spend long, chilly nights at the observatory, furthering his research and documentation. In 1938, he was awarded the Bruce Medal and, in 1940, the Gold Medal of Royal Astronomical Society. In 1942, Hubble served in the U.S. Army as head of ballistics at the Aberdeen Proving Grounds in Aberdeen, Maryland. In 1946, he received the Medal of Merit for his military service.

After the war, he returned to his research in California. He also spent time at the Palomar Observatory, helping to design and construct the 200-inch Hale Telescope. In 1948, he was the first person to use it. That year, he was featured on the front cover of *Time* magazine. The results of the nights spent in the confines of the chilly observatory had a physical effect on Hubble. In 1949, he suffered a serious heart attack. His wife, Grace, stayed by his side and was very protective, limiting his time at work. Hubble died on September 25, 1953 in Sal Marino, California at the age of sixty-three. He died of a cerebral thrombosis. At his request, there was no funeral, and the placement of his physical remains were kept secret.

Hubble never received a well-deserved Nobel Prize for his work because at that time astronomy was considered a branch of physics. Just after his death, the rules were changed, but the prize could not be awarded posthumously. NASA did honor Hubble by naming a new space telescope after him. Astronomers, including Hubble, had been aware that the earth's atmosphere limited the clarity and power of telescopes. There was an awareness that a telescope in space would provide the best observable views and photos of space. On April 14, 1990, the Hubble Space telescope was launched and orbited the earth, 101 years after Hubble's birth. The new telescope continues to offer the best views, photos, and knowledge of space for all of humankind to observe. Hubble also received honors in the naming of a newly discovered asteroid (2069 Hubble) and a crater on the moon after him.

Edwin Powell Hubble was a unique innovator with roots in Missouri. His discoveries of space have been compared in importance to that of Galileo. His contributions will continue to help our and future generations to learn more about space and perhaps the origin of our universe.

Jack Kilby
Jefferson City
Inventor

Handheld calculators, personal computers, hearing aids, digital watches, printers, microwaves, video games, store scanners, cell phones, and digital televisions are commonplace items in modern life. If you have used or are using any of these, you have benefitted from the discoveries of a man from the very heart of Missouri. He is known as the father of the integrated circuit and the microchip. His name may not be familiar, but his discoveries are internationally known.

Jack St. Clair Kilby was born on November 8, 1923, in Jefferson City, Missouri. His parents were Hubert and Vina Kilby. His father was an engineer for electric companies. Kilby was exposed early to the world of engineers.

After his early formative years in Missouri, the Kilbys moved to Great Bend, Kansas, for his father's work. Kilby's favorite subject in school was American history. When he was fourteen, he watched his father use a borrowed amateur radio to contact his business associates during a Kansas blizzard when the phone lines were down. He was fascinated with amateur radio equipment and later built his own set. He studied and received his ham operator's license from the Federal

Communication Commission. When he graduated from high school, his career interest was toward electrical engineering.

In 1941, he applied for admittance to the Massachusetts Institute of Technology (MIT). He failed the challenging entrance exam, scoring 497 of the required 500 points. After the United States entered World War II, he joined the Army and was "assigned to a radio repair shop at an outpost on a tea plantation in northeast India." He made improvements on the bulky, undependable radios carried by the troops. He made a smaller, lighter, and more dependable radio that found favorable use.

After service in the war, he was admitted to the University of Illinois, where his parents had attended college. Using his benefits with the G.I. Bill of Rights, he graduated in 1947, receiving a Bachelor of Science degree in electrical engineering. In 1948, he married Barbara Annegars, and they had two daughters. In 1950, he received a master's degree in electrical engineering from the University of Wisconsin.

While attending graduate school, he began working with the Centralab division of Globe Union, Inc., in Milwaukee, Wisconsin. He spent much time in experimentation in circuitry. In 1952, the company sent Kilby to Bell Laboratories in Murray Hill, New Jersey, to study the new innovation of the transistor. Centralab had secured a license to manufacture this newly created engineering improvement that would replace the many vacuum tubes in widespread use. The transistors were "minuscule in comparison, more reliable, longer lasting, produced less heat and consumed less power." Kilby realized that the type of experimentation needed required the facilities and resources of a larger company. He was working toward the continued miniaturization of the transistor integrated circuits.

In 1958, he moved to another Bell licensee at Texas Instruments (TI), in Dallas, Texas. In July 1958, when nearly all of the TI employees were gone on the annual two-week vacation, new employees remained to work and keep the shops operating. During this time, Kilby made great advances on the structure and manufacturing of a new "semiconductor." He would record later:

Further thought led me to the conclusion that semiconductors were all that was really required—that resistors and capacitors [passive devices], in particular, could be made from the same material as the active devices [transistors]. I also realized that, since all of the components could be made of a single material, they could be made in situ interconnected to form a complete circuit.

On September 12, 1958, he demonstrated before the TI executives the small 7/16-by-1/16-inch integrated circuit. The prototype would later be refined and modified for production. Coincidentally, several months later, at the Fairchild Semiconductor Corporation, Robert Noyce also completed work on the same concept.

The first commercial use of the integrated circuit was by the U.S. Air Force in 1961. In 1962, it "became the brains of the Minuteman Intercontinental Ballistic Missile (ICBM)." It would later be used in the Apollo Spacecraft. Although the military found important uses for Kilby's creation, TI was looking to market the product for the public use. In 1956, Kilby invented the semiconductor-based thermal printer. In 1967, Kilby designed the first integrated circuit electronic calculator, which he called the "Pocketronic." It would later be refined and produced very profitably by American and Japanese companies.

In 1970, Kilby took a leave of absence from TI to become an independent inventor. He received more than sixty patents on all of his inventions. He was interested in considering the "use of silicon technology for generating electrical power from sunlight." From 1978 until 1984, he was the Distinguished Professor of Electrical Engineering at Texas A & M University. He officially retired from TI in the 1980s.

Kilby received numerous prestigious honors for his work. In 1970, he received the National Medal of Science. In 1980, he was inducted into the National Inventors Hall of Fame. In 1989, he received the Charles Stark Draper Medal. In 1990, he received the National Medal of Technology. In 1997, TI dedicated its new research and development building as the Kilby Center. In 2000, the Royal Swedish Academy of Sciences awarded Kilby the Nobel Prize for Physics. The Kilby Awards Foundation was established by him to annually honor individuals for achievements in science, technology, and education.

It is hard to imagine the full scope of the modern applications from Kilby's inventions. Advanced medical diagnostic equipment, cell phones, digital watches, DVDs, personal computers, video games, and many other products we enjoy come from his work. The resulting international electronics market exploded from annual sales in 1961 of about $29 billion to currently over $1.5 billion.

Kilby's wife died in 1982. He died of cancer on June 20, 2005, in Dallas, Texas. This remarkable person, with such gifted innovations, was a product of Missouri.

William Lear
Hannibal
Inventor

Rarely has a man been so closely identified with his most significant creation. He was also credited with popular inventions not associated with his name. He was an innovator early in his Missouri life and never quit developing ideas into useful products.

William Powell Lear was born on June 26, 1902, in Hannibal, Missouri. His parents were Reuben Lear and Gertrude Steuber Powell. His parents had a contentious relationship that caused turmoil in Lear's life. He was a very intelligent, hardheaded, and determined child. When he was twelve years old, he told his friends that "he was going to become rich by inventing things that people wanted." He was already tearing things apart to see how they worked and then rebuilding them. He built his own radio set including earphones. He also experimented with batteries, light bulbs, and bits of wire. His curiosity found little patience with his schooling. He felt it was boring and not helpful in his personal needs in the field of engineering.

The family moved to Chicago, and the emotional turmoil within the family only increased. When Lear was in the eighth grade, he dropped out of school. He ran away from home after his parents finally separated. Lying about his age, he joined the U.S. Navy during World War I. His age did not allow him to see frontline action. He was assigned to the Great Lakes Naval Training Station. There, he was fortunate to receive his more desired formal education in electronics and radio technology.

After the war, Lear cofounded Quincy Radio Laboratory, where he built radio components. He found a practical and needed product by creating the first car radio. The growing auto industry, making cars available for the middle class, was a ripe market. Lear had problems finding financial backing for his new creation, called the "Motor-ola." In 1924, he sold the plans to the Galvin Manufacturing Corporation in Chicago. It would eventually become the Motorola Corporation. The sizeable income allowed him to expand his company and research. He also took up a hobby—flying. He had worked in various jobs at Chicago's Grant Park Airport and was interested in aviation. Later in the 1920s, his new inventions included making audio amplifiers and cases for Magnavox speakers and developing a battery eliminator as a back-up power source. Lear's reputation was also growing among industry leaders.

In 1934, Lear founded the Avia Corporation, which produced radio and navigational equipment. His company would provide equipment sales for over half of the growing industry. With increased income, in 1939, Lear founded Lear, Incorporated. He concentrated on building stereo systems and communication satellites. With the beginning of U.S. entry into World War II, his company was granted more than $100 million in government contracts to meet the aviation needs for the military. He led the company in creating other important aviation devices. He invented a new concept of autopilot flying that was capable of allowing a plane to land in low visibility. In 1950, he was recognized for this great achievement with the Collier Trophy for the most outstanding aeronautical achievement. It was presented to him by President Harry Truman.

His company expanded their creative products into new areas. He created what was then a revolutionary concept in entertainment, with the eight-track tape player. They found a ready market in homes and automobiles throughout the country.

His dream was to build the "world's first inexpensive, mass-produced business jet." The idea was rejected by his company's board of directors. He sold his interest in the very profitable company and, in 1962, founded Lear Jet. Inc., located in Wichita, Kansas. He pursued his dream, and on October 7, 1963, he demonstrated his first Lear Jet. It seated six to eight passengers. It had immediate success with many businesses wanting the prestige of owning and displaying the new jet. Lear would later answer his earlier critics by saying, "They said I'd never build it, that if I built it, it wouldn't fly; that if it flew, I couldn't sell it. Well I did, and it did, and I could."

By 1975, over 500 Lear Jets had been sold. There were some challenges with the first production models that resulted in some bad press and temporary sales slumps. Continued improvements were made in speed and dependability with the resulting Learfan Jet.

His other inventions included a brushless alternator, a new compressor, a miniaturized, hydraulic pump, and reclamation of precious ores from used materials. He would be credited with over 100 patents. In the early 1970s, Lear made an interesting observation about the future of an innovative product that we now enjoy: "I can foresee a little device which you could carry in your pocket as easily as a packet of cigarettes and it could put you in touch with any place in the world, through satellite communications systems."

His wealth was estimated to be nearly $50 million. He acknowledged that at one time he owned fourteen homes and finally narrowed them down to five—"one in Greece, two homes in Geneva, one in Los Angeles and one in Reno.

Not long after the last model was produced, Lear was diagnosed with leukemia. He died on May 14, 1978, at the age of seventy-five in Reno, Nevada. He was inducted that year into the Aviation Hall of Fame. In 1981, he was inducted in the International Aerospace Hall of Fame. In 1993, he was included in the National Inventor's Hall of Fame.

Lear's personal life was affected by his early family turmoil. His parent's divorce had an impact on his own lifestyle. He was married four times and had four daughters and three sons. He once stated that he "admitted that he liked women and whiskey." Interestingly, Lear was also a skilled pianist.

Lear did confess in an interview in the late 1970s, "Money certainly takes you away from a hell of a lot of misery but it doesn't necessarily bring happiness. What it does bring to me is the capability of doing things without having to ask somebody for the money—to see whether it can or cannot be done."

William Powell Lear was a middle school dropout and came from a poor, toxic family. He rose to great wealth and possessed a mind created for innovative inventions. He was successful in business and unsuccessful in his personal life. He rose from obscurity in his Missouri beginnings to become personal friends with U.S. presidents and international leaders. Many of the technological advances we enjoy and take for granted came from the mind of this man.

Other Missouri Innovators in Science and Technology

Thomas Akers • *St. Louis* • astronaut

Edwin W. Handler • *Columbia* • inventor *(movement detection)*

Joe Jones • *Springfield* • inventor *(Rhumba and Tertrill)*

Henry Kang • *St. Louis* • inventor *(processing image)*

Roscoe Koontz • *St. Louis* • inventor *(gamma ray camera)*

Nicholas David Caola Kullman • *Kansas City* • inventor *(optimizing voice service)*

Jerry Plunkett • *Dixon* • inventor *(specialty materials)*

Steven W. Post • *Cassville* • inventor *(furnace air blower)*

Terry Gene Rayburn • *Kansas City* • inventor *(managing applications)*

Rajesh Talwar • *Frontenac* • inventor *(friction stir welding)*

Jason R. Troxel • *Lee's Summit* • inventor *(portable imaging system)*

Joel D. Weisner • *St. Peters* • inventor *(wireless relay module)*

Roy Wilkens • *Rolla* • inventor *(fiber optics)*

Chapter Six

Politics and Military

Omar Bradley
Clark
Military

Although many figures in history claim they were born in a log cabin, such was the case with this man. He would rise from his rural Missouri beginning to become the military leader of the largest force of American soldiers under one commander. He would be praised by the nation's best and brightest military leaders. He would bring innovative concepts of battle strategy and postwar care for returning veterans.

Omar Nelson Bradley was born on February 12, 1893, about three miles west of Clark, Missouri, in a crudely built log cabin. His parents were John Smith Bradley and Sarah Elizabeth Hubbard. He was their only surviving child. His father was a schoolteacher in a series of rural, one-room schoolhouses. He received little pay, and the family lived in poverty. Bradley attended the schools where his father taught. He was a quick learner and needed more of an educational challenge. Bradley learned much from his father about respect for others, justice, hunting, patriotism, and religion.

When he was twelve years old, the family moved to nearby Higbee. There, he was able to attend an excellent public school. Three years later, in 1908, his father died. Bradley was left to provide for his mother and his two adopted cousins. He used his skill as a "crack shot" to hunt and provide some income for the family. He attended Moberly High School and excelled in sports, especially in baseball. He received a good secondary education and graduated in 1910.

After high school graduation, he began working for the Wabash Railroad. He was also trying to save some money for his planned enrollment at the University of Missouri in Columbia. His plans changed, when at the suggestion of a Sunday School teacher, he applied for admission to the West Point Military Academy. After doing exceptionally well on the competitive entry exams, Bradley was appointed by Missouri Congressman William M. Ricker to enter the military academy in the fall of 1911.

Bradley thrived in the atmosphere of military discipline. As a student, he continued his combined interest in sports and academics. His graduating class was later referred to the "class the stars fell on" because so many of them would earn their general stars. Bradley finished with a rank of 44 in a class of 164. He would apply the lessons of team building, learned in sports, in his military leadership. He graduated on June 12, 1915 as a second lieutenant of infantry.

In September 1915, he was assigned to the Fourteenth Infantry Regiment, Third Battalion at Fort George, near Spokane, Washington. His encounter with Edwin Forrest Harding proved to be a great influence on his life and leadership style. He began a lifelong study of military tactical exercises. His first exposure to military action was in the southwest United States in pursuit of Mexico's notorious Pancho Villa. He served under the command of Brigadier General John J. Pershing. With the expansion of the U.S. military forces under the National Defense Act of 1916, Bradley was promoted to first lieutenant and assigned to Yuma, Arizona. There, they awaited orders to mobilize for action in the U.S. entry into World War I. Bradley was promoted to captain.

Disappointedly, Bradley's regiment was assigned to return to the Northwest to patrol strategic copper mines in Montana. Finally in August 1918, he received orders to prepare for overseas duty, and he was promoted to major. The Fourteenth Infantry became part of the Nineteenth Infantry Division. They were stationed at Camp Dodge, near Des Moines, Iowa. Two things intervened to prevent Bradley's long-awaited desire to see combat in Europe. There was a great outbreak of influenza and the signed Armistice in November 1918. Bradley was assigned for one year to teach as an assistant professor of military science at the South Dakota State College. In September 1920, Bradley was assigned to a four-year tour of duty to teach mathematics at West Point.

The superintendent of the military academy was Douglas MacArthur. Bradley continued in his personal study of military history and tactics.

In the fall of 1924, Bradley was assigned to attend advanced courses at the Infantry School at Fort Benning, Georgia. After a brief tour of duty in Hawaii in 1928, Bradley was assigned as a student at the Command and General Staff School at Fort Leavenworth, Kansas. It was the place for upcoming officers and commanders. In 1929, he was later assigned as an instructor at the Infantry School. The assistant commander was George C. Marshall. Marshall's philosophy of simplifying tactical command procedures, especially for citizen-soldiers, was one of the most impressive lessons for Bradley. He served there for four years and made a very favorable impression on Marshall.

In 1934, Bradley graduated from the Army War College and returned to teach at West Point. In 1936, he was promoted to the rank of lieutenant colonel. In 1938, he left West Point to serve on the War Department General Staff as assistant secretary of the general staff in the Office of the Army Chief of Staff. Marshall promoted him to the rank of brigadier general and sent him to Fort Benning to command the infantry school.

At Fort Benning, Bradley established several innovative procedures. He emphasized formation and training of tank forces and the newly established airborne forces. His most significant work was the creation of an officer candidate school (OCS). The school would later produce thousands of needed military leaders for World War II.

After U.S. entry into World War II, Bradley was given command of the reinstated Eighty-Second Infantry Division. He was challenged to get the troops into acceptable physical shape while offering some means of tolerable treatment. Four months later, he was assigned to the Twenty-Eighth Infantry Division, a National Guard unit at Camp Livingston, Louisiana. His experience in getting poorly prepared troops combat ready was needed with these citizen-soldiers. Bradley accomplished his goal, and the unit was ready for combat duty overseas. Bradley was patiently waiting for the orders to take the unit into combat. But his request for combat duty would be answered in an unexpected way.

In 1943, Bradley was assigned by General Eisenhower to North Africa to build up the failing II Corps. They had suffered losses, and the British troop leaders had strong criticism of their combat abilities. Bradley provided great improvements in getting proper training as the corps commander. In April and May the corps performed well; winning battles, gaining territory, and eventually capturing more than 40,000 German prisoners. The II Corps' action paved the way for the future invasion of Italy. By August, Bradley, with Patton's Seventh Army, captured Sicily. While there, Bradley was discovered by war correspondent Ernie Pyle. Bradley's behind-the-scenes, expert, and extensive leadership was now being publicly recognized.

General Eisenhower now assigned Bradley to the crucial position of commander of the large First Army forces after their landing on D Day, called "Operation Overlord." The strategic planning required for the invasion and following operations included vital input from Bradley.

With the costly victory of the French invasion won, the U.S. troops slowly advanced toward Germany. There was strong resistance, and the German's last major advance was in the Battle of the Bulge. It found Bradley and Patton using their military tactical skills to achieve final defeat of the retreating German forces. At the end of the European operations, Bradley's Twelfth Army Group was the largest ever commanded by an American general. General Eisenhower stated that Bradley was "the master tactician of our forces" and predicted that Bradley would eventually be recognized as "America's foremost battle leader." Among the troops, Bradley's care and concern for them earned him the title of the "Soldier's General."

Following the victory over Germany, Bradley had requested a command in the Pacific from General Marshall. But Douglas MacArthur would have that assignment. To his surprise, and in recognition of Bradley's care for his troops, on August 15, 1945, President Truman appointed Bradley to direct the Veterans Administration. Returning to the United States, Bradley assumed responsibility for the postwar care of over 12 million soldiers. In typical fashion, he spent time and effort reorganizing the system to meet the many medical needs, as well as the administration of the new GI Bill for veteran education benefits.

On February 7, 1948, Bradley succeeded Eisenhower as Army Chief of Staff. He inherited a number of challenging issues: demobilization, reorganization, racial integration and unification of the military services. The growing concern over containing Soviet aggression necessitated new military strategies. Bradley also worked with Congress to provide the first increase in military salaries since the beginning of World War II.

On August 16, 1949, Bradley was assigned to the position of the first Chairman of the Joint Chiefs of Staff. On September 22, 1950, Congress promoted Bradley to the rank of General of the Army with five stars. He would be the last officer to achieve that prestigious rank. Bradley used his organizational skills to settle disputes between the military services. He helped establish the North Atlantic Treaty Organization (NATO). He was also an important adviser to President Truman during the Korean War.

On August 15, 1953, Five Star General Omar Bradley left active military service. He had served in the military for thirty-nine years, longer than any other soldier in U.S. history. He eventually moved into the business world and became the chairman of the board for Bulova Watch Company. He served in that role from 1958 until 1973.

Bradley had married his high school classmate, Mary Quale, on December 28, 1916. They had one daughter. Mary died of leukemia on December 1, 1965. He married Kitty Buhler of New York City on September 12, 1966. She was a writer for *Look* magazine. In 1974, they established the Omar N. Bradley Library and the Omar N. Bradley Foundation at West Point.

Bradley served as a member of President Johnson's "Wise Men" think tank and later was the technical adviser for the movie, *Patton*. On April 8, 1981, Bradley received the Gold Medal Award from the National Institute of Social Sciences. Ten minutes later, he died at the age of eighty-eight. He was buried with full military honors at Arlington National Cemetery.

Omar Nelson Bradley was an innovative military leader. He was very human, admitting, "Bravery is the capacity to perform properly even when scared half to death." He was a true friend of the citizen-soldier, looking out for their welfare on and off of the battlefield. He was an important international figure who built on ethics and lessons learned from his Missouri roots.

William Clark and Meriwether Lewis
St. Charles
Explorers

William Clark   *Meriwether Lewis*

Few people in the history of the United States have had their names so intertwined that they are seldom viewed as two distinct individuals. While their noted adventures took place far beyond our state's borders, they both had a significant influence on Missouri.

William Clark was born on August 1, 1770, in Caroline County, Virginia. He was the ninth of ten children born to John Clark III and Ann Rogers. His father was owner of a large, wealthy plantation with many slaves. It was located on the far western edge of the frontier. Clark's older brothers received a more formal education. In 1784, the family moved to the expanding territory in the west to Louisville, Kentucky. They built a home called Mulberry Hill. Clark was homeschooled and enjoyed learning about nature and respect for all creation.

At the age of nineteen, Clark joined the local militia and rose to the rank of captain. In 1791, he transferred to the regular army with the rank of lieutenant, serving under General "Mad" Anthony Wayne. In 1795, Clark met and served for a brief period with Meriwether Lewis, a fellow Virginian.

Meriwether Lewis was born August 18, 1774, in Albemarle County, Virginia. They were distant neighbors to Thomas Jefferson. Lewis's father was also owner of a wealthy plantation. When his father died in 1781, his mother remarried to John Marks and moved to Georgia. While there, he enjoyed learning about nature and hunting. When his stepfather died in 1787, he returned to Virginia. In 1791, he joined the local militia, and a year later transferred to the regular army. It was there that he encountered William Clark and established a lasting friendship. In 1801, Lewis became the personal secretary to the newly elected U.S. president, Thomas Jefferson.

In 1796, Clark resigned from the army and returned to Mulberry Hill to deal with struggling family financial affairs. Clark's father died in 1799, and his mother died a year later. Although not the oldest son, Clark inherited Mulberry Hill, along with the slaves and debts. In 1803, he received a letter from his former military friend, Meriwether Lewis. Clark was offered a chance to serve as co-leader of the government-sponsored Corps of Discovery. They were to explore and document findings of the newly claimed Louisiana Purchase, from the central plains to the western coast. On February 28, 1803, Congress approved $2,500 in funds for the expedition. Clark replied to Lewis, "The enterprise &c. is Such as I have long anticipate and am much pleased.... My friend, I do assure you that no man lives whith whome I would perfir to undertake Such a Trip &c.as yourself." With President Jefferson's approval, Lewis and Clark would begin their historical trip to the west. Clark sold Mulberry Hill to one of his brothers.

The two men made preparations and training for the arduous tasks. They began to enlist expedition team members with various backgrounds and practical experiences, such as "gun repair, blacksmithing, speaking multiple languages and even tailoring." The team assembled in St. Charles, Missouri, near St. Louis. On May 21, 1804, they departed from St. Charles and followed the Missouri River to the western regions. They encountered many dangerous adventures and eventually stopped at an American Indian outpost in North Dakota. They stayed with the Mandan and Hidatsa tribes during the winter of 1804. They met a French Canadian fur trapper, Toussaint Charbonneau, and his Shoshone wife, Sacagawea. The couple was hired as interpreters by the expedition party.

In the spring of 1805, the expedition party set out west and crossed the Continental Divide. In November 1805, they made it to the coast of present-day Oregon and saw the Pacific Ocean. They established a winter headquarters named Fort Clatsop. In March 1806, the party divided and made their way back east by two different routes. Clark's party went south to explore the Yellowstone River. Lewis' party went overland north of the Mississippi River. They met up in August at the Missouri River and arrived in St. Louis on September 23, 1806. They were met by an enthusiastic crowd, many of whom assumed the expedition was lost. They had traveled for twenty-eight months and over 8,000 miles. They lost only one man in their original party. They began the challenging task of documenting and organizing their findings of the long trip. Both were generously rewarded with cash and land.

Lewis returned to Washington, D. C. with their report for the president. He was appointed by President Jefferson as the governor of the Louisiana Territory, headquartered in St. Louis. While there, Lewis had difficulty with the local political leaders but made several important contributions. He helped to establish the territory of Arkansas, the first post office in St. Louis, and ordered the construction of a road between St. Louis and New Madrid, Missouri. He also, with his own funds, helped to finance the first newspaper published west of the Mississippi River, the *St. Louis Missouri Gazette*. In the fall of 1809, Lewis left St. Louis headed for Washington, D. C. He stopped overnight at an inn at Grinder's Stand, about seventy miles southwest of Nashville, Tennessee. He was found the morning of October 11, 1809, having been shot twice. He died soon after he was found. The circumstance for his death, at the age of thirty-five, has never been discovered. He was buried nearby.

After the expedition, Clark returned to Mulberry Hill before joining Lewis in Washington, D. C. In 1808, while at Mulberry Hill, Clark married sixteen-year-old Julia Hancock. They settled in St. Louis and had five children. President Jefferson appointed Clark as Commissioner of Indian Affairs. In 1813, he was also appointed as the second governor of the Missouri territory. In 1814, Clark published the book detailing the account of the famous expedition.

The year 1820 was a difficult one for Clark. His wife, Julia, died, along with a daughter and son. Clark's campaign for the first governor of the new state of Missouri ended in defeat. He continued invaluable work as Indian Commissioner for the federal government and always sought the best advantages for the interest of the American Indians. In 1821, Clark married Harriet Kennerly Radford, a widow and Julia's cousin, and they had two children. She died in 1831.

Clark continued in his position in Indian diplomacy. He "participated in treaty negotiations, negotiated intertribal disputes, drove
squatters off of Indian lands and prevented Indians from returning
to land they had given up by treaty agreements." He also persuaded
several tribes to side with the United States against the British in military conflicts. On September 1, 1838, after a brief illness, Clark died
at the age of sixty-nine in St. Louis. Recognized as a great American
hero and leader, his funeral procession in the streets of St. Louis was
a mile long. He was buried with masonic and military honors in the
Bellefontaine Cemetery.

The contributions of Lewis and Clark to the westward expansion of
the country is invaluable. Clark's expertise in Indian affairs was also
helpful in the development. His concern for the welfare of the American Indians would not be continued by future federal leaders. The
Gateway Arch stands today to honor the site location of Lewis and
Clark's return to St. Louis. It marks the spot where westward expansion was pioneered by these two explorers who are special Missourians by choice.

Enoch H. Crowder
Edinburg
Military

He was the most influential advocate general in United States military history. He was the originator of a military draft system before World War I. He came from a very simple farm family in north central Missouri.

Enoch Henry Crowder was born on April 11, 1859, in Edinburg, Missouri. He was the second of seven children born to John and Mary Weller Crowder. His father was a farmer and veteran of the Union army in the Civil War. When he was a child, public schools were not available for the entire state. Crowder was able to attend Grand River College. He graduated at the age sixteen and began to teach at a country school. He had a strong desire for additional education but was limited due to the family financial needs. His mother suggested he take the challenging entrance exam for the U.S. Military Academy in West Point, New York. He was able to finish second out of sixteen applicants. Only the first place score would be offered an appointment. Discouraged at the lost opportunity, Crowder continued his teaching career.

There are times when fate seems to intervene in a person's life in a dramatic, life-altering way. Such was the case with Crowder in 1877, when the first place scorer for the military academy resigned his appointment and Crowder was offered the position. He entered the U.S. Military Academy that fall. The courses offered were challenging for him, but he persevered and graduated on June 10, 1881. One of his classmates described him as "a boy of moderate ability and promise, displaying no special talents or even ambition." Crowder graduated thirty-first out of fifty-four cadets in his class.

He was commissioned as a second lieutenant and assigned to the Eighth Cavalry at Fort Brown, Texas. The major work of the base was to watch out for cattle thieves. He made use of his spare time by studying for a law degree and was admitted as a licensed attorney to the Texas bar. In 1884, he was reassigned to the Jefferson Barracks in St. Louis, Missouri. He was then assigned to teach military science at the University of Missouri in Columbia. Part of the instruction required the soldierly drilling of students. He continued making use of his spare time to continue his studies in law, receiving a Bachelor of Law degree in 1886. He was promoted to First Lieutenant in July 1886. He was briefly assigned to the Eighth Cavalry in pursuit of Geronimo and the Apaches throughout the American Southwest. He then returned to the University of Missouri and continued to teach until 1889.

Crowder never married but remained close to his family. He would make occasional visits with his family while in Missouri. He would become a regular correspondent when away from the state.

He received orders to go to Fort Yates, North Dakota, to suppress an Indian uprising. He was promoted to captain and assigned to the Judge Advocate General corps in the Department of Platte in Omaha, Nebraska. He gave legal advice to department heads and investigated and prosecuted courts martial. In January 1895, he was promoted to major. In 1898, with the outbreak of the Spanish-American War, Crowder was transferred to the Philippine Islands. He served as an official judge advocate, a long awaited personal goal. He helped to create a new, impartial legal system and served as an associate justice of the Philippine Supreme Court.

In 1901, Crowder returned to the United States with the rank of colonel. He was assigned to the Judge Advocate General's Department. He became the chief of the First Division of the Army's general staff. In 1904, when war broke out between Russia and Japan, Crowder was appointed as an observer from 1904 to 1905. While overseas, he developed some health issues that remained with him the rest of his life.

In the fall of 1906, Crowder was assigned to the island of Cuba. The country had become independent after Spanish control was ceded. There was a need for a provisional government with assistance from the United States. Crowder fulfilled the need by creating a new legal system and helping to establish the country's government operations. He also supervised the national elections of 1908, to ensure adherence to the new laws. He was appointed as a delegate to the Fourth Pan-American Conference in Buenos Aires in 1910.

In 1911, Crowder was promoted to the rank of brigadier general and returned to the United States. He became the head of the U.S. Army's Judge Advocate General Corps and served in that role for the next twelve years. In his position, he became an innovator of military legal standards and operations. He updated and rewrote the Army's *Article of War* and the *Manual for Court-Martial*. He was also concerned with the condition of the military prisons.

His most famous action was his drafting of the Selective Service Act. Congress passed the legislation in May 1917. With the U.S. involvement in World War I, the act allowing the federal government to order men into military, caused much public resistance. Crowder, appointed by President Wilson as Provost Marshall General, was also responsible for administering the program. Those between the ages of twenty-one to thirty years old who opposed the country's involvement in Europe's war were subject to severe penalties for failure to register for the draft. Crowder was promoted to major general in October 1917.

His concern with the condition of soldiers is exemplified in a correspondence, dated July 13, 1918, with Major-General Leonard Wood, then commander of Camp Funston, Kansas. Crowder was expressing concern that reports of medical examiners resulted in the return home of 23.7% of all "negroes" drafted. He was seeking suggestions for helping with what he called a "deplorable situation."

For all of Crowder's contributions to the United States, he was awarded the Distinguished Service Medal. In 1921, President Wilson sent Crowder to Cuba to help settle a dispute over the country's election. He returned to the United States and served a final term as judge advocate general before his retirement from the military in 1923. He had served for forty years and received numerous awards, citations, and honorary degrees from many of the nation's top colleges and universities.

President Warren G. Harding appointed Crowder as U.S. ambassador to Cuba. He served in that role until his return to the United States in 1927. He opened a law office in Chicago but was unable to continue his private law practice due to increasingly poor health. The Great Depression also found him, with many others, losing much of his financial gain. He died from liver cancer on May 7, 1932. He was buried in Arlington National Cemetery in Washington D.C. General Douglas MacArthur, Chief of Staff of the Army, was named as an honorary pallbearer.

A World War II Army Signal Corps training center in Neosho, Missouri, was named in his honor as Camp Crowder. The Crowder State Park in Trenton, Missouri, was also named in his honor. Many Missourians are familiar with the former army camp and state park but are unfamiliar with the accomplishments of this Missourian known as one of the most influential military leaders in U.S. history.

Ulysses S. Grant
St. Louis
Military/politics

He was a failure in business, accused of being a butcher in battles, and thought to have had a serious drinking problem. He is credited with having saved the Union in the Civil War. He was a two-term president of the United States, yet he died in poverty.

Hiram Ulysses Grant was born on April 27, 1822, in Point Pleasant, Ohio. He was the first son of Jesse Root Grant and Hannah Simpson Grant. His father was a tanner and businessman. In 1823, the family moved to Georgetown, Ohio. Grant was an unassuming, shy person who developed an interest in horses. He did not desire to follow in his father's tannery business. When Grant was seventeen, his father had arranged for him to be admitted to the United States Military Academy at West Point. A clerical error listed him as Ulysses S. Grant, and he made no effort to correct the mistake. He later said the "S." stood for Simpson.

Grant was only an average student at the academy. He was noted for his poor dress and tardiness. He was not excited about the educational aspects of military life. He did well in horsemanship. In 1843, he graduated twenty-first out of his class of thirty-nine. He was obligated to serve for four years of military duty.

Grant was assigned to St. Louis, Missouri at the Jefferson Barracks. There, he met Julia Dent, his future wife. After a period of courtship, Grant proposed to her, and she accepted. Before a wedding could take place, Grant was called to duty in the Mexican-American War. He served as a quartermaster, organizing the movement of military supplies. He served under Generals Zachary Taylor and Winfield Scott. Learning from the two generals, Grant was able to lead a company into combat. During his time, Grant received two medals for bravery. He also became aware that the war was for the primary purpose of gaining territory for the expansion of slavery.

In 1848, he returned to St. Louis and married Julia. They would have four children. With the family remaining in St. Louis, Grant was assigned to various locations in the Far West. In 1852, he was sent to Fort Vancouver (present-day Washington State). While there, he became involved in several failed business ventures. Because of his business failures and missing his family, Grant began to find solace in drinking. The excess of his drinking was the disputed source of much criticism that would follow him in his military career. In 1853, Grant was promoted to captain and assigned to Fort Humboldt on the northern California coast. Conflicts with his commanding officer caused him to resign from his commission on July 31, 1854.

He returned to St. Louis. His father-in-law had generously given him sixty acres of farmland, but it proved to be unproductive for Grant. He was able to build a log cabin that he called "Hardscrabble." He tried real estate and clerking but again failed. He finally resorted to selling firewood on the streets of St. Louis to support his family. In 1859, he sold the farm. In 1860, he reluctantly moved his family to Galena, Illinois, and found employment in his father's tannery business as a store clerk.

In 1861, with the outbreak of the Civil War, Grant volunteered for military service. His past service record threatened to keep him from any command, but an intervening Illinois congressman came to his defense. Grant was assigned to command a very undisciplined Twenty-first Illinois volunteer regiment. Grant was able to get them in shape and prepared for combat by September 1861. That year, Grant was promoted to the rank of brigadier general and assigned to the District of Southeastern Missouri in Cape Girardeau, Missouri.

Grant was able to capture the small town of Paducah, Kentucky. In February 1862, with coordinated action with the U.S. Navy, Grant was able to capture Fort Henry and Fort Donelson. These strategic victories in the Mississippi River were "the earliest significant victories for Union forces in the Civil War." Grant earned the nickname "Unconditional Surrender Grant." He had written the commanders of the captured forts, "No terms except immediate and unconditional surrender. I propose to move immediately upon your works." He was promoted to the rank of lieutenant general with command over all of the armies.

In April 1862, Grant faced Confederate forces in Tennessee in the infamous Battle of Shiloh. Although Grant was victorious in the two-day battle, military leaders and some members of Congress were very critical of his high number of casualties. In December 1862, Grant faced the formidable city of Vicksburg, Mississippi. Secured on the high bluffs overlooking the Mississippi River, the fortress was difficult to capture. After long maneuvers and strategical employments, Grant laid a successful siege of the city. On July 4, 1863, the city of Vicksburg surrendered to Grant. The victory was a major boost to the Union forces and morale. Grant's tactics would become the source of much study by military strategists in the years to come.

Rumors persisted about Grant's bouts with heavy drinking. These were also confused with the accounts of his severe migraine headaches, causing temporary incapacity. In October 1863, Grant was given command of the Union forces at Chattanooga, Tennessee. In November 1863, he led successful but costly campaigns at Lookout Mountain and Missionary Ridge to force the Confederate forces into Georgia.

Grant's next objective was the destruction of General Robert E. Lee's Confederate forces. He pursued General Lee in northern Virginia with encounters resulting in the loss of thousands of Union soldiers. Lee also suffered losses of fewer soldiers but with higher percentages of loss. Grant knew that replacements were available for the Union but not for the Confederacy. Finally on April 9, 1865, Lee surrendered his remaining army to Grant at the Appomattox Courthouse in Virginia. Countering the criticisms of Grant's butchery of his soldiers, Lee and the Confederate forces were treated very humanely and with the greatest respect. They were allowed to keep their horses and return home, without being taken as prisoners. He told his troops, "The war is over. The Rebels are again our countrymen, and the best sign of rejoicing is to abstain from all demonstrations in the field."

After the war, he helped to supervise some of the difficult tasks of Reconstruction. On July 25, 1866, Congress established the new rank of "four-star general" for Grant and made him the first one in U.S. history. Grant and his wife had declined an invitation from President Lincoln to attend a play in Washington, D. C. at Ford's Theater on the night of the assassination. He was deeply saddened by the nation's great loss. Grant tried to keep apart from the political turmoil caused by President Andrew Johnson's weak leadership in Reconstruction and with the eventual impeachment process. He was encouraged by both political parties to run for president in the 1868 election. He accepted the nomination of the Republican National Convention in Chicago. He chose not to campaign and spent his time with his family in Galena, Illinois.

In 1868, he was elected as President of the United States at the age of forty-six. Although Grant was a great military leader, he was not as good in selecting his administration leaders. His term was constantly embroiled in scandals but without charges of his personal involvement.

In 1872, Grant won reelection as president. During this second term, the nation faced a great financial crisis in the panic of 1873. The panic was caused by the over speculation in railroads. Grant later stated, "It was my fortune, or misfortune, to be called to the Chief Executive without any previous political training." During his administration, he was successful in the ratification of the Fifteenth Amendment and establishing the National Parks Service. He also had his own political convictions, acknowledging, "Leave the matter of religion to the family altar, the church and private schools supported entirely by private contributions. Keep the church and state forever separate."

He was asked to consider running for a third term in 1880, but the idea was not favored. In 1877–1879, Grant and his wife made an around-the-world tour without any itinerary. Everywhere, he was welcomed by large, admiring crowds. His favorite countries were Japan and Switzerland.

Grant returned to the United States with the hopes of business success. That, again, would be a failure. He borrowed money to enter into a partnership with Ferdinand Ward in a brokerage firm. In May 1884, with initial financial setbacks, Grant was asked as a business partner for a major loan of $150,000. Grant received the loan from William Vanderbilt. A few days later, Ward embezzled all of the money, and the firm went bankrupt. Grant eventually paid back Vanderbilt by selling his war trophies and uniforms.

In September 1884, Grant was diagnosed with a progressive form of cancer of the tongue. He became increasingly disabled. He wrote articles for some financial support for his now- impoverished family. He was able to negotiate a very generous contract with his friend Mark Twain to write and publish his memoirs.

Following his doctors' advice, in June 1885, he moved his family to the cooler climate of Mt. McGregor, New York. He finished his manuscript on July 19, 1885. On July 23, 1885, Grant died at the age sixty-three with his family at his side. The Grant memoirs were very successful, selling over 300,000 copies. Julia was able to receive over $500,000 from the contract.

Grant's tomb overlooks the Hudson River in New York City. His home in Galena, Illinois, is a state memorial. Near St. Louis is Grant's farm where his original log cabin, Hardscrabble, is seen by many visitors each year. He had strong ties to Missouri, where his military career began, where he found his wife, and where he tried to succeed in business. His tactics on the battlefield were innovative and helped to keep a nation united.

Carrie Nation
Belton
Politics

She was a moralist with strong convictions from her own life experiences, many of those in Missouri. She was not satisfied with just talking about her beliefs. She put actions to her words. She was both despised and praised by many for her deeds. She would leave a legacy for future generations to evaluate.

Carrie Amelia Moore was born on November 25, 1846, in Garrard County, Kentucky. Her parents were George and Mary Campbell Moore. Her father was a successful Irish plantation and slave owner. He was uneducated and a stock trader. Her mother was a relative of the religious leader and founder of the Disciples of Christ Church, Alexander Campbell. Her mother raised six children. She also suffered from some form of mental illness, eventually convinced that she was the British Queen Victoria. The family was part of the Disciples of Christ Church. At the age of ten, Nation had a dramatic conversion experience in a tent meeting.

The family experienced several moves to Kentucky, Texas, Arkansas, Missouri, and Kansas.

In 1861, with the outbreak of the Civil War, the Moore family began to fail in their share cropping plantation efforts. They lost their slaves and the farm. The family moved to Texas in 1862, in a failed attempt to start a new business. They eventually settled in Belton, Missouri, where George found employment in real estate. When the Union Army ordered them to evacuate their High Grove farm, they moved to Kansas City, Missouri. There, Nation cared for soldiers wounded after a raid in Independence. After the war, the family returned to their farm in Belton.

In 1865, the Moores took in a boarder, Union soldier Charles Gloyd, who was a local schoolteacher and doctor. He asked Nation to marry him. Her parents objected because of their knowledge of his excessive drinking. Nation ignored the warning from her parents and married Gloyd on November 21, 1867. She was twenty-one years old at the time. They moved to Holden, Missouri. Nation was soon pregnant and discovered the truth of her parents' warning about Gloyd's drinking problems. They separated soon after a few months, and she moved back to her parent's farm. Nation gave birth to her daughter, Charlein, on September 27, 1868. Her daughter developed mental problems, which Nation attributed to Gloyd's alcoholism. Gloyd died of alcoholism in 1869. Nation and her daughter moved into Gloyd's home with his mother.

Nation sold land her father had given to her and her husband's estate. She had enough money to buy a home in Holden and began studies at the nearby Normal Institute in Warrensburg, Missouri. She earned her teaching certificate in July 1872. She taught in Holden for four years. The teaching income was not adequate to support her family, and she had conflicts with the school board. When she was fired, she met Dr. David A. Nation. He was an attorney, minister, and newspaper editor. He was also nineteen years older. They were married in 1877.

The Nations purchased a 1,700-acre cotton plantation in Brazonia County, Texas. The venture met with failure, and David was forced to practice law in Brazoria, Texas. In 1880, Nation, with her daughter and mother-in-law, moved to Columba, Missouri, to successfully operate a hotel. The family later settled in Richmond, Texas, to operate a hotel. David became caught up in the political factions of the "Jaybird-Woodpecker War." In 1889, they were forced to leave Texas and settled in Medicine Lodge, Kansas. David found work as a part-time minister in a local Christian Church. In 1892, Nation claimed to receive visions from God and was baptized in the Holy Spirit, causing her to be disfellowshipped from the church. In 1893, Nation helped establish a branch of a local Women's Christian Temperance Union (WCTU). She served as a jail evangelist, taught Sunday School, and helped the needy in the community. Her help often involved allowing the homeless to stay in their house, usually without consulting her husband. The marriage would suffer as a result. The local neighborhood was also unhappy with her practices.

In 1894, Kansas voted for prohibition of alcohol, except for medicinal purposes. It was one thing to adopt prohibition but quite another thing to enforce it. Nation expressed her dissatisfaction with the lack of enforcement by getting her WCTU friends to stand outside of the saloons praying and singing hymns—both very loudly. This proved to be ineffective and the source of ridicule by the saloon patrons.

Seeking divine guidance, Nation received her divine answer on June 5, 1900:

> 'Go to Kiowa,' and my hands were lifted and thrown down and the words, 'I'll stand by you.' The words, 'Go to Kiowa,' were spoken in a murmuring, musical tone, low and soft. But 'I'll stand by you,' was very clear, positive and emphatic. I was impressed with a great inspiration, the interpretation was very plain, it was this: Take something in your hands, and throw at these places in Kiowa and smash them.

Nation responded immediately by going to Kiowa, Kansas. She gathered some rocks and entered a saloon. She announced for all to hear, "Men, I have come to save you from a drunkard's fate." She began to use the rocks to destroy the bottles and other items in the saloon. She went to two other saloons in the town and repeated the actions. Because the saloons were considered illegal, she did not face arrest. Soon after this attack, a tornado hit Kansas, and this was perceived by her as divine approval for her actions. When asked about her actions, she told others that she was "a bulldog running along at the feet of Jesus, barking at what He doesn't like."

In December 1900, in Wichita, Kansas, she entered the Hotel Carey bar room. She began her destruction of the alcohol and also a large, racy painting of Cleopatra bathing, located above the bar. She returned the next morning with a wooden club and iron bar. She began destroying bottles, mirrors, tables, chairs, and other accessories. A local detective confronted her in one saloon and said, "Madam, I must arrest you for defacing property." Her reply was, "Defacing? I am destroying!" That would be the first of many arrests in her long crusade.

Returning home after two months in jail, her husband taunted her saying that "she should use a hatchet next time to cause more damage." She responded to him saying, "That's the most sensible thing you have said since I married you." Thus began the association of Carrie Nation and the hatchet.

Nation traveled around the local communities and repeated her actions. She was now receiving local, state, and national attention for her actions. She continued her activities around the state. In the eyes of some, she was more effective at getting enforcement of prohibition than churches or other activist groups. It is reported that "between 1900 and 1910, police arrested her more than 30 times in four states for what she now called 'hatchetations.'" Often, her fines were paid by local WCTU chapters or churches. She also began to travel around the country to major cities with her crusade against alcohol by destroying saloons and even pharmacies.

In 1901, famed journalist Dorothy Dix followed Nation to cover Nation's destructive action in Nebraska. Her husband asked her to return home. She refused, and her husband divorced her on the grounds of cruelty and desertion. They had been married for twenty-four years and had no children. She began a nationwide lecture tour to raise funds for support through her speaking fees and selling miniature plastic hatchets. She also began publication of magazines, newsletters, and pamphlets.

Nation would soon lose some support from the WCTU for her excessive sexism and personal views. She said, "Men were nicotine soaked, beer besmirched, whiskey greased, red-eyed devils." She lost significant favor with many by her public approval of the assassination of President McKinley in September 1901. She told a crowd "he secretly drank and that drinkers got what they deserved."

From 1902–1906, Nation lived in Guthrie, Oklahoma. In 1905, she published her biography, *The Use and Need of the Life of Carrie A. Nation*. That same year, Nation found it necessary to commit her daughter, Charlien, to the Texas State Lunatic Asylum. Nation continued her lecture tours to the East Coast. She made an attempt to do a lecture tour in Europe, but after being hit with an egg in Scotland, she gave up on the tour and returned to the United States.

Eventually, dealing with poor health, Nation moved to Eureka Springs, Arkansas. She set up house known as "Hatchet Hall," for her "National College." It was not a college nor did it offer any college courses, but it did provide some limited educational instruction. In January 1911, during a speech in a local city park, Nation collapsed. She was taken to the Evergreen Place Hospital, a mental health facility, in Leavenworth, Kansas. After months of care, Nation died on June 2, 1911. She was buried in Belton, Missouri in her family's burial plot. Some time later, the WCTU made a headstone for her grave. It was inscribed, "Faithful to the Cause of Prohibition, She Hath Done What She Could." In the 1950s, her home in Medicine Lodge, Kansas, was bought by the WCTU, and it was declared a U.S. National Historic Landmark in 1976.

Carrie Amelia Nation has a lasting mixed legacy as a reformer and an unstable activist. When once asked about her occupation, she replied, "Destroyer of the works of the Devil by the direct order of God." She had important life events in Missouri, and she used her innovative crusade activities to lay the groundwork for the Eighteenth Amendment some seven years after her death.

Thomas J. Pendergast
Kansas City
Politics

He never held a major elected government office but became one of the strongest political powers in Missouri. He rose from poverty to great riches. He was benevolent and treacherous in his treatment of others. He helped many Missourians to endure the financial hardship of the Great Depression.

Thomas Joseph Pendergast was born on July 22, 1872, in St. Joseph, Missouri. He was the ninth child of Michael and Mary Reidy Pendergast. They were immigrants from County Tipperary, Ireland. His father worked as a teamster. Thomas received formal education through the sixth grade. He found work in St. Joseph as a laborer, clerk, and wagon driver. He continued there until he was eighteen years old.

His older brother, James, had left St. Joseph and found work in Kansas City, Missouri. James found success in organizing political alliances in the city in the West Bottoms industrial area among the poorer working class. In the saloons bordering the Kansas border, he developed a strong political machine that provided needed services to the citizens in exchange for political favors. His influence expanded to the North End of the city. The city was divided into wards. In 1892, James was elected alderman of Kansas City's First Ward.

Two years earlier, 1890, Pendergast left St. Joseph and moved to Kansas City as a bookkeeper for James. Pendergast learned valuable lessons from his brother. He saw the good that James had done for the citizens, as well as the less honorable activities, such as financial gain through the protected vice industries. In 1894, James saw the promise and allegiance of his younger brother and appointed Pendergast as a deputy constable of the First Ward city court. In 1896, Thomas Pendergast was appointed deputy constable in the county court. In 1900, Kansas City mayor James A Reed (a supporter of James) appointed Pendergast to a two-year term as superintendent of streets. It was a powerful political position with the ability to offer lucrative city contracts in exchange for political support.

Pendergast began to have great influence beyond the city and county borders. In 1902, he was unanimously elected as a delegate to the Democratic National Convention.

That same year, James' health began to suffer, and Pendergast provided assistance for the aldermanic duties. In 1911, James died. Pendergast ran for his brother's alderman position and won the election to the city council. He began to strengthen his grip on city power but faced competition with Joseph Shannon, leader of the Ninth Ward. The two developed a "Fifty-Fifty" compromise that split control of political favors to be offered to supporters.

During this time, Pendergast appointed a young Harry S. Truman as one of the three Jackson County judges in the Eastern District. The position was more as a road contractor than anything else. The relationship between the two men remained steady over the years. Over time, the earlier compromise fell apart and the political power struggle was won by Pendergast in 1925.

Pendergast expanded his political control with appointments of powerfully obligated men. He also learned from his brother the importance of meeting the physical needs of his constituents. His machine organization helped to organize and finance food, coal, and clothing distribution to the needy residents of the First Ward. He established the practice of charitable activities, especially on holidays. The Thanksgiving and Christmas meals for the poor were legendary. It was reported, "At a typical holiday meal in 1930, more than three thousand homeless men of all races formed a line of several blocks." Many of these projects were supported by the continued profits from the protected vice industries and Pendergast-controlled business operations. The most prominent was the Ready-Mix Concrete Company. It was estimated that "Pendergast received over $30 million annually from gambling, prostitution and narcotics profits in the 1930s."

During the Great Depression, when many in the city could not find work, Pendergast created work positions to offer meaningful financial assistance to the unemployed. This strengthened the political support for his organization that was now expanding into western Missouri.

Pendergast, aware of reaching out to the growing middle class of the city, began to provide benefits for them. He controlled the city's nightlife. The nightclubs provided a home to popular jazz musicians, for which the city is known. William "Count" Basie, Bennie Moten, and Charlie "Bird" Parker all found successful careers building in the city. Pendergast also organized extravagant social events for the richer ethnic citizens excluded from the country clubs.

His influence was growing statewide in power, reaching to the Missouri governor's office. Governor Guy Brasfield Park's mansion was called "Uncle Tom's Cabin." In 1934, Pendergast was influential in the election of Harry Truman as the U.S. Senator. With support from President Franklin Roosevelt, many saw the election as an attempt for Pendergast to gain influence on a national level; history has shown that Truman maintained an honest and respectable role as senator.

Not all of Pendergast's appointees proved to be forever loyal to him and his political machine. The one proving most disastrous was the appointment of Lloyd C. Clark as governor in 1936. Clark desired the position of Truman in the U.S. Senate. He knew that to have a chance at that, he needed to discredit Pendergast.

For the next few years, Pendergast faced a barrage of criminal charges from federal prosecutors, often with Governor Clark's assistance. Evidence was discovered of the Pendergast machine's involvement in voter fraud. After a series of trials, 278 people were indicted with over 200 serving prison time. Pendergast himself was found not guilty, but the findings angered many Missourians outside of the Pendergast machine's control. President Roosevelt and Senator Truman remained at a distance from any public support of Pendergast. Further investigation led to the "Insurance Scam." A lawsuit in 1935, between the State of Missouri and private insurance companies, was settled by Pendergast's intervention for a profit of $750,000. Other findings discovered other kickbacks to Pendergast for another half a million dollars in 1936. None of the income was reported on federal income returns. Pendergast was charged with federal income tax evasion. He pleaded guilty and was sentenced to one year and three months in prison with a five-year probation period following. He also paid a $10,000 fine.

While in prison, Pendergast's machine lost some of its political power. The appointment of a former Federal Bureau of Investigation agent as chief of police and John B. Gage as mayor led to reforms. The major influence of the Pendergast machine ended by the late 1940s.

Still in his probationary period, Pendergast died from a heart attack in Kansas City on January 26, 1945. It was just a few days after the election of Harry S. Truman as vice president of the United States. Pendergast was seventy-two years old. He was buried in Forest Hills Calvary Cemetery in Kansas City.

Unfortunately, Pendergast was not the only political boss over a city machine in a major U.S. city during that time period. He was a powerful political figure for Missouri with many direct and indirect influences on state leaders. His name is forever associated with political corruption and with charitable actions. He was a unique character in Missouri history.

John J. Pershing
La Clede
Military

He was a farm boy from north central Missouri who would become the highest ranking soldier in the U.S. military since George Washington. He would leave the farm and have command of the largest military combat force in the U.S. history. His mediocre grades were in no way indicative of his brilliant combat strategies.

John Joseph Pershing was born near Laclede, Missouri, on September 13, 1860. He was the first of nine children born to John Fletcher Pershing and Ann Thompson Pershing. His father was a successful farmer, land speculator, postmaster, and owner of a general store in Laclede. His early education was in a special school for intelligent youth. In 1873, the nation experienced a great economic depression. Pershing's father lost most of his wealth and experienced the bank foreclosing on his properties. His father was forced to take a job as a traveling salesman. At the age of fourteen, Pershing, as the oldest son, was expected to keep the farm profitable while his father traveled.

Pershing kept at his farm responsibilities and was able to graduate from high school. Unable to afford a college education, Pershing accepted a teaching position on the basis of his high school diploma. In 1878, he taught at a school for African Americans in Prairie Mound, Missouri. With enough money saved, he continued his education at the State Normal School at Kirksville, Missouri in the summers. He completed the requirements for a teaching certificate and graduated in 1880. He returned to teach at Prairie Mound with the goal of returning to the State Normal School to work toward a degree in law.

In 1882, he applied for entry at West Point because of its promise to provide a free, elite, college-level education. His sister helped him to study for the rigorous, competitive entry exam. He received the highest test score among the applicants. In 1882, his acceptance led to an interest in the military and an opportunity for career advancement. He was a mediocre student and very popular with the other cadets. He was voted class president four years in a row. He graduated from West Point in 1886, ranked thirtieth out of a class of seventy-seven.

Pershing was assigned to the 6th Cavalry at Fort Bayard, New Mexico. He took part in several campaigns against the rebellious Native American Apaches and Sioux. Pershing was cited for his bravery and meritorious service. In 1887, he was transferred to Fort Stanton, where he excelled in rifle marksmanship. In 1890, he was transferred to South Dakota to put down the last of the Sioux uprisings. In 1891, Pershing accepted a position at the University of Nebraska as professor of Military Science and Tactics. Dismayed at the apathy shown by students, faculty, and community, Pershing was fighting against the "accepted recipe for army-making" by then-Secretary of State William Jennings Bryan that "a million men (would) spring to arms overnight." Pershing fought against the popular tide of thought and successfully developed an award-winning, military drill company. He also completed studies for a law degree, graduating in 1893.

In 1895, Pershing was assigned to the Tenth Cavalry, one of the first all-black "Buffalo Soldier" regiments, at Fort Assiniboine in Montana. There he again led troops rounding up renegade Creek Indians and transporting them to Canada. He became a strong spokesman for African American troops. In 1897, he was assigned to West Point as an assistant instructor in tactics. Because of his rumored strict disciplinary actions, the cadets began referring to Pershing as "Black Jack." In 1898, at the request of his superior officers, Pershing was assigned to duty in Washington, D. C., as director of the newly developed Division of Customs and Insular Affairs. After recovering from a bout of malaria, he began his duties providing military government for the new insular positions of the United States: Cuba, Puerto Rico, the Philippines, and Guam. In 1899, he was ordered to Manila in the Philippines as part of the Eighth Army Corps. For two years, Pershing participated in rounding up the insurrecting native groups. His distinguished service and actions caught the attention of his superiors, even the Secretary of War, Elihu Root. In 1901, Pershing was eventually transferred to the Fifteenth Cavalry unit in the Philippines. There, he became knowledgeable of the area and people. He learned to speak the Moro language. This aided his assignment as intelligence officer and proved successful in assisting him with responding to attacks on Camp Vicars where he was stationed. In 1903, Captain Pershing was ordered back to the United States. In Washington, D. C. Pershing met and eventually married Miss Helen Frances Warren, daughter of a Wisconsin senator, Francis E. Warren, who served as chairman of the Senate Military Affairs Committee.

In 1904, Pershing was assigned to duty in Oklahoma City as assistant chief of staff, Southwest Division. In 1905, at the request of President Theodore Roosevelt, Pershing was a military attaché to Tokyo and served as an observer of the Russo-Japanese War.

In 1906, Pershing was promoted by President Roosevelt from captain to the rank of brigadier general, over the heads of 862 more senior officers. This controversial promotion created political and military enemies, especially in light of his relationship with the Wisconsin senator. That same year, Pershing was reassigned to the Philippines at Fort McKinley near Manila. Pershing was instrumental in establishing peace with the continually rebellious Moros. He had learned their language and customs. In 1913, he was assigned to Fort Bliss, Texas, commanding the Eighth Brigade. During this time, Pershing was dispatched to Mexico to challenge the Mexican revolutionaries led by Pancho Villa. In 1915, as Pershing was preparing to bring his family to the Southwest, he received word that fire had destroyed his family home, killing his wife and three of his four children. Only his son Warren remained. After the funerals in Cheyenne, Wyoming, Pershing returned to Fort Bliss to lead the "Punitive Expedition" to capture Pancho Villa. Pershing described the frustrating mission as "a man looking for a needle in a hay stack with an armed guard standing over the stack forbidding you to look in the hay." Although the primary objective was not accomplished, Pershing's command and tactics attracted the interest of a young first lieutenant, George S. Patton.

In 1917, the United States declared war on Germany, and Pershing was ordered back to Washington, D. C. He was eventually assigned the duty of commander of the American Expeditionary Forces (AEF). While the title of the command was impressive, the reality was very different. The United States at that time had only a regular army of 25,000 men under command. There were no reserves, as such, except for the sparsely-numbered, trained men from officer's training camps of the Plattsburg Movement (established by General Leonard Wood). It was estimated that 500,000 men were needed to complete the necessary military organization. Pershing's responsibility was to establish a separate United States Army in Europe. He was also to persuade the British and French forces that the United States would not provide men to fill their military commands. It took months of recruitment and training in the United States to send men to Europe. Pershing took the responsibility for special training and involvement of the U.S. troops in European actions. The integration of the U.S. troops in the Allied war efforts brought heavy casualties but eventual victory over a two-year period.

Pershing informed the president that additional forces were needed, and the U.S. forces would swell to over two million combat soldiers in Europe. His troops were involved in the difficult and pivotal military conflicts of the war. He faced German troops in the battle of Cantigny, the Meuse-Argonne offensive, and the battle of St. Mihiel. His AEF forces succeeded in cutting off the German supply lines, forcing them to surrender.

With the Armistice signed on November 11, 1918, Pershing had commanded troop strength of over two million men. He was a returning war hero who wisely left war reconstruction activities and policies to the politicians.

Upon his return in 1919, Congress authorized the new rank of General of the Armies and promoted Pershing as the only general with that rank. The last military soldier to receive that rank was General George Washington. In 1920, some Republicans wanted Pershing as their candidate for president. He refused to campaign but offered to serve if nominated. Because of his close association with Democratic president Woodrow Wilson's policies, he did not gain strong support. In 1921, he was appointed chief of staff of the United States Army. In 1924, he retired from military service and became a private citizen. In

1932, he won the Pulitzer Prize for his memoir, *My Experiences in the World War*. He continued as a strong advocate for military preparedness for the United States. As he followed the deteriorating actions in Europe, he strongly supported the aiding of Britain in preparation for the Second World War. Pershing was able to see the United States' involvement in World War II and the eventual Allied victory in 1945.

John Joseph Pershing continued to be recognized and honored by a grateful nation. He died at Walter Reed Hospital in Washington, D. C., on July 15, 1948. Pershing was honored in a lying-in-state ceremony in the U.S. Capitol Rotunda, seen by an estimated 300,000 people. He was buried at Arlington Cemetery. During his military assignments, Pershing commanded such future leaders as fellow Missourian Harry Truman, George Patton, George Marshall, and Douglas MacArthur. He had earned the title as "one of America's most influential military leaders."

There were many tributes of honor paid to him in the United States and around the world. The Pershing missile and Pershing tank were named after him. His Laclede birthplace is a Missouri State Historic Site. In 1941, arguments were made to name the new military base near Waynesville in his honor. This great man of history came from humble Missouri beginnings.

Phyllis Schlafly
St. Louis
Activist

She was seen by some as the messenger from God to deliver America from the moral abyss. She was seen by others a messenger from a different divine source as an obstacle to women's rights. But no one could deny her ability to influence and activate her loyal, national followers from her Missouri base.

Phyllis McAlpin (Stewart) Schlafly was born on August 15, 1924, in St. Louis, Missouri, to John Bruce Stewart and Odile Dodge. Her father was a lawyer, and during the Great Depression in the 1930s, he lost his job. Her mother, a teacher with two college degrees, also worked as a librarian to provide family income. Schalfly, the oldest of two daughters, grew up in a poor family setting but was able to attend the Catholic schools in St. Louis. She began college at a very young age. She attended Maryville College of Sacred Heart and then transferred to Washington University in St. Louis. She graduated Phi Beta Kappa in just three years with a B. A. degree in 1944, at the age of nineteen. She also supported her college expenses by "working nights full-time in a World War II defense job testing explosives."

After graduation, Shlalfly went to Harvard University and earned her master's degree in political science in just one year. She took a job in Washington, D. C. with the American Enterprise Association. Unhappy with the federal government bureaucracy, she returned to St. Louis and worked as a bank researcher. She also became involved in Republican political activities. On October 20, 1949, she married John Fred Schlafly, Jr. He was from a very wealthy family and was a successful lawyer. She was twenty-four, and he was thirty-nine. They moved to home across the Mississippi River in Alton, Illinois. Her marriage into wealth would later become a target of criticism for her positions on women and marriage.

In 1952, she won the Republican primary for Congress but lost in the general election. She was an active member and leader in the Daughters of the American Revolution and a staunch anti-communist. She was a delegate to the 1956 and 1960 Republican National Conventions. She was president of the Illinois Federation of Republican Women from 1956 to 1964. She used these positions to build a strong base of contacts and support. In 1958, she and her husband started an organization to educate Catholics on the dangers of communism. In 1962, she hosted a fifteen-minute radio program, *America Wake Up*. It focused on national security was carried by twenty-five radio stations in Illinois. In 1963, she received the Woman of Achievement Award.

In 1964, she attracted attention, positively and negatively, with her book, *A Choice Not an Echo*. She challenged the traditional rigged process of selecting Republican presidential nominees by "small group of secret kingmakers from the elite East coast." Her book had a strong influence as an estimated 3.5 million copies were sold. Schlafly was a strong supporter of Senator Barry Goldwater at the 1964 Republican National Convention. With his landslide defeat to President Lyndon Johnson, Schlafly became identified with losing causes. She lost other attempts at a congressional seat in Illinois in 1967 and 1970.

From 1964 through 1976, Schlafly wrote five books on defense and nuclear policy with retired Rear Admiral Chester Ward. In 1967, she lost a heated campaign for president of the National Federation of Women. That same year, she started publishing a newsletter, *The Phyllis Schlafly Report*. It was nationally targeted to serve the interest of politically conservative women.

In 1972, Schlafly would achieve her biggest challenge on a national scale in her strong opposition to the Equal Rights Amendment (ERA). By the end of 1971, the ERA had been approved in the House of Representatives and was ratified by thirty of the required thirty-eight states for adoption. Momentum seemed for certain for approval. In February 1972, Schlafly organized "STOP-ERA." The name was an acronym for "Stop Taking Our Privileges." The volunteer organization began a strong lobbying effort in the remaining states to defeat ratification of the ERA. She became the avowed enemy of feminism. In her writings and speeches, she denounced the ERA, claiming it would "undermine traditional families, remove legal protections of wives, subject women to the military draft, remove barriers to women in combat, promote abortion on demand, open the way for homosexual marriage and require that public bathrooms be unisex." While many of the clams were unfounded, they were effective in rallying her base of supporters. Even with a deadline extension through June 1982, the ERA fell short of adoption by just three states.

Schlafly was a national voice of women on the conservative right of many issues. In 1973, with the U.S. Supreme Court decision on the legalization of abortion, the conservatives found an issue that would serve them well in future presidential races. Schlafly became a national celebrity, much in demand as a speaker and guest on numerous television and radio programs. Her volunteer organization of STOP-ERA was transformed into the new ultra-conservative organization, the Eagle Forum.

In 1978, with her husband's misgivings, she returned to Washington University in St. Louis to complete requirements for a law degree. She became a strong supporter and favorite speaker for Ronald Reagan in his run for the presidency in 1980. She wrote books and articles supporting many of Reagan's policies. She maintained her status as a very divisive and controversial political figure with her outlandish quotes. She stated, "Sex education classes are like in-home sales parties for abortions" and "The atomic bomb is a marvelous gift that was given to our country by a wise God."

In 1992, Schlalfly was confronted with a very personal family issue. It was publically announced that her son was a homosexual. Interestingly, that same year, she would be named Illinois Mother of the Year. On July 13, 1993, her husband died, and she moved to the suburbs of St. Louis.

She continued her conservative and sometimes controversial writing and speaking during the contentious, and even more divisive, political elections of the 1990s and 2000s. In 2011, she spoke out for "shotgun marriages" as the solution to unwanted pregnancies. She was also active in defeating an attempt to revive the ERA. She continued in her controversial statements, "By getting married, the woman has consented to sex, and I don't think you can call that rape." She was a strong supporter of Donald Trump's presidential ambitions. Her last book, printed after her death, was *The Conservative Case for Trump*, coauthored by Ed Martin and Brett Decker.

Phyllis Schlafly died on September 5, 2016 in St. Louis. She was survived by her six children and many grandchildren. She authored eighteen books and coauthored five other books. Her supporters said, "Phyllis Schlafly stands for everything that has made America great and for those things which will keep it that way." She was also called the "first lady of the conservative movement." Feminists said "it was her husband's wealth—he was a lawyer from a rich Illinois family—that had liberated her to politick." Liberals had to concede, "Schlafly has to be regarded as one of the two or three most important Americans of the last half of the 20th century although every idea she had was scatterbrained, dangerous and hateful."

She was a major force in American politics and still has ideological influence today. She was a Missourian who brought innovative and controversial ideas into her political activities. She was an acknowledged leader with a strong following.

Dred Scott
St. Louis
Activist

His case was fought for over twelve years in the legal system from the city of St. Louis all the way to the United States Supreme Court. His goal was personal freedom for his family in the midst of a national conflict over slavery. The results of his historic court case would be one of the sparks that ignited the War Between the States.

Dred Scott was born in 1795, in Southampton County, Virginia. He was a slave owned by Peter Blow and his wife, Elizabeth. He grew up in the slave quarters and tended to the Blows and their six children. Soon after his birth, the Blow family and their slaves moved to Huntsville, Alabama, to a cotton plantation. Scott worked for the growing family with two more children born. In 1830, unsatisfied with the farming experiences, the Blows moved the family to St. Louis, Missouri. They ran a boarding house called the Jefferson Hotel.

In 1831, Elizabeth Blow died. The next year Peter died. Before his death, Blow sold Dred Scott to Dr. John Emerson, an assistant surgeon in the army stationed at Jefferson Barracks in St. Louis. Scott would become Emerson's personal valet. On December 1, 1833, Scott traveled with Emerson to Fort Armstrong, at Rock Island, Illinois. It was the first time that Scott was living in "free" territory. He remained there for three years, serving Emerson's personal needs. On May 4, 1836, Fort Armstrong was closed, and Emerson and Scott transferred to Fort Snelling in the Wisconsin Territory on the upper Mississippi River.

At Fort Snelling, Scott met Harriet Robinson, a slave from Virginia who was fifteen years younger than Scott. Robinson's owner was Major Lawrence Talifeero, an Indian agent and a justice of the peace. In an unusual ceremony for blacks at that time, in 1836 or 1837, Scott and Harriet were officially married by her owner. Wanting to keep the couple together, Emerson was given ownership of Harriet.

In April 1838, Emerson was transferred to Fort Jesup in Louisiana. Harriet was pregnant but made the long trip south with Scott. On February 6, 1838, Emerson had married Eliza Irene Sanford. For unknown reasons, the Scott family was sent to St. Louis and then back to Fort Snelling. Their daughter, Eliza Scott, was born on the free waters on the steamer, Gipsey. They would remain there for two years. In 1840, Emerson was transferred to Florida where his medical services were needed during the Seminole War. Scott and his family were sent back to St. Louis. As was customary then, the Scotts were hired out to others while the Emersons collected their wages.

In 1843, Emerson died. His wife, Irene, assumed the Scotts as her property. She returned to St. Louis on her proslavery father's plantation. For the next three years, the Scotts again worked for other people while Irene collected their wages. On April 6, 1846, the Scotts each filed petitions for their freedom from Irene Emerson. It is very likely that they had some assistance from the children of the Blow family. The Scotts claimed that they had lived in free states and should be considered as freed slaves. Irene challenged their petition in the St. Louis Circuit Court. After numerous delays, the case was dismissed on June 30, 1847, due to a technicality. Irene immediately got approval for the Scotts to be placed in the custody of the local sheriff. He would be responsible for hiring out the Scotts and collecting and keeping their wages. After additional delays, on January 12, 1850, the case was heard, and the jury of twelve white men ruled in favor of the Scotts, granting their request for freedom. But while the case was on appeal to Missouri Supreme Court, the Scotts remained in the custody of the sheriff.

Irene Emerson moved to Springfield, Massachusetts, and married Dr. Calvin Chaffee, an antislavery congressman. He was not aware at that time of Irene's court battle to maintain custody of the Scotts. On

March 22, 1852, the Missouri Supreme Court, in a 2–1 decision, reversed the earlier ruling, keeping the Scotts in slavery. With help of the Blow family, the decision was appealed to the United States Supreme Court. The Blows used their influence and contacts to hire attorney Roswell Field, a well-known lawyer in Washington, D.C. He enlisted Montgomery Blair, a prominent Missouri national politician, to present the Scott's case before the Supreme Court. The case was heard during the national controversy over the slavery issue with political and economic interests in the outcome. Seven of the nine Supreme Court justices were appointed by pro-slavery presidents from the South. Five of those were from slave-holding families. On March 6, 1857, the Supreme Court ruled against the Scotts in the landmark case. Chief Justice Roger B. Taney, presenting the majority opinion, ruled that Scott, "because of his race was not a citizen of the United States. He had no right to bring suit in a federal court." The entire Scott family, including the children, were to remain in slavery under the ownership of Irene Emerson Chaffee.

The court's decision added to the growing division among the states and the U.S. Congress. Because of Dr. Chaffee's political position, the decision was too controversial to be allowed to stand. Shortly after the decision was announced, Dr. and Mrs. Chaffee transferred their ownership of the Scotts to Taylor Blow in St. Louis. Chaffee was relieved to release the Scotts from their possession, but Irene would only agree if she was able to collect her declared eight years of back wages from the Scotts of about $750.

On May 26, 1857, the Scotts received their emancipation from papers drawn up by Taylor Blow. Judge Alexander Hamilton, of the St. Louis Circuit Court, was the judge who originally declared their freedom seven years earlier. The Scotts were celebrities in St. Louis from the national attention given to their Supreme Court case. Following their freedom, Scott worked as a porter at Barnum's Hotel in St. Louis. At their home on Carr Street, Harriet took in laundry.

Only a year after gaining his freedom, Dred Scott died on September 17, 1858, from tuberculosis. Taylor Blow had Scott buried in the Wesleyan Cemetery at Grand and Laclede avenues. After that cemetery became abandoned, Blow had him reburied in Calvary Cemetery in North St. Louis. His headstone marker reads, "In Memory Of A Simple Man Who Wanted to Be Free." Harriet survived Scott by eighteen years. She died on June 17, 1876, and was buried in Section C of Greenwood Cemetery in St. Louis County in Hillsdale, Missouri. She was able to experience President Lincoln's emancipation of all slaves in the United States.

Harry S Truman
Lamar/Independence
Politics

One of the most familiar and significant Missourians, whose influence transcended all national boundaries, held only a high school diploma. He was a reluctant farmer and failed businessman whose rise in politics led him to become the most powerful military leader in the world. His thick glasses, which he had to wear since childhood, did not hinder his ability to see human needs and develop international programs to meet those needs. He was an idealistic supporter defending the spread of democracy around the world.

Harry S. Truman was born May 8, 1884, to John and Margaret Truman, in Lamar, Missouri. He was the first of three children. Many myths have been created regarding his middle initial. The reality was simple. His parents thought he needed a middle initial. The respected grandparents were named Solomon and Shippe. Not wanting to offend either one, they simply gave him the middle initial "S" without any period. Later in his political life, he was confronted by English scholars who chided him for the lack of a period after his middle initial. They told him it was a poor example for children in school. He was then willing to add a period after his middle initial.

His father was a livestock trader who struggled to make a modest living for his family. His mother was an industrious housewife with a strong appreciation for the arts and a strong dedication to the Christian faith. After he was born, the family moved to Harrisonville, Missouri, and then moved again to Belton. In 1887, they finally settled on his grandfather's farm in Grandview, Missouri. Truman grew up a "momma's boy" but struggled to gain the respect of his father. He learned to read from his mother by using the family Bible but had difficulty reading the fine print. His mother took him to an eye doctor in Kansas City who discovered that Truman had what he called "flattenned eyeballs." He prescribed expensive eyeglasses with very thick lenses. This seemed to change Truman's world. The fear of breaking the glasses prevented him from participating in rough boyhood activities in his neighborhood.

When Truman was six years old, the family moved to Independence, Missouri, so he could attend a regular school. It was said that he read every book in the Independence Public Library. He also became a good musician. He would get up twice a week at 5:00 a.m. to practice piano.

Truman grew up with experiences in both the Baptist and Presbyterian churches. He identified himself as a "lightfoot Baptist." His dedication and active membership did not appear to be very strong. Truman would be inclined to remain happily removed from denominational practice and politics.

As a young man, Truman worked in the fields and with the farm animals. He experienced the joys of a good harvest and the devastation of cruel weather-related failures. He became aware of the dependency on agricultural production and the great economic challenges facing farm families. Truman grew up knowing the hard labor and risks of working the land.

In his home and at high school, reading was promoted. He had access to great literary works. In 1901, Truman graduated from Independence High School.

Truman continued to be self educated and never lost his thirst for learning. His poor eyesight caused limitation in the normal physical pursuits of other youth but allowed him to explore the world of literary and artistic appreciation. Even with limitations due to the demands of the farm, his eyesight, and family finances, Truman never lost sight of his personal dreams. When his eyesight prevented him from achieving an education at West Point, he continued in the pursuit of serving his country through the military. He was able to join a local national guard unit that had lower qualifications for eyesight.

After high school graduation, Truman would become involved in additional jobs away from the farm to assist with the limited family income. He experienced early employment as a drug store custodian, mailroom clerk, and railroad construction crew timekeeper, as well as various positions in the banking business. Unhappy with business life and the family needing his help, in 1906, Truman returned to the family farm in Grandview. He would work there for the next eleven years.

Although Truman worked hard on the family farm, he was constantly drawn to other areas of interest. He found limited success in his non-agricultural, business ventures. There may have been another interest drawing Truman away from the family farm—his growing attraction to Bess Wallace. At those times when Truman seemed to be settled comfortably in business ventures, the family farm demanded his attention. Crop failures, family illnesses, and deaths seemed to keep drawing Truman back to the farm. He would be in his late thirties before he was finally able to escape the demands of the farm and live an independent life.

Even when Bess's family disapproved of her interest in Truman— she was thought to be marrying down—he never lost sight of his dream regarding their relationship. When Truman experienced failure in business interests in Oklahoma and Kansas City, he continued his dream for success. That sense of keeping the dreams in spite of obstacles would carry him throughout his life, even in the presidency.

As World War I began and the nation prepared for combat, National Guard units were transformed into the mobilized armed services. Truman was able to sneak his way into the military ranks. He completed his military training at Camp Doniphan at Fort Sill in Lawton, Oklahoma. He eventually commanded the Battery D of the Second Battalion, 129th Field Artillery that saw fierce action in France. Before the war, he had proposed to Bess Wallace but did not receive her positive response. After the war, Truman was promoted to colonel in the Army Reserves. He also made a second marriage proposal to Bess Wallace, which she accepted. They were married in Independence on June 28, 1919. They would have one daughter, Mary Margaret.

Joining with an army buddy, Truman opened a haberdashery store in downtown Kansas City. After several years of success, the store faced the national economic crisis of 1921. The store closed with remaining debts that Truman paid in full by 1934. Another army buddy, who admired Truman's ability to bring into line an undisciplined army command, recommended Truman for a political position in Jackson County. In 1922, the local party machine boss, Thomas Pendergast, made him judge of the County Court of the eastern district of Jackson County. The position was more administrative than judicial. He lost an election in 1924, due to his opposition of the Ku Klux Klan. In 1926, he was made the presiding judge for the court. He led a significant program with a Ten Year Plan that aided in expanding the city's economy and increased his popularity. He had also established a reputation for honesty and efficiency.

His rise to national prominence came in 1934, when he ran for the U.S. Senate. Successful in his campaign with strong Democratic support, Truman became an outspoken proponent fighting against corporate greed and its influence over national policies. He played a significant role in the passage of the Civil Aeronautics Act of 1938 and the Transportation Act of 1940. In 1940, he narrowly won reelection as U.S. Senator, influenced in some degree by his election as Grand Master of the Missouri Grand Lodge of Freemasonry in September 1940.

After reelection, Truman was appointed chairman of the important Senate Special Committee to Investigate the National Defense Program. As the country was preparing for aid and entry into World War II, defense contractors were under criticism for overpricing inferior military supplies. Truman became personally involved with site visits to military camps being constructed, and it is estimated that the committee's actions saved the nation more than fifteen billion dollars and many lives.

In the 1944 presidential campaign, the Democratic party and President Franklin Roosevelt reached a compromise on his running mate. Truman was recommended, and he reluctantly accepted the position. On January 20, 1945, he was sworn in as vice president. As with other former vice presidents, Truman was not involved in the details of national or foreign policies. Eighty-two days after his election, President Roosevelt died in Warm Springs, Georgia. On April 12, 1945, a stunned nation watched a nervous Truman being sworn in as the thirty-third President of the United States. In 1945, Truman was named *Time* magazine's Man of the Year.

During Truman's first term, he was supported by Roosevelt's cabinet and political leaders. He was committed to completing many of Roosevelt's "New Deal's" immediate and long term goals. The first challenge was bringing World War II to a successful conclusion. With the Allies now in control in Europe and winning decisive battles in the Pacific, decisions had to be made about peace and the war's aftermath. In Europe, justice was needed for the war atrocities of the Germans and support for the war refugees. In the Pacific, crucial decisions had to be made regarding Japanese surrender. With the Japanese tradition of no surrender, drastic measures had to be taken to save as many lives as possible. It had been estimated that over half a million men would be lost in trying the invade the Japanese islands. Truman had not been made aware of the prior creation of an atomic bomb. But when he faced the options, he confidently made his decision to use its force. He later said, "Think of the kids that won't be killed! That's the important thing." It took two demonstrations of this powerful weapon, but the Japanese finally surrendered and the long and devastating war was over. British Prime Minister Winston Churchill said of Truman, "You, more than any other man, have saved Western Civilization."

There were also serious problems on the domestic front. The transfer from a war economy to a peacetime economy created many conflicts for business leaders and labor. Debilitating national strikes threatened the stability of the national economy. Truman acted decisively with some successes and some setbacks. The employment of the vast number of returning veterans was also faced with decisive action through the GI Bill and hiring incentives.

The new Cold War era presented unique challenges for Truman. He was able to follow through on Roosevelt's plan for the United Nations and creation of the Central Intelligence Agency, the North Atlantic Treaty Organization and the National Seciurty Council. Truman also dealt with the modernizing of the military structure and issued four unpopular civil rights executive orders, including integration of the military. In addition, he presented his own economic plan he called the "Fair Deal."

With all of these responsibilities, Truman now faced a decision about his own political future. He had a public approval rating of only 36%. Assured by many of his inevitable defeat, Truman plotted out his own campaign strategy by going directly to the people. He began his famous "whistle stop" campaign across the country. It proved an effective campaign tactic that would be copied later by other candidates. He won reelection and was sworn in on January 20, 1949. His second inauguration speech was the first one to be televised to the nation.

With Truman's surprising election victory in 1948, all areas of national politics were caught off guard. It was also a time of change within the administration's organizational structure. The international situation was challenging because of human suffering in war-ravaged countries. Communist aggression was also of paramount concern to the free world leadership. This would lead Truman to create his most innovative concept in his second administration.

The U.S. State Department was undergoing change with General Marshall's declining health. Truman's Budget Bureau Director, James Webb, was moved to the State Department as undersecretary of state. Truman wanted his 1949 Inaugural Address to send a message of international immediate concern and help. As president, Truman had seen firsthand the ravages of war in Europe. He made a point to tour a destroyed Germany at the Potsdam Conference. With State Department infighting trying to protect existing but inadequate programs, there was very little assistance in trying to meet Truman's proposed international policies. Inclusion of the fourth point in Truman's 1949 inaugural address came about with secretive and dedicated assistance from Benjamin Hardy. After the 1949 inaugural address, there were strong favorable reactions, especially to the fourth point. Truman now had the monumental task of getting the program operable. It needed to be approved in Congress, accepted in the State Department, and adequately funded and staffed.

He sidestepped the State Department for his new Point Four international program, and appointed Dr. Henry Garland Bennett, president of Oklahoma A & M College, to be the new director in late 1950. Bennett had been very successful in leading his school to provide technical assistance programs in various countries.

Truman's attitude toward the State Department was best communicated to his former business partner, David Morgan, in a letter dated January 28, 1952:

> The State Department is a peculiar organization, made up principally of extremely bright people who made tremendous

college marks but who had very little association with actual people down to the ground. They are clannish and snooty and sometimes I feel like firing the whole bunch but it requires a tremendous amount of education to accomplish the purposes for which the State Department is set up. In a great many key places I have men of common sense and we are improving the situation right along.

The present Secretary of State is one of the best that has ever been in office, but on lower levels we still have the career men who have been taken out of college without any experience with the common people.

As Bennett began his leadership in developing this bold new program, he traveled widely, becoming very much a hands-on director. He evaluated needs, national leadership, and necessary personnel. After his travels, he often returned to Washington, D. C., to consult with key leaders. He met with Oklahoma Senator Robert S. Kerr, State Department personnel and with Truman.

Truman was facing tremendous opposition at home from a number of sources. On April 10, 1951, Truman fired General Douglas MacArthur from his Far Eastern military command. At that time, the national polls indicated a 69% approval for MacArthur. At the same time, Joseph MacCarthy was publicly attacking Truman administration officials as being part of a communist conspiracy. The Korean War was going badly with great loss of American soldiers, as well as loss of support at home.

Personally, Truman was also facing great pressures. On November 1, 1950, two Puerto Rican nationalists attempted to assassinate Truman outside of the Blair house. On December 5, 1950, Truman's longtime friend, Charlie Ross, advisor and press secretary, died at his White House desk. When Truman made the announcement, he broke down and was left in tears. That same evening he and Bess attended daughter Margaret's concert at Constitution Hall. The next day, *Washington Post* music critic Paul Hume panned the performance and later received a harsh letter of attack from Truman. Other great losses for Truman were the deaths of Henry Bennett and Benjamin Hardy on December 22, 1951. His public response was personal and emotional. He knew that besides the loss of valued friendships was the loss of effective leadership for his promising international assistance program. Another aspect of the tragedy was losing the continuing effectiveness of fulfilling the international humanitarian dreams of Truman, Bennett, and Hardy. Truman would realize that he alone could not fulfill these dreams—it took a cooperative effort and talents of committed leaders.

In 1952, Truman faced the decision whether to run for a third term. Although a new constitutional admendment prevented any future president to have the opportunity for a third term, Truman was still eligible. With further declining poll popularity and the absolute reluctance of his family to continue living in Washington, D. C., Truman decided not to run. In January 1953, he returned home, personally driving himself and his family, to Independence, Missouri. For the next twenty years, he enjoyed his new status as "Mr. Citizen."

He continued to lead a very productive life. He was offered substantial pay for product endorsements but refused the offers, stating that "the presidency was not for sale." He certainly needed the additional income, as his only income source was a World War I officer's pension. There was no presidential retirement salary offered then. He wrote his memoirs, served as advisor to the Democratic party, and received many honors. In 1953, he received awards from the Four Freedoms Foundation, the Sidney Hillman Foundation, and the American Jewish Congress. On May 29, 1964, the "premiere of Greece unveiled a 12-foot golden statue of Truman at Athens as a measure of thanks for the aid program Truman had offered in 1949." On his 80th birthday on May 8, 1965, he was honored at a luncheon in Kansas City in which leaders from around the nation world sent checks, used to establish a chair of history in his name at the Westminster College in Fulton, Missouri. On July 30, 1965, Truman was honored by President Lyndon Johnson coming to Independence. In Truman's new presidential library, Johnson signed into law the new Medicare bill. Truman had proposed such a bill when he was president. Johnson said, "It was really Harry Truman of Missouri who planted the seeds of compassion and duty which have flowered into care for the sick and serenity of the fearful."

On December 20, 1972, Harry S. Truman died in the Kansas City Medical Center and Research Hospital at the age of eighty-eight. His wife, Bess, died in 1982 and was buried next to her husband in the center courtyard of the Truman Presidential Library in Independence, Missouri.

People who knew Truman wrote of his dreams and unselfish desires to help all peoples of the world. Ken Hechler, an administrative aid in Truman White House office, noted, "If I had to pick Mr. Truman's one trait that made me proudest of all to work for him, it was that he never lost the common touch and was determined to use the awesome power of the president to help bring peace and justice to average people all over the world." The day after Truman died, Mary McGrory, wrote a tribute to him in the *Washington Star*. She wrote that "He was not a hero or a magician or a chess player, or an obsession. He was a certifiable member of the human race, direct, fallible, and unexpectedly wise when it counted." She continued:

> He did not require to be loved. He did not expect to be followed blindly. Congressional opposition never struck him as subversive, nor did he regard his critics as traitors. He never whined.
>
> He walked around Washington every morning—it was safe then. He met frequently with reporters as a matter of course, and did not blame them for his failures. He did not use the office as a club or a shield, or a hiding place. He worked at it. . . . He said he lived by the Bible and history. So armed, he proved that the ordinary American is capable of grandeur. And that a President can be a human being....

Many years after Truman's death, other authors would rediscover the dreams and impact of this great man. David McCullough, in his wonderful biography of Truman, summarized that—

> Ambitious by nature, he was never torn by ambition, never tried to appear as something he was not. He stood for common sense, common decency. He spoke the common tongue. As much as any president since Lincoln, he brought to the highest office the language and values of the common American people. He held to the old guidelines: work hard, do your best, speak the truth, assume no airs, trust in God, have no fear. Yet he was not and had never been a simple, ordinary man.... He was the kind of president the founding fathers had in mind for the country.

Robert Ferrell, in his biography of Truman, concluded in similar expressions that—

Harry Truman was a farm-boy President who had come up the hard way through the army and through years as a local official.... he had a reserve of salty language, and a ready wit. He could say things that were too quotable. Sophisticates saw him as gauche and uninstructed; they were embarrassed by a President who would play the piano in public—and so obviously enjoy himself. Now his owlish spectacles and rumpled suits, his simple habits and fatherly pride, his passion for history, his pungent humor, his love for Bess all are part of a charm that reminds us that a good President and a good person can be one.

When Truman left office in 1953, he was ranked one of the lowest approval percentages ever. Today, in every list ranking the American presidents in order of importance and quality, Truman is nearly always ranked in the top ten. He was content to let history record his place and the significance of his decisions as president. In the year 2000, a C-Span Poll ranking of all U.S. Presidents was conducted by fifty-eight historians and scholars, Harry S. Truman ranked fifth behind Lincoln, Franklin D. Roosevelt, Washington, and Theodore Roosevelt.

His decisions as president were certainly significant: commanding and ending a world war, dropping the first and second atomic bombs, maintaining a war and peace-time national economy, saving a starving Europe from destruction, stopping communist aggression in Europe, supporting a United Nations organization, commanding a war in Korea, organizing a technical assistance program to help underdeveloped countries of the world, defending his administration leaders of false charges, integrating the American armed services, and just ignoring public opinion polls and doing what he felt was right.

Truman found deep roots in the land, the common people and a higher purpose for existence than personal wealth or power. He loved his country and all its citizens. He had great dreams for the peoples of the world—especially the suffering and uneducated. He found avenues for the practical application of his dreams. Missouri will always be associated with Harry Truman.

Other Missouri Innovators in Politics and Military

William T. Anderson • *Huntsville* • military
John Ashcroft • *Springfield* • politics
Enoch Crowder • *Edinburg* • military
John C. Fremont • *St. Louis* • military/politics
William Fulbright • *Sumner* • politics
Dick Gregory • *St. Louis* • comedian/activist
Tim Kaine • *Kansas City* • politics
Rush Limbaugh • *Cape Girardeau* • commentator
Sterling Price • *Keytesville* • military
Ike Skelton • *Lexington* • politics
Maxwell Taylor • *Kansas City* • military
Jim Webb • *St. Joseph* • politics
Roy Wilkins • *St. Louis* • activist
George Allison Whiteman • *Longwood* • military

Chapter Seven

Sports

Henry Armstrong
St. Louis
Boxing

He was the only boxer to hold world titles in three weight classes simultaneously. He was a small man with a history of being bullied because of his size. He came from a very poor family, accumulated great wealth, and lost it later in his life. He was born out of state but had his childhood, youth, and education experiences in Missouri.

Henry Jackson, Jr., was born on December 12, 1912, in Columbus, Mississippi. He was the eleventh of fifteen children born to Henry Jackson and America Jackson. His father was a mix of American Indian, Irish, and black heritage. He was a sharecropper and a butcher. Henry Jr.'s mother was half-Cherokee Indian. When Jackson was four years old, the family moved to St. Louis, Missouri. His father found work at the Independent Meat Packing Company. His older brothers also found work there. A year later, in 1918, his mother died, and Jackson was left under the care of his paternal grandmother at the age of five. She had hopes that he would consider a career in the ministry, but Jackson was too much of a free spirit for such a discipline.

He attended L'Overture Grammar School in St. Louis. He was nicknamed "Red" by his classmates because of his hair color. He had to learn how to defend himself from the bullying and taunting of his classmates. In spite of this, Jackson was a good student and earned good grades.

Jackson attended Vashon High School in St. Louis. He was elected class president. He found work outside of school shining shoes and also as a pinboy in a bowling alley to help support his family. He also is reported to having run the eight miles to school, improving his athletic abilities. Another side of Jackson was demonstrated when, as valedictorian, he read an original poem at his graduation ceremony. He graduated at the age of seventeen.

His father's health was failing, and Jackson was needed to supply additional family income. He lied about his age, claiming he was twenty-one years old, and got a job working as a section hand on the Missouri Pacific Railroad. Considering his own future, Jackson found a discarded newspaper and read about a boxer named Kid Chocolate who had earned $75,000 for just one bout. That was the motivation that Jackson needed to change the course of his life.

He met a local former boxer, Harry Armstrong, who became his friend and mentor. Receiving training much needed, Jackson adopted the name Melody Armstrong. In 1929, he competed in his first amateur fight in St. Louis at the Coliseum. He won his bout with a knockout in the second round. Confident of his ability, he tried competing in professional bouts in other cities with only moderate success.

In 1931, Jackson and Armstrong left St. Louis on freight trains and traveled to California. He was introduced to fight manager, Tom Cox, and introduced himself as Harry Armstrong's brother, Henry. He became known afterward as Henry Armstrong. He signed a contract with Cox for three dollars. For the next year, Armstrong fought over 100 bouts, winning most by knockouts and losing none. He narrowly lost the opportunity to represent the United States in the 1936 Olympics in Berlin. In 1932, Cox sold the contract to Wirt Ross for $250. The Great Depression era produced small winnings for a fighter, and Armstrong supplemented his income by operating his shoeshine stand from 1931 to 1934. He began to earn a reputation as a unique "whirlwind" boxer, with titles such as Homicide Hank, Perpetual Motion, and Hurricane Henry.

In 1934, Armstrong met and married Willa Mae Shony. They had one daughter, Lanetta. The marriage soon ended in divorce. Armstrong would attempt a successful marriage several other times.

In 1936, Armstrong won the local featherweight championship. Watching the fight was the famous singer Al Jolson. Jolson convinced New York manager Eddie Mead to take on Armstrong. Jolson paid the $5,000 for the contract, with assistance from actor George Raft. Immediately, the management team of three set out to win the three world weight titles.

Armstrong did not disappoint them. On October 29, 1937, he defeated Petey Sarron and won the featherweight world championship title. On May 30, 1938, he defeated Barney Ross for the welterweight world championship title. Armstrong was outweighed but dominated the fight. He said, "I carried him the last four rounds. I was asked to do it, and he thanked me." On August 17, 1938, he defeated Lou Ambers and won the lightweight world championship title. It was a brutal fight for Armstrong, with a loss of Armstrong's blood that nearly stopped the fight. Armstrong actually tried for a fourth title, middleweight, on March 1, 1940, but lost in a controversial decision.

Armstrong struggled to maintain his championships but would eventually lose them within a year. Holding three different weight titles at the same time is still an accomplishment unmatched by any other boxer. He took off for sixteen months and traveled to China, Burma, and India with George Raft as a member of a troupe to entertain the soldiers. Returning to the United States, he tried unsuccessfully for a comeback. After several more years of moderate success, he announced his retirement in 1945, at the age of thirty-two. It is estimated that Armstrong had earned as much as one million dollars in winnings. But by the time of his retirement, most of it was squandered. Armstrong was also facing a personal fight with alcoholism.

He tried his hand as a boxing manager, but his growing addiction to alcohol led to his arrest in Los Angeles. In 1949, Armstrong, at the depth of despair, experienced a profound religious conversion. He turned his life around, and he was ordained as a Baptist minister in the Morning Star Baptist Church in Los Angeles in 1951. He had fulfilled the early desire of his paternal grandmother. His preaching was dynamic, attracting large crowds. He turned his attention to helping at-risk youth. He established the local Henry Armstrong Youth Foundation. Two books were written to help finance the organization, *Twenty Years of Poem, Moods, and Meditations* in 1954, and in 1956, *Gloves, Glory, and God.*

In 1972, Armstrong returned to St. Louis. He established the Henry Armstrong Youth Foundation and also directed the Herbert Hoover Boys Club. He also served as assistant pastor of the First Baptist Church.

With failing health and suffering from early dementia, Armstrong returned to Los Angeles in 1980. The famous boxer was now financially dependent on his $800 monthly social security income. On October 22, 1988, he died in Los Angeles at the age of seventy-five. He was survived by his wife, Gussie; one daughter; and one grandson.

In 1990, he was inducted into the Boxing Hall of Fame. His record was listed as 151 wins (97 knockouts), 21 losses, and 9 draws. He is considered one of the three best boxers of all time, along with Jack Dempsey and Joe Louis.

Yogi Berra
St. Louis
Baseball

"It ain't over 'til it's over" and other malapropisms are attributed to this most unique sportsman from Missouri. He came from an Italian immigrant family and was the most popular player in America's greatest pastime. His professional accomplishments were as innovative as his name.

Lawrence Peter Berra was born on May 12, 1925, in St. Louis, Missouri. His parents had emigrated from Italy to an Italian-American community in south St. Louis known as "The Hill." He was the fourth of five children born to Pietro and Paolina Berra. His father was a worker in a brickyard. The family lived across the street from the Garagiola family. Their father worked with Berra's father in the same brickyard. Berra became lifelong friends with the Garagiola's son, Joe. The entire neighborhood youth enjoyed playing baseball on a nearby vacant lot. The neighborhood formed a YMCA team called "The Stags." On Saturdays, local sponsors took the boys to see the St. Louis Cardinals play ball. The Cardinal team, known as "The Gashouse Gang," won the World Series in 1934.

Berra's older brothers were so enthused with baseball that they wanted to pursue it as a career. This desire was quickly denied by their father, who required the older sons to get jobs to help with the family income.

Berra attended Wade Grammar School and South Side Catholic School in St. Louis. He had little interest in academics and quit school in the eighth grade. He went to work immediately to help with family finances. He worked at a series of jobs in a coal yard, drove a delivery truck, and pulled tacks in a shoe factory. He was unable to stay at any job very long because of absences due to playing baseball. Berra developed an unusual stance of squatting with his arms folded, causing a childhood friend to say he looked like Yoga, a Hindu holy man. He was stuck from then on with the nickname "Yogi."

When Berra was fourteen, he began playing left field for the Stockham Post American Legion Junior team. He developed his fielding and batting skills. His brothers convinced their father that Berra was capable of pursuing a career in baseball. In 1942, Berra and his friend, Joe Garagiola, both tried out for the St. Louis Cardinals. Both were offered contracts, with Garagiola offered a signing bonus of $500. Berra was offered a signing bonus of only $250. Deeply offended, Berra turned down the contract offer. Looking at other baseball teams, Berra signed a contract with the New York Yankees in 1943. He did get a signing bonus of $500. He began playing for the Norfolk Virginia Tars and eventually traded up to the Yankee's Kansas City farm club.

In 1943, at the age of eighteen, Berra did not report to Kansas City because he was drafted into the U.S. Navy. He trained as a gunner. He saw heavy action in World War II in North Africa and in the D-Day invasion of France. As a Seaman First Class on the Coast Guard transport *Bayfield*, he fired rockets and machine guns from a small landing craft for the fifteen-day operations. He was transferred to a naval base in Groton, Connecticut. While there, he joined a baseball squad and played against semi-professional baseball teams. He displayed unusual skills, especially in batting, catching the attention of professional baseball scouts.

After his military duties were completed on May 6, 1946, the New York Giants offered the Yankees $50,000 for his contract. Their offer was denied. Berra began playing on the Yankee farm team in New Jersey. His hitting was so good that he was called up to play for the Yankees. He played his first major league game on September 22, 1946. He hit a home run at his first time at bat and another in his second game. Berra had a habit of swinging at all pitches, including bad ones. He was able to hit those pitches and seldom struck out. He rotated with the catching staff and had a very successful first full year with eleven home runs and fifty-four runs batted in (RBIs). In the 1947 World Series, with the Yankees against the Brooklyn Dodgers, Berra became the first player to hit a pinch-hit home run in a postseason major league game.

1948 was an important year for Berra's career. The New York Yankees hired Casey Stengel as manager. Sensing Berra's needs in fielding as a catcher, Stengel brought in former catcher, Bill Dickey, to help Berra. Berra was able to improve his skills in fielding and throwing. He also improved on calling for the right pitches in game situations. Berra developed a common practice of constant conversation with opposing batters, often disrupting their concentration. Ted Williams was the only player to ever tell him to shut up (which he never did). His friend Joe Garagiola tells the story of Berra's encounter at bat with Hank Aaron: "When Aaron came up to bat, Berra noticed that the trademark on the bat was facing the pitcher. 'Henry,' Berra said, 'you don't want to break your bat. Better turn it around, so you can read the trademark.' Aaron replied, 'I didn't come up here to read.'" Berra's improvements in catching found him selected for the first of fifteen consecutive All-Star games.

In his personal life, 1948 was also an important year. At a St. Louis steakhouse, he met a young woman from Salem, Missouri, named Carmen Short. The two became immediate friends and were married on January 26, 1949, at St. Ambrose Catholic Church on the Hill. They set up housekeeping there until resettling in New Jersey in 1951. They had three sons.

The 1949 season saw the growing strength of the Yankees. That year they would win a string of five straight World Series victories until 1953. Berra's contributions were significant. He led the Yankees in RBIs for seven straight years. For five years, he had more home runs than strikeouts. In 1950, he became one of four catchers to have an error-free season. In 1951, he won the Most Valuable Player award (MVP). In 1952, Berra hit a career-record thirty home runs. In 1954, Berra drove in a career high 125 runs and won his second MVP award. 1956 was a banner year for Berra. He not only helped the Yankees to win another World Series, but he also called the only perfect game for pitcher Don Larson. He recalled, "You knew that he was pitching a no-hitter, but the game was so close you couldn't worry about anything but winning the game."

The physical toll on Berra was beginning to affect his ability as a catcher and he was moved to starting in the outfield. He helped his replacement catcher, Elston Howard, (the first African American to play for the Yankees) who was also from St. Louis. The early 1960s found Berra considering retirement as a player. In 1963, he officially retired as a player, leaving behind a very unique legacy. Over seventeen seasons, he played in fourteen World Series, winning ten of those. He holds the "World Series record for most games (75), at-bats (259), hits (71) ... and is third for most home runs (12) behind Babe Ruth and Mickey Mantle."

In 1964, Berra took over as the manager for the New York Yankees. He led the team to a World Series championship. After being defeated by the St. Louis Cardinals in the seventh game, Berra was fired as manager. He then became the assistant manager for the cross-town rival, the New York Mets under manager Casey Stengel. He was a player-coach and became the manager of the Mets in 1972, replacing ailing Gil Hodges. He led the Mets to a World Series championship, becoming one of only a few managers to have championship teams from the American and National Leagues. He was inducted into the Baseball Hall of Fame in 1972. His new three-year contract with the Mets ended early in 1975 when he quit because of management problems, not of his doing.

In 1976, he returned to the Yankees as a coach. The team would win two more championships in 1977 and 1978. Berra turned down two offers from controversial team owner George Steinbrenner. After equally controversial manager Billy Martin was fired, Berra agreed to take over as manager in 1985. His son Dale had become a part of the Yankees' team. He had had his own confrontations with Steinbrenner as a coach, and his time as manager was cut short after a poor early team record. When Berra was fired in the early season, he was able to take his first summer vacation in forty-three years.

After his harsh experience with George Steinbrenner, Berra vowed never to return to Yankee stadium. In 1986, Berra accepted the position as a bench coach with the Houston Astros. He served admirably for seven years. He was described as "a breath of fresh air ... a relief from the lies and the posturing and the greed of today's sports." He officially retired from baseball in 1992. His career in baseball spanned forty-six years, with twenty-nine of those coaching.

He devoted much of his retirement years to pursuits of philanthropy. In 1996, he received an honorary doctorate degree from Montclair University. Two years later, at the university, Berra established the Yogi Berra

Museum and Learning Center. A baseball stadium was also named after him. To support his programs, he continued his pitchman ads for various products and made guest appearances on radio and television.

In 1999, Berra ended his fourteen-year feud with George Steinbrenner after Steinbrenner's apology. Berra became a regular visitor to the clubhouse and tutored several of the players. That year Berra was elected to Major League Baseball's All-Century Team. On March 6, 2014, Carmen died after suffering a stroke. She was eighty-five. On September 22, 2015, at the age of ninety, Berra died at home in his sleep. The Associated Press, in announcing his death, sent out the first wire report: "New York Yankees Hall of Fame catcher Yogi Bear died. He was 90." A cartoon character from Hanna-Barbera was created using Berra's name. Several newspaper websites reported the wire before it was corrected and resent.

On November 24, 2015, two months after his death, President Barack Obama posthumously presented him with the Presidential Medal of Freedom. Obama used one of Berra's famous quotes to describe him, "If you can't imitate him, don't copy him."

Besides a legacy in baseball, he also left an unforgettable string of quotes referred to as "Yogisms." These spontaneous pronouncements are often quoted. Among the most popular are the following:

"When you come to a fork in the road, take it."
"You can observe a lot by just watching."
"No one goes there nowadays, it's too crowded."
"Baseball is 90% mental and the other half is physical."
"A nickel ain't worth a dime any more."
"Always go to other people's funerals, otherwise they won't come to yours."
"The future ain't what it used to be."
"It gets late early out here."
"If the people don't want to come out to the ballpark, nobody's going to stop them."
"He hits from both sides of the plate. He's amphibious."
"I'm not going to buy my kids an encyclopedia. Let them walk to school like I did."
"It ain't the heat, it's the humility."
"It ain't over 'til it's over."

Yogi Berra made baseball fun. He was an entertaining and talented player and also a model for family faithfulness in sports figures. He was forever tied to his Missouri roots and will always be an important innovator in Missouri's history.

Bob Costas
St. Louis
Broadcaster

He was not an athletic figure of note. He even failed to make his high school basketball team because of his size. He was a feisty guy with a good voice and a journalistic heart. He owes the beginning of his professional career to his experiences in Missouri.

Robert Quinlan Costas was born in Queens, New York, on March 22, 1952. He was born to John George and Jayne Quinlan Costas of Greek and Irish heritage. His father was an electrical engineer and moved several times for his work. The family settled in Commack, Long Island, where the teenaged Costas was raised. He and his father shared a love for sports. He attended Commack High South School.

In 1970, he enrolled at Syracuse University for a communications degree. By the second year, he was announcing the school's basketball and football games on campus radio station WAER. His voice quality and descriptive announcing caught the attention of local radio station WSYR. They offered him a job broadcasting the games of Syracuse's local minor league hockey team, the Syracuse Blazers. In spite of knowing very little about the sport, he accepted their offer. He dropped out of college in his final year before graduation.

In 1974, at age twenty-two, Costas sent a demo tape to popular radio station KMOX in St. Louis. He applied to broadcast the games of the Spirits of St. Louis basketball team of the American Basketball Association (ABA). He was successful as an announcer, but his job was terminated after four years because of the folding of the ABA.

He found work announcing games for the University of Missouri and other regional assignments for the National Football League and the National Basketball Association.

In 1979, Costas, briefly employed by CBS, did the play-by-play announcing for the Chicago Bulls basketball team on station WGN-TV. In 1980, he was employed by NBC as a sports announcer. There were concerns about his youthful appearance, but those concerns quickly vanished with his "meticulous preparation" and polished performance before the camera. His arrival in sports broadcasting brought new innovative dimensions to the profession. He was credited with "reinventing sports broadcasting by imparting levels of articulation, intelligence, polish, insight, and wit."

His popularity reached beyond the traditional sports area. In 1982, he was invited to appear on *Late Night with David Letterman* to announce occasional dog-sled and elevator races. That year he was paired up with veteran announcers to broadcast *NBC's Game of the Week*. In 1985, at the age of thirty-three, he became the youngest winner of the Sportscaster of the Year Award.

His personal life found a new commitment in 1983. He married Carole Randall Krummenacher. They would have two children. Their marriage ended in divorce in 2001.

He maintained some personal traits, such as carrying a vintage Mickey Mantle baseball card in his wallet. In his broadcast he added some memorable quotes. During the 1989 baseball playoffs, he quipped, "Elvis has a better chance of coming back than the Blue Jays." Regarding football star Terrell Owens' four-million-dollar house on the market, he noted, "I think that any Philadelphia resident would rather buy the deed to the Bates Motel."

His talents allowed him to expand to many other sports assignments—figure skating, horse racing, football, and others. In 1986, *Sports Illustrated* pronounced their evaluation of his attributes:

> Costas is able to pull together an audience. He appeals to the Tommy Dorsey crowd because he can talk about the DiMaggios, worships the old Ballparks, and knows when to be reverent.... But he also pulls in the baby-boomers because he's one of them, and knows when to be irreverent.

Costas added regular weekly talk shows to his agenda and was able to have very informal conversations with noted guests from the world of politics, entertainment, and sports. In 1988, Costas would reach many new viewers with his announcing the Winter Olympic Games on ABC. This was the first of many Olympic coverages. He was greatly influenced by the longtime Olympic coverage of sports announcer Jim McKay. His coverage currently continues with the only break in 2014. After announcing the beginning of the games, he was forced to drop out due to a case of pinkeye.

Throughout the 1990s, Costas continued his multi-sport announcing, regular weekly talk shows, and international coverage of the Olympic Games. In 2000, he wrote the book *Fair Ball: A Fan's Case for Baseball*. It was on the *New York Times* Best Seller list for several weeks.

With his growing popularity, he found opportunities to expand into cameos for movies and hosting television special programs. He also was able to conduct important and respected interviews with sports figures caught up in national controversies.

After his divorce in 2001, he maintained a single life until 2004. He married Jill Sutton on March 12. They maintain and keep two homes in St. Louis and New York.

In January 2009, Costas was ranked 6th by the American Sportscasters Association in its list of the Top 50 Sportscasters of All-Time. In 2012, he was inducted into the National Sportswriters and Sportscasters Association (NSSA). Throughout his career, he has earned numerous awards and honors. He won eight National Sportscaster of the Year. Awards. He also has won a record twenty-six Emmy awards in the fields of news, sports, and entertainment.

Bob Costas has a unique career in professional broadcasting that began in Missouri. He continues to keep his Missouri ties and already has a permanent place enshrined in television history.

Joe Garagiola
St. Louis
Baseball

He gained more respect and popularity after retiring from his professional sports career. He had a self-deprecating humor that endeared him to a large broadcasting audience. He was born in Missouri and never was far from his Missouri roots.

Joseph Henry Garagiola, Sr., was born in St. Louis, Missouri, on February 12, 1926. He was the son of Italian immigrants. He grew up on Elizabeth Avenue in the western section of the city known as "The Hill." His father was a brickyard worker. He lived across the street from a lifelong friend, Yogi Berra, who was nine months older. It was an enthusiastic baseball neighborhood with weekly games in a vacant lot. He struggled in school, especially with English classes. With no advanced academic ambitions, Garagiola set his sights on a career in baseball.

When he was sixteen, he tried out for the hometown St. Louis Cardinals with his friend, Yogi Berra. He accepted their offered contract with a signing bonus of $500. Berra was only offered a $250 signing bonus and refused their contract. Much later, Garagiola said, "Not only was I not the best catcher in the Major Leagues, I wasn't even the best catcher on my street!" His father had misgivings about his career choice of playing games.

At the age of seventeen, Garagiola was the youngest player to play for the Cardinals' farm club, the Columbus Red Birds. On April 24, 1944, he was called into military service. He did his basic training at Jefferson Barracks, Missouri. He then was sent to Fort Riley in Kansas. He played for the base team, the Centaurs. In 1945, he was sent to the Philippines. There he played baseball for Kirby Higbe's Manila Dodgers. He was discharged in early 1946 and joined the Cardinals as a catcher at the age of twenty. He made his major league debut on May 26, 1946.

1946 was a very good year for the Cardinals and for Garagiola. The Cardinals won the World Series in seven games against the Boston Red Sox. During the series, Garagiola caught five of the seven games and batted 6-for-19, a better average than competitor Ted Williams. That would be the height of his career stats. On September 11, 1947, Garagiola was involved in a collision at home plate with Jackie Robinson. It caused a serious shoulder injury that affected his catching and batting abilities. He played with the Cardinals for five years and was traded to the Pittsburgh Pirates. After two seasons he was traded to the Chicago Cubs. Lasting a season there, he was again traded to the New York Giants. He retired from playing professional baseball in 1954, after nine seasons. Garagiola said of his decision to retire, "[I] knew it was time to retire when I was catching, and his ex-teammate Stan Musial stepped into the batter's box, turned to Joe and said, 'When are you gonna quit?'" He also quipped that he thought, after playing for four of the eight National League teams, that "he was just modeling uniforms for the National League."

In 1949, Garagiola met and married Audrey Dianne Ross. She was the organist at the St. Louis Cardinals' ballpark. They would have two sons and a daughter. Later, there would be eight grandchildren in their family.

In 1955, he began a new career for the next seven years, calling games for the Cardinals on radio station KMOX. He worked alongside famed Cardinals announcers Harry Caray and Jack Buck. Garagiola provided many human-interest stories and humorous self-deprecating stories. His grew a loyal and loving national fan base. In 1961, he was selected by NBC to broadcast several nationally televised baseball games. He provided play-by-play coverage from 1965 to 1967 for the New York Yankees. During that time he was able to call Mickey Mantle's historic 500th home run.

In the 1960s and 1970s, Garagiola expanded his national popularity by hosting several television games shows. From 1967 to 1973 and again from 1990 to1992, he found the opportunity to serve as a regular panelist for *The Today Show*, conducting a number of significant personal interviews. He also authored a book, *Baseball Is a Funny Game*. Two other books would follow, *It's Anybody's Ballgame* (1980) and *Just Play Ball* (2007).

In 1968, he returned to NBC and shared play-by-play duties with Curt Gowdy until 1976. He then continued in the role on a full-time basis. In 1973, he received the Peabody Award for his work with NBC. Later, joined by Vin Scully, the pair called many nationally televised games throughout the 1980s. After calling the 1988 World Series games, Garagiola resigned from NBC sports over future contract agreements. He also wanted to spend more time with his family.

In the 1976 U.S. Presidential campaign, Garagiola became a good friend and strong supporter of President Gerald Ford. On election night, Garagiola was invited to spend the night with President Ford watching the disappointing election returns.

From 1988 to 2012, he gave part-time color commentary for the Arizona Diamondbacks. His son, Joe Garagiola, Jr., was the team's general manager. Joe., Sr," said "his fondest memory was the 2001 season when the Diamondbacks, with his son, Joe Garagiola Jr., as the team's general manager, beat the New York Yankees in the World Series."

He guest hosted *The Tonight Show Starring Johnny Carson*. He became a strong advocate against the all-too-common use of chewing tobacco. He had used it early in his playing career but quit cold turkey in the late 1950s. He helped work with families of players suffering from oral cancer related to the addiction.

An interesting deviation from his baseball career happened in 1994 when he hosted the Westminster Kennel Club Dog Show at Madison Square Garden in New York City. He continued as its host for nine years until 2002.

He received a number of important recognitions. In 1991 the Baseball Hall of Fame presented him with the Ford C. Frick Award for outstanding broadcasting accomplishments. In 1988, he received the Children's MVP Award from the Jim Eisenreich Foundation for his work with kids. In 2004, he was inducted into the National Sportscasters and Sportswriters Hall of Fame. On December 4, 2013, he was named as the 2014 recipient of the Buck O'Neil Lifetime Achievement Award, noting his advocacy against smokeless tobacco and founding the Baseball Assistance Team, which provided grants to needy members of the baseball community.

Garagiola had earlier suffered a stroke and continued in ill health until 2013, when he suffered a heart attack. He died on March 23, 2016, in Scottsdale, Arizona. He was ninety years old. His funeral mass was held on April 13 in St. Louis at St. Ambrose Catholic Church, the same church where he was baptized. He was interred at Resurrection Cemetery in St. Louis.

He was very humble in describing his career accomplishments. He wrote:

Each year I don't play, I get better. The first year on the banquet trail I was a former ballplayer, the second year I was just great, the third year one of baseball's stars, and just last year I was introduced as one of baseball's immortals. The older I get the more I realize that the worst break I had was playing.

Joe Garagiola reminds us of a time when competitive professional sports was fun. He also reminds us of the importance of the strong moral influences and friendships in our early lives. His unique life is a proud reminder of those early beginnings in Missouri.

Stan Musial
St. Louis
Baseball

A statue honoring him is found just outside of Cardinals stadium in downtown St. Louis, Missouri. He played only for the Cardinals for twenty-one years. He was the first Cardinal to have his jersey number retired. He was recognized for his batting accomplishments, as well as his gentlemanly relationship with players and fans.

Stanislaw Francizek Musial was born on November 21, 1920, in Donora, Pennsylvania. He was the fifth child born to Lukasz and Mary Lancos Musial. His father was a Polish immigrant steelworker who loaded freight cars with bales of wire at the American Steel and Wire Company. His mother, a Czech-born immigrant, worked as a domestic servant. During the Great Depression, family finances were very tight, often dependent upon donations from local food pantries. Adding to the difficulties of the family was Musial's father's struggle with alcoholism.

When Musial started school, he had his name anglicized to Stanley. He was only an average student and worked at odd jobs to help with the family income. He spent his free time playing baseball. He remembered his mother making baseballs for him from bits and pieces of any available scraps. At the age of eight, he announced his plans to become a professional baseball player. In high school, he was recognized as a talented ball player, but his first sport was actually gymnastics. He was an accomplished tumbler whose skills proved helpful in his later baseball career.

On September 29, 1937, at the age of seventeen, Musial signed a contract with the St. Louis Cardinals for $65 a month. The contract was kept secret, so he could continue playing high school basketball his senior year. He was the only member of his family to graduate from high school.

After graduation, Musial spent the next two baseball seasons with the Class D Mountain State League in Williamstown, West Virginia. He started as a mediocre pitcher who occasionally played in the outfield. He was a natural left-handed hitter and thrower. His increasingly poor pitching nearly led to his release. When a team outfielder was injured, Musial was moved to the position on a regular basis. He began to focus on his batting skills and made very noticeable improvement. His over .300 batting averages secured his position on the team. In 1940, after being moved to another Class D League in Daytona Beach, Florida, Musial suffered a serious shoulder injury while playing centerfield. Fortunately, that ended his pitching career. But as his batting continually improved, in 1941, he was moved to a Class C farm team in Springfield, Missouri. His twenty-six home runs and .379 batting average led to his being moved in mid-season to a Class B Farm club in Rochester, New York. In September, Musial was called up to the Cardinals team and was an immediate success. With the season winding down, in his twelve-game play, Musial batted .426 and in a doubleheader game had six hits. He was given the starting position in left field for the 1942 season.

In 1937, Musial had met Lillian Susan Labash. The high school sweethearts were married on May 25, 1940, in Daytona Beach. The couple would produce four children and remain married for seventy-two years. He would become the first grandfather to hit a home run in the major leagues.

Musial hit .315 in his rookie years and now helped his team win the 1942 World Series. In 1943, Musial was named the National League Most Valuable Player (MVP) Award, the first of the three MVP awards he would earn. He helped his team win a second World Series in 1944. In 1945, Musial was drafted into the military in the final months of World War II. He joined the Navy and was assigned to Pearl Harbor and Philadelphia doing ship repair. He spent his spare time playing baseball with the service teams. He was honorably discharged and returned to St. Louis to once again play with the Cardinals.

In the 1946 season, he stepped right in to his old patterns and won his second MVP award, helping the Cardinals to win their third World Series title in five years. That year, when he played against the Brooklyn Dodgers, fans shouted as he came to bat, "Here comes the man." He was forever after dubbed "Stan the Man."

An example of his gentleness and considerate nature was demonstrated, in 1947, when Jackie Robinson became the first African American to play in major league baseball. While others, including some of Musial's teammates, demonstrated their disrespect, Musial was kind and explained that "he had no trouble with integration" because of his history playing sports with African Americans in his high school days.

In 1948, Musial accomplished one of the best record-setting hitting seasons of any player. He led the National League in runs, hits, doubles, triples, RBIs, and batting average (.376). He received his third MVP award.

In 1949, Musial opened his own restaurant in St. Louis. It became an important gathering place for local and visiting dignitaries. He enjoyed visiting and hosting the patrons. He showed the same personality on and off the ballfield. He was never thrown out of a game and enjoyed the bantering in the dugout.

Musial continued to create a masterful baseball record. From 1942 to 1958, he batted over .300. Joe Garagiola once remarked, "He could have hit .300 with a fountain pen." On May 13, 1958, Musial hit his 3,000th career hit. Failing to hit .300 in 1959, Musial considered retiring but was placed in left field and continued to play for four more years. His age and injuries forced him to sit out some games.

On September 29, 1963, Musial, who earlier had announced his plans to retire, played his last game. At pregame ceremonies, Musial was honored. Major League Commissioner Ford Frick said, "Here stands baseball's perfect warrior. Here stands baseball's perfect knight." Musial served as vice president of the Cardinal organization from 1963 to 1966. In 1967, he served as general manager for the team. On August 4, 1968, a statue of Stan Musial was placed outside of Busch Memorial Stadium.

In 1969, Musial was elected to the National Baseball Hall of Fame in his first year of eligibility. His total career accomplishments in baseball are amazing. He had 3,630 hits with 1,949 runs scored, 725 doubles,

1,951 RBIs, and 1,377 extra base hits. He played in 3,026 games and batted 10,972 times.

Musial devoted his retirement years to his growing family, local restaurant, national charities, and political activities. He had campaigned actively for fellow Catholic presidential candidate John F. Kennedy. President Lyndon Johnson named Musial as special consultant for the National Council on Physical Fitness. He served as chairman in that capacity from 1964 to 1967 as chairman.

In 1964, Musial wrote his autobiography, *Stan Musial: "The Man's" Own Story as Told to Bob Broeg*. One of Musial's unlikely interests was playing his harmonica. He became quite accomplished and "in 1994 he recorded 18 songs and he sold the recordings along with a harmonica-playing instruction booklet."

In 1999, Musial was named a member of the Major League Baseball All-Century Team. On February 15, 2011, President Barack Obama awarded Stan Musial the Presidential Medal of Freedom, the highest honor a civilian can receive. President Obama remarked, "Stan matched his hustle with humility. Stan remains, to this day, an icon, untarnished; a beloved pillar of the community; a gentleman you'd want your kids to emulate."

Soon after receiving that prestigious award, Musial developed Alzheimer's disease. His wife, Lil, died in May 2012. Musial died eight months later on January 19, 2013, at his home in St. Louis County. He was buried in Resurrection Cemetery in Affton, Missouri. Famed Sportscaster Bob Costas said, "All Musial represents is more than two decades of sustained excellence and complete decency as a human being." In light of today's professional baseball players, that description and example is all too rare.

Satchel Paige
Kansas City
Baseball

He became the first black pitcher in professional baseball. He was the first black baseball player inducted into the Baseball Hall of Fame. He rose from being in a state reformatory school in his early teen years to prominence in the world of professional baseball at a time of desegregation controversy in American life.

Leroy Robert Page was born on July 7, 1906, in Mobile, Alabama, in a section called "South Bay." He was the middle child of twelve children born to the family of John and Lula Page. His father was a gardener and spent little time with the family. His mother worked as a washerwoman and was the dominant parent in the household. All the children were expected to contribute as best as they could as early as they could to the family income. Leroy searched the alleys for empty bottles to redeem for cash. He later delivered ice to homes for tips. He found better income by working at the Louisville and Nashville Railroad station. He carried bags for passengers for tips of ten cents each. Realizing that the handling of individual bags was time-consuming and providing little income, he developed a system of attaching multiple bags to a long pole balanced on his shoulder. This allowed for more tips per trip. The story developed that from that creative exercise he earned the nickname "Satchel." His mother changed the family name from Page to

"Paige." Paige would later confess that "My folks started out by spelling their name 'Page' and later stuck in the 'i' to make themselves sound more high-tone." Soon after the name change, his father died.

Two weeks before his twelfth birthday, Paige was arrested for repeated petty theft and truancy from his school. He was sent to an Alabama reform school, the Industrial School for Negro Children in Mount Meigs, Alabama. He had grown even then to 6'4" and stood out as a great prospect for sports. As a child, he had developed a love for baseball. He was very fortunate to have had a good school baseball coach, Edward Byrd, who took a personal interest in developing Paige's potential in the sport. Byrd concentrated on Paige's ability at pitching. Taking advantage of his physical size, Byrd taught him to kick his foot high and move his pitching hand far enough forward in the throw to disguise what kind of pitch was being thrown and the speed of the ball. He was also taught to analyze the batters by observing their knees and their batting stance. He experimented with various types of pitches and created his unique "hesitation pitch." He later reflected that he "gave up five years of freedom to learn how to pitch."

Paige was released from reform school six months early in December 1923, at the age of seventeen. He joined an all-black semi-pro team, the Mobile Tigers, where his older brother Wilson was already pitching. He earned a dollar a game. He found another opportunity for additional income by pitching for batting practice with local white minor league teams. In 1925, he was discovered by Alex Herman, player/manager of the Chattanooga Black Lookouts of the Negro Southern League. Herman's offer of $50 a month was delayed until Paige's mother was assured of her cut of the salary. He began to pitch for the team in June 1926. His first game was a big loss, but he found an opportunity to improve his pitching style when he was loaned out to various clubs around the country. For the next three years, he pitched nearly every day for teams in Birmingham, Baltimore, Cleveland, Pittsburgh, and Kansas City. He became known for his strong strikeout record and was nationally recognized in the Negro League baseball circles.

In 1930, Paige was offered $100 a game to join the Cuban Santa Clara team. He lasted only eleven games before returning to the United States because of the strict moral requirements for players in the Cuban league. Paige continued his rapid pace of hiring out for various teams and playing nearly every day. In 1931, he was offered $250 a game to finish out the season for the Baltimore Black Sox. The team, with Paige's assistance finished the season with an amazing record of ninety-eight wins and thirty-two losses. The Negro Leagues did not keep accurate records of individual player's statistics. But Paige's accomplishments were noticed by many and not just in the Negro Leagues.

Throughout the 1930s and early 1940s, "barnstorming" was often more profitable than the regular season play. Various All-Star teams were created to play against each other and occasionally with major league teams. Paige had the opportunity to pitch against some of the stars of major baseball with memorable results. When Paige played against the famous Cardinal pitcher Dizzy Dean, Dean said, "If Satch and I were pitching on the same team, we'd clinch the pennant by the fourth of July and go fishing until World Series time." He also noted that Paige was "the pitcher with the greatest stuff I ever saw." Famous New York Yankee star Joe DiMaggio said of Paige that he was the best pitcher he had ever faced.

On October 26, 1934, Paige married his longtime girlfriend, Janet Howard. The marriage lasted only several years, ending when she supposedly had Paige served with divorce papers while he was walking to the pitcher's mound at Wrigley Field. The divorce was finalized on August 4, 1943. In 1946(?), he married another longtime girlfriend, Lahoma Brown. They would have seven children together.

In 1937, Paige was offered a contract to play for a Dominican Republic team, the Dragones, in Santiago. He helped the team to win their league championship. Paige returned to the United States to face a ban on the players who had left their teams to play for international clubs. He formed his own All-Star team to barnstorm the country. For the next two years, Paige played for the Club Agrario of Mexico City and the Puerto Rican Guayama Witch Doctors. He had consistently good records but was always ready to return to the United States.

In 1940, Paige returned to play for the established Travelers, a barnstorming team for the Kansas City Monarchs. His continued good pitching record allowed him to be called to play for the Kansas City Monarch team on September 12, 1940. Crowds from Kansas City and other ballparks increased the attendance whenever it was announced that Paige would be pitching. Because of that, the Monarchs, continuing to hire out Paige, purchased a DC-3 airplane to fly him to other ballparks. He pitched successfully against the New York Black Yankees before 20,000 fans at Yankee Stadium. In 1941, he helped the Monarchs to win their third consecutive Negro League championship. On August 1, 1941, Paige made his first appearance in the East-West All-Star Game.

World War II found many of the players in all baseball leagues drafted for military service. Paige was deemed too old for recruitment. He continued to serve the Monarchs well in his performances. In 1946, with many of the drafted professionals returning to baseball, Bob Feller organized a barnstorming team and asked Paige to create a team from the Negro League to compete against him. They scheduled thirty-five games in thirty-one cities in seventeen different states to be played in twenty-seven days. Travel would cover 13,000 miles. The events gave Paige more exposure to appreciative baseball fans of all races.

In 1946, the color barrier was broken when Branch Rickey hired Jackie Robinson to play for the Brooklyn Dodgers. Additional black players were added to various clubs. Paige received his long awaited opportunity when Bill Veeck offered Paige a contract on July 7, 1948, to finish the season for the Cleveland Indians. On July 9, 1948, Paige, on his 42nd birthday, became the oldest rookie and the seventh black player to play in major league baseball. As he helped the team win the American League Pennant race, Paige also became the first black pitcher to pitch in the World Series. He played his second year for the Indians before being released at the end of the 1949 season. He continued his barnstorming play and then signed for three years to play for the St. Louis Browns until they disbanded in 1953. During that time, he earned two All-Star game selections.

For the next few years, Paige traveled with the barnstorming teams, drawing large audiences at various ballparks. Looking toward retirement, Paige discovered that he lacked three innings of play for a major league team to qualify for a professional baseball pension. In 1965, Charles O. Finley, owner of the Kansas City Athletics, signed Paige to pitch for one game. At age fifty-nine, Paige became the oldest player in major league history. He pitched three shutout innings against the Boston Red Sox. He needed just twenty-eight pitches to get the nine outs. As he left the pitcher's mound, he received a standing ovation from the crowd. The stadium lights dimmed, and the fans lit matches and cigarette lighters while singing, "The Old Gray Mare."

The following years, Paige served as a batting coach for the Atlanta Braves and as an executive for the minor league Tulsa Oilers. He pitched in his last game in organized baseball in 1966. He had already settled down in Kansas City with his second wife and their now eight children.

In 1966, Ted Williams, being inducted into the Major League Baseball Hall of Fame, urged that Negro league players be considered for entry into the Hall of Fame. It was originally determined that two separate wings be established for white and black players. But it was finally agreed that there should be no separation from these honored players. On February 9, 1971, Satchel Paige had the honor of being the first Afro-American member of the Major League Baseball Hall of Fame.

Paige wrote two autobiographies, *Pitchin' Man* in 1948 and *Maybe I'll Pitch Forever: A Great Baseball Player tells the Hilarious Story Behind the Legend* in 1962. His often quoted Mark Twain's line was "Age is a question of mind over matter. If you don't mind, it doesn't matter."

He made his last public appearance in Kansas City on June 5, 1982. The wheelchair-bound man with an oxygen tube strapped to his face thanked the crowd for the honor of having a local baseball stadium near his home named after him. He said, "I am honored with the stadium being named for me. I thought there was nothing left for me. I've been in Kansas City 46 years and I can walk down the street and people don't know me." On May 31, 1981, a made-for-television movie, *Don't Look Back*, explored Paige's life story. In 1999, he was ranked 19th on *Sporting News'* list of the 100 greatest baseball players.

He died at the Truman Medical Center in Kansas City on June 8, 1982, less than a month before his seventy-fifth birthday. On July 28, 2006, a statue of Satchel Paige was unveiled in Cooper Park, Cooperstown, New York, commemorating the contributions of Negro leagues to baseball. The Satchel Paige Elementary School in Kansas City is named after him.

It is impossible to create a cumulative record of all of Paige's baseball statistics. Larry Tye, writing for the Society of American Baseball, summed up his life best:

> The truth is that Satchel Paige had been hacking away at baseball's color bar decades before the world got to know Jackie Robinson. Satchel laid the groundwork for Jackie the way A. Philip Randolph, W. E. B. DuBois, and other early Civil Rights leaders did for Martin Luther King, Jr. Paige was as much a poster boy

for black baseball as Louis "Satchmo" Armstrong was for black music and Paul Robeson was for the black stage —and as much as those two became symbols of their art in addition to their race, so Satchel was known not as a great black pitcher but a great pitcher. In the process Satchel Paige, more than anyone, opened the opportunity for blacks in the national pastime and changed his sport and this nation

Missouri is honored to lay claim to having a significant part of this great innovator's life and career.

Casey Stengel
Kansas City
Baseball

He was a fair baseball player but found his real fame as an outstanding manager in professional baseball. He was a showman, prankster, and quarreler. He tested the limits of other managers and league commissioners. But none could deny his distinguished record of accomplishments.

Charles Dillon Stengel was born on July 30, 1890, in Kansas City, Missouri. He was the youngest of three children born to Louis and Jennie (Wolff) Stengel. His father was a German immigrant and an insurance salesman who also ran a city street sprinkler to keep down the dust on the unpaved city roads. Stengel was raised in a comparatively middle-class home and neighborhood. He was originally nicknamed "Dutch." He was very active early on in community sandlot baseball games. He carried his interest and talents in sports to Kansas City's Central High School. His basketball team won the city championship. His baseball team won the state championship. He struggled about his career choice. He had an interest in dentistry but could not deny his love for baseball.

In 1908, he dropped out of high school and joined with the Kansas City Red Sox minor-league baseball team. He earned a dollar a day and traveled around the country. In 1909, he was offered a contract to play

with another minor-league team, the Kansas City Blues. He was offered $135 a month, which was more than his father's salary. His father
had to sign the contract for him since Stengel was underage.

Stengel reported to spring training in 1910 at Excelsior Springs,
Missouri. He began as a pitcher but found better success playing in
the outfield. He was transferred to the Kankakee Kays of the Class D
Northern Association. The league folded in July. He was then transferred to another Class D team, the Shelbyville Grays, which became
the Maysville Rivermen. He returned to the Kansas City Blues by the
end of the season. In the off seasons, Stengel was undecided about his
career choice and enrolled in the Western Dental College. Being left-
handed, he struggled in dental school, having to use dental tools designed for right-handed persons. The Blues sold Stengel to the Aurora
Blues of the Class C Wisconsin-Illinois League. There, he caught the
attention of a scout for the Brooklyn Dodgers, and they purchased his
contract on September 1, 1911.

In 1912, the Dodgers assigned Stengel to the Montgomery Rebels of
the Class A Southern Association. He performed well, but his on-the-
field antics led one scout to describe him as "a dandy ballplayer, but it's
all from the neck down." He returned to the Dodgers' team and made
his major league debut at Brooklyn's Washington Park on September
17, 1912. He started in center field. He played very well, and the team
was impressed. He earned his nickname of "Casey" when he labeled
his ball bag with hometown initials: "K. C." Stengel.

Stengel began an irritating habit, before each season, of holding out
for a better salary before signing the contract. It worked fine for a few
times but became very irritating to owners and other players. For the
next four seasons, Stengel played well for the Dodgers. Charles Ebbets,
the club owner, was very unhappy with Stengel's annual contract hold-
outs. Before the 1917 season, he once got back an unsigned contract
from Stengel with the comment that Stengel thought Ebbets had made
a mistake and sent him the contract for the batboy! Stengel also complained about the poor hotel accommodations while they were on the
road. On January 9, 1918, Ebbets traded Stengel to the Pittsburgh Pirates.

Pittsburgh's club owner, Barnet Dreyfuss, wisely told Stengel he had
to prove himself on the field before there would be any consideration
of any salary increase. Stengel did not impress the team when he was

ejected from a game for arguing with the umpire and fined for taking off his shirt. Stengel decided to take a break from major league baseball for a while, and in the summer of 1918, he joined the U.S. Navy. He managed and played for the Brooklyn Navy Yard's baseball team.

After the war, Stengel returned to play for the Pirates. He continued his antics on the field, causing growing dissatisfaction from Dreyfuss. On August 9, 1919, he was traded to the Philadelphia Phillies. His request for a raise was refused, and Stengel went back to Kansas City. He sat out the rest of that season, creating a barnstorming baseball team. He returned to play in the 1920 season for the Phillies but was continually hampered with injuries. At the end of that season, he was traded to the New York Giants.

He developed an immediate friendship with Giants' manager John McGraw. His value as a player was again threatened because of injuries. McGraw began to use Stengel as an assistant coach to train the newer players. Seeing only limited playtime, after the season in 1922, Stengel and other major leaguers formed a barnstorming team and toured Japan and the Far East. In 1923, Stengel continued limited play with the Giants. But his continued antics on the field, such as arguing with the umpires, led to ejections and even suspensions. McGraw patiently continued to gain control of Stengel's good coaching relationship with the younger players. Stengel's one distinctive play was in the 1923 World Series. In the first game played in the just-opened Yankee stadium, Stengel, despite a serious leg injury, hit the first home run in the new stadium. It was not just a home run, but an inside-the-park home run! In the third game, Stengel again homered, and as he rounded third base, he blew kisses to the Yankee crowd and thumbed his nose at the Yankee bench. Baseball commissioner Kennesaw Mountain Landis saw the incident and fined Stengel. Landis was quoted as saying, "Casey Stengel just can't help being Casey Stengel." That was enough for McGraw, and at the end of the season, Stengel was traded to the Boston Braves.

In 1924, Casey met Edna Lawson. They were married in August in St. Louis, Missouri. They would have a long, enjoyable marriage of fifty-one years. There were no children. After the baseball season, Edna joined Stengel in a barnstorming team in a tour of Europe. Stengel met King George V and the Duke of York. Edna sipped tea with Queen Mary. That winter, upon return to the United States, Edna's father had a new house built for them in Glendale, California. They would live there for the rest of their lives.

Stengel would end his major league playing experiences in 1925. The Braves sent him to Worcester, Massachusetts, as a player/manager. He was noted for entertaining the fans with his arguments with umpires and tantrums on the field. He also developed a reputation for rambling media interviews and strange quotations, referred to as "Stengelese." He had a chance to take over as manager for the Toledo Mud Hens, a position he really wanted. The team was under the franchise of McGraw and the Giants. But the Braves were unwilling to release him. In a very creative move, Stengel used his multiple job titles to accomplish his goal. As the team manager, he released himself as a player, and then as team president, he fired himself as manager. He was now free to secure the job that McGraw had wanted him to take.

Stengel stayed with the Mud Hens as manager for six years. He led the team to a championship season in 1927. He had missed part of the year, being suspended by the league for "inciting fans to attack the umpire after a close play during the first game of a Labor Day doubleheader." Eventually, the Great Depression and team's faltering wins led to Stengel's firing as the manager.

Sportswriters and some baseball players were convinced that the clowning of Stengel and his poor record with the Mud Hens would prevent any return to major league baseball. But when the Brooklyn Dodgers fired Max Carey as manager, they unexpectedly hired Casey Stengel as manager on February 24, 1934. McGraw died the next day. The Dodgers did not fare well in the next season, and Stengel was fired during the 1936 World Series. With another year of salary on his contract, he left baseball in 1937 and began investing in oil wells. He became very wealthy and was able to invest in the Boston Braves baseball team and was asked to serve as manager in late 1937. He accepted and served the team for the next six years until 1943. His team did not do well in any of the years under his management.

Stengel spent the next few years managing minor-league teams in Milwaukee, Kansas City, and Oakland. The Oakland team would win their pennant race in 1947. In 1949, the New York Yankees, under new ownership and under new general manager George Weiss, made the surprising announcement of Casey Stengel as the new Yankee manager. Weiss had been suggesting Stengel for a number of years, but Stengel's clowning on and off the field and a comparatively poor past win record had led many to believe his time had passed.

Stengel began his long association with the New York Yankees with his "platooning" of the team's players, mixing up the positions played and batting order. He found the good results and proved himself an effective manager. He helped the Yankees to win the 1949 World Series and was awarded Manager of the Year by *Sporting News*. Both would be repeated in 1953 and 1958. When asked the secret to his managerial skills, he said, "Keep the five guys who hate you away from the five who are undecided." Stengel, aided in his championships with players like Yogi Berra, Mickey Mantle, and Joe DiMaggio, was the only manager to win five consecutive World Series pennants, from 1949–1953.

The Yankees just missed the league championship until 1957 and 1958. They were primarily a team of veteran players who at times resented Stengel's tight control of their lives. They also had difficulties accepting Stengel's advice for improving their play and batting. Rumors began to spread in the 1959 season that Stengel was going to be fired. With the "youth movement" on the Yankee roster, the 1960 season fulfilled the rumors. He was fired at the end of the 1960 season after their loss in the World Series to the Pittsburgh Pirates, ending his eleven-year run with the Yankees. When asked about how he felt to be let go because of his age, he replied, "I'll never make the mistake of being seventy again."

Stengel returned to his Glendale home and worked as vice president in Edna's family's Valley National Bank. A severe back injury prevented him from accepting other managerial offers of major league teams. In the fall of 1962, Stengel's old friend, George Weiss, persuaded him to accept the manager position of the newly established New York Mets. The team was a collection of error-prone athletes. They finished their first year with a major league season record of 120 losses. However, the fans loved the team, as well as Stengel and his continued on and off-the-field antics. The attendance at their games soared to nearly one million. The second year was another flop, with the team again finishing last in the league.

In 1964, the Mets began play in their new Shea Stadium. The new stadium did little to improve their play or their standing at the end of the season. Stengel quipped, "We are a much improved ball club, now we lose in extra innings!" Growing criticism questioned Stengel's ability to manage. He broke his wrist in a fall on ice but continued managing, not missing a game. In 1965, Stengel fell off of a barstool and broke his hip. At his wife's urging, Stengel announced his retirement as manager of the team on August 30, 1965. He was assigned by the Mets as their West Coast scout.

On March 8, 1966, Stengel was elected to the National Baseball Hall of Fame in Cooperstown, New York. In 1969, he received an award for the greatest living baseball manager. The award was presented by President Richard Nixon at the White House. That same year the Mets won the World Series. In 1970, the Yankees retired his jersey number 37, followed later that year by the Mets. Stengel continued public life, speaking at banquets and giving interviews. He summed up his career in typical "Stengelese": "There comes a time in every man's life and I've had plenty of them."

Stengel's wife, Edna, suffered a stroke in 1973 and was moved to a nursing home. Stengel stayed at their Glendale home until September 29, 1975, when he died at the age of eighty-five of lymphatic cancer. Edna lived for another two-and-a-half years. They were buried beside each other in Forest Lawn Memorial Park in Glendale, California.

As a player, Stengel compiled a record of 1,277 games played, , 575 runs scored, 1,219 hits, 60 home runs, and 535 runs batted in, as well as a career batting average of .284. As a manager, he won 1,905 games, lost 1,842 games, and played or managed on eight World Series championship teams.

On July 30, 1976, a plaque was dedicated in his honor at Yankee Stadium's Monument Park. Mickey Herskowitz, writing in the *Houston Post*, said of Stengel, "It is fashionable to say that successful people, in any field, could have been whatever they wanted. But you could not picture Casey Stengel being anything else but what he was, the greatest showman baseball has ever known."

He brought his unique personality and skills to major league baseball. He was an innovative manager who earned the devotion of the players and fans. He was another person from Missouri who brought pride to the state and the country.

Helen Stephens
Fulton
Track

She was known as the "Fulton Flash." She won two track and field gold medals in the 1936 Summer Olympics in Berlin, Germany. Afterward, she had a very uncomfortable personal audience with Adolf Hitler. She had several exhibition races against track and field star Jesse Owens. She held many American track and field records for several decades.

Helen Herring Stephens was born on February 3, 1918, on a farm outside of Fulton, Missouri. Her parents were Frank Elmer and Bertie Mae Herring Stephens. She had a younger brother. Stephens worked very hard with chores on the family farm. She later recalled the significance of her childhood activities: "From the time I was a small child I was training, only I didn't know it. I was walking, running, doing chores, building up my body, my lung capacity, my wind, my endurance, everything people have to train for today." She remembered that, when she was eight years old, she had a dream that she would be the fastest runner in the world.

Stephens attended the Middle River School, a one-room school in Callaway County. She then graduated from Fulton High School. None of her schools had any athletic programs for women in that day. Fortunately for her, the physical education teacher at her high school, Coach W. Burton Moore, recognized her exceptional running abilities. He was well acquainted with training athletes in track and field. He volunteered to help her with improving her running skills, often on the roads near the high school. He would become her personal trainer in the years ahead.

In 1934, Stephens was fifteen and six-feet-tall. Coach Moore clocked her performance in the 50-yard dash and was astounded when she completed the dash in a world record time, 5.8 seconds. On March 22, 1935, Coach Moore took her to St. Louis to compete in her first official race. One of her opponents was Stella Walsh, a Polish gold medalist from the 1932 Olympics. Stephens won the fifty-yard race at 6.6 seconds, a new indoor record on a dirt track. She was a celebrity in the track and field world and especially at her high school.

In the summer of 1936, Stephens and the other Olympic team members sailed for Germany. The IX Olympiad was held in Berlin. Her friends strongly encouraged her to not participate as a protest against Adolph Hitler's treatment of the Jews. She decided to go ahead and compete as an obligation to her team and country. On August 4, 1936, Stephens raced in the 100-meter race and won with a new world record of 11.5 seconds. That record would stand until broken twenty-four years later by American Wilma Rudolph. On August 9, Stephens ran the anchor leg of the 400-meter relay team that also set a new world record time of 46.9 seconds. She received a gold medal for each of the events and had fulfilled her childhood dream of being the fastest runner in the world. She also caught the attention of the German Chancellor Adolf Hitler.

Stephens later told of their personal meeting after the races. She said that he came into the room and gave her a Nazi salute. She responded with a "good, old-fashioned Missouri handshake." She then recounted that "he got hold of her fanny and began to squeeze, pinch and hug me, saying 'You're an Aryan type. You should be running for Germany.'" He later asked her to spend the weekend at Berchtesgaden, to which she quickly refused.

Stephens returned home and attended William Woods College in Fulton. She earned her degree and began playing for the All-American Red Heads Basketball Team. She would later become the first woman to "create, own, and manage her own semi-professional basketball team," known as the Helen Stephens Olympics Co-Eds. They would play from 1938 until 1952, with a break during World War II. She also ran in several exhibition races against another 1936 track and field star, Jesse Owens.

During the war, Stephens worked in the Curtis-Wright aircraft plant in St. Louis. She enlisted in the Women's Reserve of the U.S. Marines. After the war, she joined the Federal Civil Service, working for many years in the Research Division of the U.S. Aeronautical Chart and Information Service in St. Louis, Missouri. She retired from work in 1976, at the age of fifty-eight. She moved to Florissant, Missouri, just outside of St. Louis. She helped coach at her alma mater, William Woods College.

She continued her personal involvement in track and field Senior Olympics events. At the age of sixty-eight, she ran the 100-meter dash in 16.4 seconds, just 4 seconds slower than when she was eighteen. Stephens, who never married, died on January 17, 1994, at the age of seventy-six. She was buried in Fulton, Missouri.

Helen Stephens is recognized in the National Track and Field Hall of Fame, the United States Track and Field Hall of Fame, and the Women's Hall of Fame. Her accomplishments would provide the opening for many schools recognizing the value of an organized women's sports program. She never wavered in her devotion and love for her home state of Missouri.

Other Missouri Innovators in Sports

Bill Bradley • *Crystal City* • basketball/politics

Dan Faurot • *Mountain Grove* • football

Elston Howard • *St. Louis* • baseball

Cal Hubbard • *Keytesville* • baseball

Hal Irwin • *Joplin* • golf

Bob Orton • *Kansas City* • wrestling

Mike Shannon • *St. Louis* • baseball

Payne Stewart • *Springfield* • golf

Tom Watson • *Kansas City* • golf

Earl Weaver • *St. Louis* • baseball

Kellon Winslow • *St. Louis* • football

Chapter Eight

Others

Daniel Boone
Defiance
Pioneer

He was the greatest American frontiersman. He was a family man. He was captured by American Indians. He was cheated out of his property by a state and the federal government. He found his final peace and freedom in the early wilderness of Missouri.

Daniel Boone was born in a log cabin on November 2, 1734, near Reading, Pennsylvania. His father, Squire Boone, Sr., was a blacksmith and a weaver. His mother, Sarah Morgan, had recently emigrated from England before meeting and marrying Squire Boone, Sr. Boone was the sixth of eleven children born to the couple. He had little formal education, but he received a basic education from his Aunt Sarah. His life skill education came from his father, who acquainted him with surviving in the wilderness. Boone got his first rifle at the age of twelve and quickly developed successful hunting skills. Boone also learned wagoner skills from his father.

At age fifteen, Boone moved with his family to Rowan County, North Carolina. Eager to avoid large settlements and having an interest in exploring the wilderness, the Boones made numerous moves to new locations. Boone set up his own hunting business. With the encroaching

French and Indian War, Boone joined with General Edward Braddock as a wagoner in 1755. He met a lifelong friend, John Finley, who shared tales of the great wilderness in Kentucky with Boone. While Braddock attempted to capture Fort Duquesne, the company was attacked by an ambush of French and Indians. Boone escaped on horseback.

On August 14, 1756, Boone married his Irish sweetheart, Rebecca Bryan. They settled in North Carolina and started a family, resulting in ten children. Boone felt that he now had all that a man needed: "a good gun, a good horse, and a good wife." But ever the adventurer, Boone began a trek west to the mysterious wilderness of Kentucky.

In 1767, Boone, with several other adventurers, set out for Kentucky. He was the first to lead an expedition to explore eastern Kentucky and found that the hunting met his expectations. Two years later, he was joined by his friend John Finley and two others to explore farther west in Kentucky. They cleared a 300-mile path through the Cumberland Gap that became the main highway for future travelers. Boone encountered American Indians, having both some friendly and hostile experiences.

He returned home and was hired by Richard Henderson and the Transylvania Company to lead a small group of settlers to colonize Kentucky. He reached the site of what became Boonesborough in April 1775. He returned back home to bring his family to the new settlement. Forts were constructed for protection from the American Indians who were unhappy with the uninvited neighbors. Boone was given the rank of major in the local militia. In July 1776, his daughter Jemima was captured by the Shawnee and Cherokee tribespeople. He was able to rescue her. Boone took the settlers' money to invest in speculative land permits but was robbed on his trip to make the purchases. The settlers were angry with him, and he promised to repay them. It would take many years, but he did keep his promise.

In 1778, Boone himself was captured by the Shawnee tribe. The chief adopted Boone as his son and was told of the tribe's plans to attack and destroy Boonesborough. Fearing for his family's welfare, Boone escaped and traveled alone 160 miles back to Boonesborough to warn the settlement. His family had returned to North Carolina, and the attack was successfully defended. Boone traveled to his family and returned with them back to Kentucky in 1780. Boone became a lieutenant colonel of Fayette County, a legislative assistant, and sheriff.

There were continued engagements with hostile Indians. In 1872, at the "Battle of Blue Licks," Boone's two sons fought along with him. One son was killed and the other seriously wounded. In 1786, Boone moved with his family to Maysville, Kentucky. He continued as an elected state legislator. In the state's survey of land ownership, Boone's lands were called into question. A court ruled against him, and much of Boone's land investments were lost. Angry at how the state had treated him despite being an early explorer and trailblazer, Boone left Kentucky.

In 1788, Boone and his family settled in what is now Point Pleasant, West Virginia. In 1789, he was appointed lieutenant colonel of Kanawha County and served as a legislative delegate in 1791. Growing dissatisfied with politics and the increasing number of neighbors, Boone was ready to head west once again.

In 1795, Boone and family moved to the Spanish territory that would become Missouri. The Spanish government appointed him commandant of the Femme Osage district, along with a grant of 8,000 acres. He continued his hunting and enjoyed the beauty and challenges of the new wilderness. The Spanish held lands had been passed on to Napoleon in France. In 1803, the United States bought what was called the Louisiana Purchase. The territory of Missouri was now in federal hands and ownership. When land surveys were made, it was determined again that Boone had no legal claim to the lands granted to him by the Spanish. After an appeal was made, Boone was granted 850 acres.

In 1810, Boone returned briefly to Kentucky to pay off his outstanding debts to the early settlers of Boonesborough. He had received some income from books he wrote about his wilderness experiences. He was left with only fifty cents. He returned home and spent several years of peaceful life, enjoying his hunting. In 1813, his wife, Rebecca, died. Boone would spend the rest of his life in his son's home in St. Charles, Missouri.

He died on September 26, 1820, at the age of eighty-six. He was buried next to his wife west of Defiance, Missouri, on a hilltop overlooking the Missouri River. In 1845, Boone's family had the bodies exhumed for reburial in Frankfort, Kentucky, just a few miles from the fort of Boonesborough. Substantiated rumors abound that Boone was buried at his wife's feet, and they dug up the grave next to her, leaving Boone still buried in Missouri.

Since his death, many books have been written about the Daniel Boone. These have added to the myths and legends about the undisputed greatest woodsman in American history. He found his final peace and rest in the early wilderness of Missouri.

He was a frontiersman, soldier, Western guide, trapper, and Indian agent. His time in Missouri was productive and instructional in his career. He achieved national acclaim and was the subject of numerous magazine stories, books, and movies.

Kit Carson
Boone's Lick
Pioneer

Christopher Houston, "Kit" Carson was born on Christmas Eve, 1809. He was born in a log cabin in Madison County, Kentucky. He was born two months premature, which may have affected his physical growth. He was the sixth of ten children to Lindsey Carson and Rebecca Robinson Carson. His father was a soldier in the American Revolutionary War and a wilderness farmer. In 1810, the family moved west to Howard County, Missouri, and bought land from Daniel Boone's family in Boone's Lick, near the Missouri River. Young Carson would grow in a community faced with the challenges of the frontier wilderness. He was able to play with the friendly American Indian children and learned to fear the hostile local Indians. He learned from his father the skills of hunting and trapping.

In 1818, when Carson was just nine years old, his father died when a burning branch fell on him. As one of the older children still at home, Carson assumed responsibility to try and provide for the family needs. He said, "I jumped to my rifle and threw down my spelling book." He never received a basic education and could neither read nor write. It was a cause of much embarrassment throughout his life.

Carson's mother remarried, and differences developed between Carson and his stepfather. In 1824, at the age of fourteen, Carson was apprenticed to a saddlemaker in the village of Franklin, Missouri. His other brothers had traveled west, following the Santa Fe Trail through the Rocky Mountains. Sitting still, cutting leather, and mending harnesses were not exciting to Carson. Two years later, in August 1826, he ran away. As required by law, the saddlemaker had to publicly report the runaway apprentice. An advertisement was printed in the October 6, 1826 edition of the *Missouri Intelligencer:*

Notice is hereby given to all persons, that Christopher Carson, a boy about 16 years old, small of his age, but thick-set; light hair, ran away from the subscriber, living in Franklin, Howard County, Missouri, to whom he had been bound to learn the saddler's trade, on or about the first of September last. All persons are notified not to harbor, support or assist said boy under penalty of law. One cent reward will be given to any person who will bring back said boy.

Carson had quickly fled far from Missouri. He joined with a caravan of merchants, Bent's wagon train, heading west to Santa Fe, New Mexico. He worked as laborer, tending to the needs of the accompanying herds. He settled in Taos, New Mexico, which was a headquarters for fur-trapping expeditions throughout the area. Carson joined with them and learned valuable lessons in wilderness living. Carson was "five foot four and 135 pounds of solid muscle." He worked for the Ewing Young trappers, traveling in Arizona and California. He also worked for Jim Bridger's Hudson Bay Company. He worked as a hunter for William Bent at Bent's Fort. He also lived among several Indian tribes. He was married twice to two Indian women, one Arapahoe and the other Cheyenne. Neither marriage lasted, but they resulted in the birth of two daughters. Carson took a steamboat to St. Louis, Missouri, to take one of his daughters to a convent for schooling. In spite of his lack of formal education, he was a quick to learn and became fluent in Spanish, French, and several Indian dialects. He had a working vocabulary of Apache, Arapahoe, Blackfoot, Cheyenne, Comanche, Crow, Navaho, Paiute, Shoshone, and Ute. He also could communicate in the universal Indian sign language.

In 1842, on one of his trips back to St. Louis to visit his daughter, he met the explorer John C. Fremont. Fremont had come to the city looking for a guide on his mapping trip to the Wind River in Wyoming in the far West. Carson convinced Fremont of his knowledge of the land and his ability to translate languages that would be encountered. The two men would become good friends and business associates for the next several years. The first expedition took them through the southern pass of the Rocky Mountains. In 1843, the second expedition took them to the Great Salt Lake area in Utah and even farther west to Fort Vancouver in the Pacific Northwest. In 1845–46, another expedition led them to California and Oregon. Fremont made regular reports of the back to Washington, D.C., with glowing comments about Carson and his valuable wilderness skills. Carson became a popular national figure when the reports were printed for the American public. Ten thousand copies of Fremont's reports became the "pioneer's guide for the Oregon Trail."

In 1843, Carson married his third wife, Maria Josefa Jaramillo, the daughter of a prominent Taos family. He purchased a home in Taos where his family lived while Carson continued his travels. They would eventually have eight children.

In 1846, skirmishes with the Mexican troops in the Southwest led to military combat. Carson was asked by Fremont to assist General Stephen W. Kearny in New Mexico. They engaged in battle against Mexican forces near San Pasqual, California. Kearny's troops were overwhelmed and Carson, with two others, managed to escape the surrounding forces. They traveled to find reinforcements and led them back to rescue Kearny's troops. They would win further battles in San Diego, San Gabriel, and Los Angeles. Carson's heroic efforts were reported to President James Polk, who appointed him lieutenant in the mounted rifle regiment. The appointment was later rejected by a defiant U.S. Senate.

In 1849, Carson returned to Taos and began life as a farmer and occasional scout for the military. Concerned about fair treatment for the American Indians, Carson became an agent in the Office of Indian Affairs and later served as a superintendent of Indian Affairs for the Colorado Territory. He became most active in working for the Utes and the Jicarilla Apaches. He saw the encroaching white settlements' effect on the Indian population and advocated for the creation of reservations to protect the Indian interests. In 1858, Dr. De Witt C. Peters wrote a book, *The Life and Adventure of Kit Carson, the Nestor of the Rocky Mountains.* This added to the popularity and legends about Carson.

In 1861, with the beginning of the Civil War, Carson left his position with Indian Affairs and was appointed a lieutenant colonel, leading the First New Mexico Volunteer regiment. From 1861–1865, he fought invading Confederate soldiers, as well as rebelling American Indian tribes. One of his assignments was to relocate the Navajos to Bosque Redondo, a reservation located near Fort Sumner, New Mexico, by "any means necessary." The tribe was forced to march 300 miles in a journey known as the Long Walk. It was a sorrowful experience with hundreds of Navajos losing their lives.

In 1865, he was appointed as brigadier general of volunteers. He left the army in 1867. He returned home to Taos, hoping to expand his ranching enterprise. His wife, Josefa, died on April 23, 1868, from complications after giving birth to their eighth child. Devastated, Carson was taken to Fort Lyon, Colorado, where he died one month later on May 23, 1868 from an abdominal aortic aneurysm. Carson and his wife were eventually taken to Taos, New Mexico, for burial together in what became known as the Kit Carson Cemetery.

His house in Taos would become a museum. Carson's autobiography, *Kit Carson's Own Story*, was published in 1927. Carson City, the capital of Nevada, was named in his honor.

Kit Carson, although a famed frontiersman and trapper, was also an accomplished soldier. His kind nature is also acknowledged in his innovative concern with the welfare of Native Americans. His early life experiences in Daniel Boone's wilderness territory provided needed life skills. He made frequent trips to St. Louis to visit and check on his daughter's education, in spite of his lack of a formal education.

Jesse and Frank James
Kearny
Outlaws

Jesse James

Frank James

They were products of the conflict of political forces in the Civil War and the location of its most cruel and violent actions. They were sons of a Baptist pastor and would become the most widely known American outlaws, even in their early years. They would also be divisive characters in local and national culture with myths and legends.

Frank and Jesse James were born on a farm in Clay County near Kearny, Missouri, to Reverend Robert Sallee and Zerelda Elizabeth Cole James. Their father was a well-educated Baptist minister and helped to found William Jewell College in Liberty, Missouri. The James family, with help from neighbors, built a log cabin in the Centerville area of Clay County. It would later become known as Kearny. Reverend James was a pastor of a small Baptist Church outside of Kearny. His wife, "Zee," was six-feet-tall and a hard worker on the farm. Franklin "Frank" James was born on January 10, 1843. Another son, born two years later, died within a month. Jesse Woodson James was born on September 5, 1847. A sister was born in 1849.

In 1850, Reverend James agreed to serve as chaplain for a wagon train headed to California in search of gold. Soon after arriving, Reverend James contracted a fever from drinking contaminated water. He developed cholera and died on August 18, 1850, at Placeville, California and was placed in an unmarked grave.

Back in Missouri, Zee was left to run the farm. Frank was only seven years old and Jesse was four. On September 10, 1852, Zee remarried a neighboring farmer named Benjamin Simms. Simms despised the James boys and often punished them very harshly. Zee could not tolerate his abusive behavior and sought a divorce. However, Simms was killed on January 2, 1854, in an accident.

The next year, Zee married for the third time to Dr. Archie Reuben Samuel. The kind doctor allowed Zee to run the family and handle discipline of the children. Dr. Samuel was able to provide income for the purchase of additional land to the family farm. Eventually, slaves were purchased to help with the farming needs.

Frank had made use of his late father's large library and read many of the traditional literary works. He was well read in the Bible and considered becoming a schoolteacher. Jesse was very different, leaning more toward the prankish antics of his youth. The boys loved their stepfather and valued the skills he taught them in horseback riding and shooting. It appeared to be a very normal, enjoyable family life.

As would happen to many families in 1861, the start of the Civil War created turmoil and division within communities—especially in Missouri, a border state. The James family, with their slaves and strong family backgrounds from Confederate states, was found in political conflict with some of the Unionist families in the community. Missouri had voted to align with the Union, but many loyalties remained committed to Confederate sympathies. On May 4, 1861, Frank, age eighteen, joined the Missouri State Guard to fight for the Confederacy. Jesse, age fourteen, remained at home but was much in the Confederate corner. Frank was involved in the early battles of the Civil War in Missouri at Wilson's Creek and Lexington.

After these battles, Frank returned home briefly. He was arrested there by Union forces and released only after signing a statement of allegiance to the Union. The commitment was short-lived, as in July 1862, Frank joined the Missouri Partisan Rangers of William Clark Quantrill. The band of guerillas fought in the Border Wars, attacking Union forces in Missouri and Kansas. The gang grew with new and even more vicious volunteer raiders. The horrific attack on the town of Lawrence, Kansas, on August 21, 1863, marked the group members as criminals and outlaws.

Three months after the attack on Lawrence, Union soldiers came to the Samuel farm in search of Frank. When questioned about Frank's location, fifteen-year-old Jesse refused to answer and was severely horsewhipped. Dr. Samuel, denying any knowledge of Frank's location, was taken to the yard and repeatedly hanged close to death before his family. He would survive the ordeal, but it made a lasting impression on Jesse.

The next year, Quantrill's band divided over leadership control. Frank sided with the more verocious faction led by "Bloody" Bill Anderson. Sixteen-year-old Jesse was able to join the group, serving alongside of his brother. The group began a series of hit and run raids, trying to assist General Sterling Price's raids in the autumn of 1864. A failed attack on a federal blockhouse in Fayette, Missouri, resulted in the wounding of both James brothers. There is some question as to whether the brothers had recovered enough to participate in Anderson's cruel raid on the small town of Centralia, Missouri, on September 27, 1864. A train was robbed and the town burned. Aboard the train were twenty-four unarmed Union soldiers. They were "dragged off the train by the frenzied ruffians and were murdered in front of the horrified citizens of the town."

Feeling the pressure of Union forces in hot pursuit, the group divided with Frank going with Anderson to Kentucky and Jesse staying in Missouri under a subordinate of Anderson. Both of the divided groups came under heavy attacks from Union forces. Anderson was killed in Kentucky, and Frank escaped to return to Missouri. Jesse's group was also surrounded by Union troops. In September 1865, Jesse rode into Lexington, Missouri, under a white flag to surrender to the Union forces. He was shot in the chest and taken to Rulo, Nebraska, for recuperation. He made his way to Kansas City to live with his aunt, the sister of Robert James. Her daughter and Jesse's first cousin, Zee (named after Jesse's mother), nursed him back to health. Zee and Jesse fell in love, and a long courtship began.

The Civil War ended, but the hatred for the Union continued with the James brothers. On February 13, 1866, Frank went to Liberty, Missouri, with a band of his own. With some standing guard, Frank and two others walked into the Clay County Savings Association Bank. It had been selected because the bank's president was said to have aided the Union forces who had attacked the Samuel farm years earlier. They robbed the bank, killing a student of William Jewell College, escaping with over $60,000. There is some question as to whether Jesse was involved in the robbery, but the brothers were able to live a comfortable life with the stolen money.

In December 1866, the James brothers did make another "revenge" bank attack in Gallatin, Missouri, killing a cashier they mistook for an informer. No money was taken. They also robbed a Kansas City Exposition ticket office, accidently shooting a young girl. This time, various companies offered rewards for the capture of the two—dead or alive. Posses continued to search for the pair, coming close, at times, to capturing them.

In 1866 and 1867, the James brothers' fame attracted national attention through the writings of John Newman, an alcoholic ex-Confederate soldier and editor of the *Kansas City Times*. In newspaper articles and "dime novels," Newman presented the two as Robin Hood-type heroes:

> These men are bad citizens, but they are bad because they live out of their times. The nineteenth century with its Sybaric civilization is not the social soil for men who might have sat with Arthur at the Round Table, ridden at tourney with Sir Lancelot, or won the colors of Guinevere.... What they did, we condemn. But the way they did it we can't help admiring.

Newman would receive letters of appreciation from the James brothers, often defending the rationales for their actions.

In 1874, the brothers and their new gang robbed a stagecoach in Malvern, Arkansas. They also conducted the first peacetime train robbery in Missouri at Gads Hill. These actions found the involvement of the new Pinkerton detective agency, hired by the railroads, to pursue the brothers. Their first several assigned agents were found murdered. Reward money began to increase rapidly with combined offers from the banks, railroads, and the state.

That same year, the brothers took the opportunity to begin family life. On April 24, after nine years of courtship, Jesse married his cousin, Zee. Several months later, Frank married Annie Ralston. The two couples enjoyed a leisurely honeymoon in Texas financed by their robbery loot.

The Pinkertons, wanting revenge for their murdered agents, followed rumors of the brothers' location at the Samuel farm. On January 25, 1875, they arrived at the farm, broke a window, and threw in an incendiary device. It rolled into the fireplace and exploded. In the house were only Dr. Samuel, Zee, and thirteen-year-old Archie, the James's half-brother. Dr. Samuel was unharmed. Zee's hand was mutilated and required amputation. Archie was killed. The incident, published in Newman's discrediting newspaper articles, only increased sympathy for the James brothers and cast the pursuers as uncaring child killers.

On September 7, 1876, the James brothers and their gang attempted a bank robbery in Northfield, Minnesota. It was a failure, with some gang members being killed or captured. The James brothers barely escaped, but the incident frightened them and their wives. The two couples decided to go to Tennessee where they took on aliases and settled as farmers. Their actions and habits raised the suspicion of the townspeople. Jesse left for New Mexico Territory to find new gang members. The ones willing to join were inexperienced and not very good followers.

The new gang began another series of crimes throughout the Midwest. They robbed a train at the Glendale station, just south of Independence, Missouri. They stole about $6,000. But the crime also caused the United Sates Express Company to offer a $25,000 reward. At the same time, the Chicago and Alton railroad added another $15,000. With the already existing reward offer, it was a very tempting sum for anyone.

By now, the gang had been reduced in number. Wanting to plan another big train robbery, two new gang members were recruited, Bob and Charlie Ford. At the same time, in 1879, Missouri Governor Thomas Crittenden was under strong pressure from the citizenry for protection and action. He persuaded the railroads to offer an additional $50,000 reward.

The gang traveled with the James brothers to St. Joseph, Missouri, and then on to the Samuel farm in Kearny. At this time, Bob Ford met secretly with Governor Crittenden to capture Jesse James. Attracted by the large reward and frightened of the James brothers' suspicious nature, Bob agreed to offer his service to end Jesse James' career.

On April 3, 1882, the Fords and Jesse sat in the James' rented home in St. Joseph, Missouri. As Jesse stood on a living room chair to adjust a picture on the wall, Bob Ford snuck up behind him and shot Jesse James in the back of his head. James, age thirty-four, died immediately. People in the state were incensed at the cowardly actions of the Fords. They were arrested and charged with murder, but Governor Crittenden pardoned them. They would go on to become celebrities, often reenacting their actions in the James' home, to mixed reviews. Jesse's body was put on display for the many visitors curious about the hero/criminal.

Frank James was living a quiet life in Virginia. After word of Jesse's death reached him, he decided to surrender to Governor Crittenden and face a trial. The jury did not convict him, on the basis of little actual evidence of his crimes. He left imprisonment to return to his quiet life. He died on February 18, 1915, in Clay County, Missouri.

Zee Samuel buried Jesse James on the family farm. A monument was placed over his grave. She sold tickets to visit the grave and offered to relate stories of the brothers' lives and exploits. Jesse's son, Jesse, Jr., made a silent Western movie in which he played his father.

The mixed perception of Frank and Jesse James remains. Some see them as avengers for the wrongs done to them and their family. Others see them as uncaring criminals and killers. The picture portrayed of them as modern-day Robin Hoods is an exaggeration as no record has been found of them ever giving money to the poor. They were Missourians and unique in their place in the state's and nation's history.

Calamity Jane
Princeton
Pioneer

She was born Martha Jane Canary on May 1, 1852, in Mercer County, near Princeton, Missouri. Her parents were Robert Wilson and Charlotte M. Canary. She was the oldest of six children. Her father was a successful farmer who had a gambling problem. Her mother "wore bright-colored clothes, drank, cursed, and smoked cigars." She was also a prostitute. Jane spent much of her time in the outdoors riding horses. She never received any formal education and at times even misspelled her name, adding an extra "n" in Canary. She would often wear men's clothing for comfort.

In 1865, her father was accused of stealing. He sold the farm and joined a wagon train heading west for the gold fields of Virginia City, Montana. Jane helped with the trip, learning the skills associated with riding and shooting. On the five-month-long journey, her mother died of pneumonia in Blackfoot, Montana. In the summer of 1866, after arrival in Virginia City, her father took the family to Salt Lake City, Utah. As her father tried his hand at farming, Jane was left in charge of the household and the younger children. She did learn new skills, one being able to snap a thirty-foot bullwhip. In 1867, her father died. Jane took the children in a wagon to Fort Bridger, Wyoming Territory. They arrived in May 1868. The family lived in a boarding house operated by Mrs. Ed Alton, where Jane babysat for Mrs. Alton. When Mrs. Alton heard that Jane was found in a dance hall wearing men's clothing, Jane was fired.

The family then left Fort Bridger by Union Pacific Railroad and arrived in Piedmont, Wyoming. Still needing to support her large family, Jane found a variety of work—"dishwasher, cook, waitress, dance-hall girl, nurse and ox team driver." She seemed to disappear from the historical record in the early 1870s. There are some accounts that she had signed on as a scout for General George Armstrong Custer in his conflicts with the Native Americans. She also began a part-time experience as a prostitute at the Fort Laramie Three-Mile Hog House. It was about that time she was named "Calamity." She assured any of the men who offended her that a calamity would come their way. That is the more plausible story of the several stories of how she got her name.

In 1875, Jane went with General George Crook's expedition against the Sioux in the Black Hills of the Dakota Territory. She served as a scout and bullwhacker ("Bullwhackers walked beside the long teams of Oxen that pulled the lines of freight wagons carrying anything from railroad ties to baskets of potatoes."). Her skills as a horse rider and sharpshooter were well used.

That same year, Jane accompanied the Newton-Jenney Party into Rapid City. She took an excessive liking to alcohol and roughhousing with the men. Jane eventually settled down in the nearby city of Deadwood in the Black Hills area of the Dakota Territory. She became good friends with the legendary Wild Bill Hickok. She claimed that they later married and had a daughter. Both statements lack any credible proof. Hickok was murdered in August 1876.

She became an important part of the interest in the Wild West due to writers such as Ned Webster. In 1877, he began a lengthy series of *Deadeye Dick* dime novels. Calamity Jane was a popular figure as a cursing, cigar-smoking heroine.

Stories of her more positive nature became known when she saved passengers on a runaway stagecoach being chased by Plains Indians. In 1878, she was noted for her nursing smallpox victims in the epidemic in the Deadwood area. In 1880, Jane held a benefit performance as storyteller to raise money for a young child she claimed as her own to be educated at a Catholic boarding school, St. Martin's Academy in Sturgis, South Dakota. After the benefit, Jane used some of the large proceeds to enjoy a night of drinking.

In 1881, Jane bought a ranch west of Miles City, Montana. She kept an inn. She married Clinton Burke. They moved to Burke's hometown of Boulder, Colorado, where Jane attempted running another inn. They lived together for about six years. In 1887, she gave birth to a daughter, Jesse, who was later adopted by foster parents.

In 1893, her storytelling and national reputation caught the attention of Buffalo Bill's Wild West traveling show. She told stories of her exploits and performed sharpshooting skills astride a horse. In 1896, she also published her own inaccurate autobiography, *Life and Adventures of Calamity Jane by Herself*, which she sold after her performances. She was irregular in her performances due to drunkenness and fighting. She was fired in 1901.

She retired near Deadwood and died on August 1, 1903, at the age of fifty-one. She was found in the Calloway Hotel in Terry, suffering from pneumonia and alcoholism. Calamity Jane was buried in Deadwood's Mount Moriah Cemetery, next to Wild Bill Hickok.

Several decades later, Jane would become the subject of numerous films, plays, and television shows. There would continue to be books written about her with the questionable legends.

Martha "Calamity" Jane Canary was a Missourian influenced by her unstable home life. She was a unique figure in her special talents and persona. Although many of the legends created about her life are not verified, the stories are entertaining and exciting.

She was a national legend born in Missouri. She was a celebrated frontierswoman with often exaggerated accounts of her life, self-proclaimed and published. She was the subject of numerous books, plays, and movies.

Charles Lindbergh
St. Louis
Aviator

Charles Augustus Lindbergh, Jr., was born on February 4, 1902, in Detroit, Michigan. He was the only child of Charles Augustus Lindbergh, Sr., and Evangeline Lodge Land. His father was a Swedish immigrant. His mother was from a prominent family in Detroit. After a house fire in 1905, the family moved to Little Falls, Minnesota. Unusual in that time, his mother had graduated from the University of Michigan with a degree in chemistry. She earned her master's degree from Columbia University in New York. She was a school teacher at the Cass Technical High School in Detroit and later at Little Falls High School in Minnesota. His father was active in politics and became a United Sates Congressman from Minnesota from 1907 until 1917. He lost favor with voters after his refusal to support the entry of the United States in World War I.

Lindbergh spent most of his childhood in Little Falls and Washington, D. C. He much preferred the outdoor life of Minnesota to the city life of Washington, D. C. In 1909, his parents separated. His mother began a new teaching position at Redondo Beach, California. With all of his traveling between states, Lindbergh attended numerous schools for very brief periods of time. He was not a good student, with interest only in anything mechanical. He was able to graduate from Little Falls

High School on June 5, 1918. At his parents' urging, Lindbergh enrolled at the University of Wisconsin-Madison in late 1920, majoring in mechanical engineering. Due to poor grades and a lack of interest, Lindbergh dropped out of college in the middle of his sophomore year.

In March 1922, Lindbergh went to Lincoln, Nebraska, to work for Nebraska Aircraft Corporation and to study airplane flying. The company bought old military planes and repaired them for sales to the public. Lindbergh became very knowledgeable in airplane mechanics and developed working relationships with the local pilots. He even joined in the barnstorming tours, stepping out on airplane wings as the planes flew into towns. In May 1923, he went to Souther Field in Americus, Georgia. He made his first solo flight and was able to buy a World War I surplus Curtis JN-4 "Jenny" biplane for $500. Lindbergh began a series of barnstorming flights across the Southern states.

On March 19, 1924, Lindbergh joined the Army Air Service. He began his training at San Antonio, Texas. Of the 104 cadets who started the program, only 18, including Lindbergh, would remain. On March 25, 1925, he graduated first in his class. He earned his Army pilot's wings and a commission as Second Lieutenant in the Air Service Reserve. He joined the 110th Observation Squadron, Thirty-fifth Division, Missouri National Guard that was stationed in St. Louis, Missouri. He would eventually receive the rank of captain in July 1926. That move would prove to be very fortunate for his career.

In October 1925, Lindbergh was hired by the Robertson Aircraft Corporation at Lambert-St. Louis Flying Field in Anglum, Missouri. He was assigned the job of preparing for new Contract Air Mail Route #2 from St. Louis to Chicago. He was the chief pilot with responsibilities for hiring other pilots. There were scheduled stops in Springfield and Peoria, Illinois. On April 13, 1926, he took the Post Office Department's Oath of Office. Two days later he began his route. Encounters with bad weather, mechanical problems, and fuel consumption proved to be invaluable experience for his next big venture.

In 1919, Frenchman Raymond Orteig had offered a $25,000 prize for the first pilot to fly nonstop across the Atlantic Ocean from New York to Paris. Several pilots from the United States and France had tried unsuccessfully with tragic results. Lindbergh felt he was up to the challenge but faced difficulties in financing such a risky venture. He had savings of only $2,000. He was able to convince two St. Louis businessmen to help him obtain a bank loan of $15,000. His Robertson Aircraft Corporation donated another $1,000. The total of $18,000 was far less than the other potential pilots had available.

In Mid-February 1927, Lindbergh left for San Diego to oversee the design and special construction of a plane for the overseas trip. At the suggestion of the businessmen, the airplane was named the *Spirit of St. Louis*. The total cost for the plane was agreed to at $10,580. It was a "fabric-covered, single-seat, single-engine, 'Ryan NYP,' high-wing monoplane with registration N-X-211." On May 10, Lindbergh flew the plane first to St. Louis and then on to Roosevelt Field on New York's Long Island. Lloyds of London was giving odds of ten-to-one for Lindbergh's successful attempt.

On May 20, 1927, at 7:52 am, twenty-five-year-old Charles Lindbergh took off on a muddy, rain-soaked runway. His 2,710-pound plane had a 450 U.S. gallons of fuel. The trip would cover 2, 610 miles and take 33.5 hours. During the flight, he experienced wintery weather challenges, for which his earlier mail route had prepared him. He fought fatigue, keeping the windows open to prevent falling asleep. He landed at Le Bourget Airport in Paris on May 21, 10:22 pm. A crowd of an estimated 150,000 were waiting and enthusiastically welcomed Lindbergh. He was carried on their shoulders for half an hour. It was noted that people were "behaving as though Lindbergh had walked on water, not flown over it." He became an overnight international hero. The President of France presented him with the French Chevalier Legion of Honor medal. Upon his return to the United States, he was widely welcomed with military honors. A tickertape parade was held for him in New York City. At the White House, President Calvin Coolidge presented him with the Congressional Medal of Honor and the Distinguished Flying Cross. On June 16, 1927, Lindbergh was awarded the official prize money. On July 18, 1927, Lindbergh was promoted to the rank of colonel in the Air Corps of the Officers Reserve Corps of the U.S. Army.

Lindbergh received numerous awards, parades, honors and job offers. He was gracious in his acceptance of assignments flying around the country in his plane to make himself available to the American audience. He wrote his book *We* in 1927, which became an immediate best seller. He continued to promote his interest and support of aviation. He soon began a tour of Latin American countries. In Mexico

City, he met the daughter of the American ambassador to Mexico, Anne Spencer Morrow. They developed an ongoing relationship and were married May 27, 1929, in Englewood, New Jersey. They would have six children.

The couple would find their only quiet time together in the plane. Lindbergh taught Anne to fly, and together they worked to map air routes for the major airlines. They even flew to Asia, mapping routes to China. By 1931, they had flown over 30,000 miles, mapping additional ocean routes. Hoping to escape from the public spotlight, the Lindberghs moved to an estate in Hopewell, New Jersey. Their world would be shattered forever with an event that happened in March 1, 1932.

Their firstborn son, Charles Augustus, Jr., just twenty months old, was kidnapped from his nursery at the house. The crime made international news. A $50,000 ransom note was received and paid. A nationwide manhunt was underway. Sadly, just a few weeks later, the child's body was found in woods near the home. Ransom money was traced back to an immigrant carpenter, Bruno Hauptmann. After a very public trial, in an almost circus-like atmosphere, Hauptmann was found guilty and electrocuted on April 3, 1936, at Trenton State Prison.

Out of concern for his remaining children and to escape the continued public interest, in 1935, Lindbergh quietly moved his family to Europe, first in England and then in Brittany, France. While in Europe, Lindbergh had several eventful experiences. He worked with Dr. Elexis Carrel to develop the first glass perfusion pump, allowing a heart and to beat and lungs to breathe while undergoing surgery. He was also able to report on the growing military force of the German army with experimentation in rocket warfare. A controversy erupted over Lindbergh's receiving the Service Cross of the German Eagle from Nazi leader Hermann Goering. Lindbergh would face accusation of being a Nazi sympathizer during the outbreak of World War II. He and his family returned to the United States in 1939, amid mixed opinions about his patriotism.

In 1941, Lindbergh joined the America First Committee that opposed any U.S. involvement in World War II. He truly believed from his firsthand observations that the German war machine was unbeatable. The attack on Pearl Harbor December 7, 1941, found Lindbergh quiet in the committee's activities. His attempt to reenlist in the military was refused. He went to the Pacific war area as an advisor, and as a civilian, he flew in over fifty combat missions.

After the war, he served as a consultant for the chief of staff of the U.S. Air Force. He and his family lived in Connecticut and also built homes in Switzerland and Hawaii.

In 1953, Lindbergh wrote an expanded account of his 1927 flight in the book, *The Spirit of St. Louis.* The book won a Pulitzer Prize in 1954. That year, President Eisenhower restored Lindbergh's commission and appointed him a brigadier general in the Air Force. He later served as a consultant to Pan American Airlines and helped to design the Boeing 747 jet. He continued his avid support for aviation, remembering his appreciation of his friends in Missouri. He promoted the importance of St. Louis' new Lambert International Airport as a major airline hub. In 1959, Trans World Airlines began offering Boeing 707 services from Lambert Field. Later he supported the growth of McDonnell-Douglas Aircraft, which had merged with Boeing in 1977.

Through the 1960s, Lindbergh became a very vocal proponent of conservation of the natural world. He moved his family to live in Hawaii on the island of Maui the last few years of his life. They built a home in the jungle a mile away from a church he helped to restore. He had developed lymphatic cancer. He helped to plan the details of his memorial service and burial. He died on August 26, 1974 and was laid to rest at the Palapala Ho'omau Church in Kipahulu, Maui. His grave marker displayed a quote from Psalm 139:9: "If I take the wings of the morning, and dwell in the uttermost parts of the sea, even then your powerful arms would guide and protect me." His gravesite on a hill overlooks the Pacific Ocean and is visited annually by many visitors. His wife Anne retired to Darien, Connecticut, and continued to publish his books from letters and diaries.

His years in Missouri were comparatively few. His aviation experiences and personal connections were vital to his career. Charles Lindbergh received much from Missouri and returned much more. He was an innovator in aviation and forever associated with "the Spirit of St. Louis."

Although his time in Missouri was limited, he is forever associated with the city of St. Louis. He received financial backing from Missourians for his historic venture that vaulted him into American legend status.

William Quantrill
Albany
Outlaw

When legends and unsupportable accounts dominate a person's history, it is difficult to establish a credible biography. Although his life covered only twenty-seven years, it was filled with violence and murder. His legacy is one of the greatest acts of brutality in the American Civil War. He used Missouri as his base for vengeful deeds. Even in death, he is a mystery, with his remains buried in three difference gravesites.

William Clarke Quantrill was born on July 31, 1837, in Canal Dover, Ohio. He was the oldest of eight children born to Thomas Henry and Carline Cornelia Clarke Quantrill. His father was a tinker and a school principal. His father had a mean side and fought with his neighbors and also embezzled school funds. Accounts indicate that young Quantrill also had a very mean side. He "enjoyed nailing snakes to trees, shooting pigs through the ears just to make them squeal." He was also reported to have tied the tails of cats together to watch them fight and scratch each other to the death. His father also beat him in public for no apparent reason. His mother remained a strong supporter of his, even considering his many problems.

By the age of sixteen, Quantrill was able to get a job teaching in Mendota, Illinois. That same year, 1854, his father died of tuberculosis. In 1857, he ran away from his teaching assignment to avoid horse theft charges against him. He arrived in Kansas for a brief time, and in 1858, he joined an army provision train to Utah. Along the route, he encountered gamblers and other nefarious characters who influenced his darker side. In Salt Lake City, he became a professional gambler and was tied to a series of murders and thefts at Fort Bridger. With a warrant out for his arrest, he fled again to Lawrence, Kansas, where he again taught school. Kansas was at the center of the slavery issue dividing the country.

Quantrill had grown up in a strongly pro-Union, antislavery family. But in his travels, he encountered proslavery proponents who had an impact on his own views. He initially joined an antislavery force in Kansas and turned on them, participating in their murders. He discontinued his custom of communicating with his family and changed his political allegiance. It may have been a case of what was best for him financially as opposed to any personal conviction.

When the Civil War broke out in April 1861, Quantrill joined the Confederate forces. He fought in the first formal military skirmish of the war under General Sterling Price in the Wilson's Creek Battle just outside of Springfield, Missouri. He participated in several other skirmishes in northern Missouri. He became dissatisfied with the required military discipline and the apparent inability of the Confederate Army to deal with Union troops to his satisfaction. By the end of 1861, he left the regular Confederate force to create his own guerilla force. Their small militia found satisfaction murdering Union forces from Kansas who were crossing into Missouri on raids. His band began to raid pro-Union communities, robbed mail coaches and supply wagons, and attacked Union supporters. The success and notoriety of his activities increased the numbers of his gang.

Quantrill and his men found some refuge with local, pro-Confederate families. On one such occasion, in Blue Springs, Missouri, Quantrill met thirteen-year-old Sarah Katherine King. They were secretly married, and she remained with him at their camps until his death.

By 1862, the gang caught the attention of Union leaders. They declared the gang, now known as "Quantrill's Raiders," as outlaws. The ongoing border wars between Kansas and Missouri also attracted others to Quantrill's band. Among these were Frank and Jesse James, William T. "Bloody Bill" Anderson, and the Younger brothers. The group had now grown to over 400 men. The gang led successful attacks on August 11, 1862, on the Union-controlled city of Independence, Missouri. On October 17, 1862, the group attacked Shawnee, Kansas. The commander of the Department of Missouri, Major General Henry W. Halleck, ordered that "guerillas such as Quantrill and his men be treated as robbers and murderers, not normal prisoners of war." Quantrill would respond by no longer allowing the surrender of Union supporters or soldiers.

Union forces began to gather and imprison the pro-Confederate activist families along the Kansas-Missouri border. Many family members of Quantrill's gang were imprisoned. One group was placed in a makeshift jail in Kansas City. The three-story building was not very stable, and on August 13, 1863, the building collapsed, killing and injuring many prisoners. Among these were members of "Bloody Bill" Anderson's immediate family. At this time, the city of Osceola, Missouri, was burned by Union forces. These two incidents were the motivation to exact revenge on the city of Lawrence, Kansas.

The most notorious event of Quantrill and his raiders would take place on August 21, 1863, in Lawrence, Kansas. The town was the known center for the antislavery activists in Kansas. At 5:00 a.m., Quantrill led his band of 450 raiders down from Mount Oread and into the town of 3,000 people. They indiscriminately killed 183 men and boys. Stores and the one bank were looted, and the town structures set on fire. One survivor, the Rev. H. D. Fisher, described the scene:

> With demoniac yells the scoundrels flew hither and yon, wherever a man was to be seen, shooting him down like a dog. Men were called from their beds and murdered before the eyes of wives and children on their doorsteps. Years, entreaties, prayers availed nothing. The fiends of hell were among us and under the demands of their vengeful black leader they satiated their thirst for blood with fiendish delight.

In response to the vicious attack on Lawrence, Union General Thomas Ewing, Jr., issued General Order No. 11. It required that three counties along the Kansas border be evacuated. Citizens were forced to leave their homes and marched by Union forces with them, facing houses, fields, and buildings being burned and livestock being killed. The area became known as the "Burnt District."

There was also growing disapproval among Confederate supporters and leaders with Quantrill's Raiders' sadistic action. After participating in a few skirmishes in northern Missouri, Quantrill moved his men to Texas.

In Texas, Quantrill's men, well financed with loot from the raids, tried to associate with the regular Confederate forces. But their continued practices of robbery and mayhem caused the local residents to bitterly complain to the Confederate leaders. Eventually, the local Confederate commander, Brigadier General Henry McCullough, tried to mediate the situation. But Quantrill and his men were uncooperative, and on March 28, 1864, the commander had Quantrill arrested. He escaped and returned to find his gang in turmoil. Various factions were either unhappy with the violence or wanted more power and control. Quantrill was forced out of the camp. He took about twenty followers and traveled through the Indian Territory and returned to Missouri.

Anderson led the majority of Quantrill's Raiders back to Missouri. He continued the harsh treatment of Unionists on September 1864, repeating the tactics of the Lawrence Raid, in town of Centralia, Missouri. One month later, Anderson would be killed in a battle near Orrick, Missouri.

Quantrill, with his small force, set out for Washington, D. C. in an attempt to assassinate President Abraham Lincoln. In November 1864, he left with his raiders from Lafayette County, Missouri. He encountered large troops of Union forces near the Mississippi River and had to abandon his plans. In early 1865, he led his group of thirty-three men into Kentucky with their customary raids. Dressed in federal uniforms, Quantrill's Raiders were able to pass themselves off as Union troops. With the surrender of Confederate forces, guerilla bands on both sides of the conflict began roaming the countryside.

Federal authorities commissioned a guerilla leader and former Union leader, Captain Edwin Terrell, to hunt down Quantrill and his band. On May 10, 1865, Quantrill and his men had stopped for rest at the farm of James H. Wakefield near Taylorville in Spencer County. Terrell's men discovered their location and made plans to capture the gang. A witness of the incident stated, "The men of Captain Terrell went briskly up to the lane, and, rising the swell, charged down upon the barn, unslinging carbines and getting pistols in hand. Coming in range, fire was opened and yells set up to terrify the Missourians." Quantrill's men scrambled for their horses while Quantrill was asleep in the barn loft. His horse had bolted before he could reach it and Quantrill set out in a run after his men. Quantrill was shot in the back and became paralyzed. He was transported to a military hospital in Louisville, Kentucky. He was reportedly converted by a Catholic priest. In considerable pain, on June 6, 1865, he died at the age of twenty-seven.

He was initially buried in St. John's Cemetery in Louisville. Legend says that later in 1889, his skull was buried by his mother in the Fourth Street Cemetery in his hometown of Dover, Ohio. The rest of his remains were interred on October 24, 1992, at the Confederate Memorial State Historic Site in Higginsville, Missouri.

Among those who escaped the ambush at the farmhouse were Frank and Jesse James. The lessons they learned from Quantrill would be used in their own raids and robberies. Quantrill's wife, Sarah, lived until 1930.

Quantrill's unique style of warfare was abhorred by the Union forces and eventually detested by the Confederate forces. He was described as a pathological killer and by others as a hero for the cause of states' rights. But whatever one's viewpoint, none can deny his impact on the states of Kansas and Missouri.

Belle Starr
Carthage
Outlaw

She was an unusually well-educated woman for her time. She was raised in a well-to-do family and had all of the material benefits of a talented child. She would become one of the most notorious outlaws of the Old West, known as "the Bandit Queen of the Old West."

Myra Maybelle Shirley (called May) was born on February 5, 1848, on her father's farm near Carthage, Missouri. Her father, Judge John Shirley, had been married twice before settling with Elizabeth Pennington, relative of the famous Hatfields who fought with the McCoys. May was the middle child of seven children born to Shirley from his multiple marriages. As an earlier homesteader, her father sold an 800-acre farm and moved to Carthage, where he purchased a hotel and livery stable on the town square. His wealth allowed for May to receive a classical education, including training in piano at the Carthage Female Academy. With help from her father's extensive home library, May completed her studies in "reading, spelling, grammar, arithmetic, manners, Greek, Latin, Hebrew and music." She was described as bright but strong-willed.

Growing up, her best friend was her brother, Bud. Six years older than May, Bud taught her skills in horse riding and firing a pistol and a rifle. The lives of the family would change with the start of the Civil War. Caught in the area of the Kansas-Missouri Border Wars, the Shirleys were sympathizers with the Confederate forces. At the age of twenty-one, Bud rode away to join William Quantrill's guerilla army. Among the neighbors and friends nearby were Cole Younger, Frank James, and Jesse James. May vowed to do all she could to support the Confederate cause against the Union. She even assisted as informer for Quantrill's army in attacking a neighboring house used as a barracks for Union soldiers. Soon after, in 1864, Bud and another gang member were eating in the home of a Confederate sympathizer. Union forces surrounded the home, and when Bud tried to escape, he was shot and killed. His death devastated the family. May was under suspicion of aiding the Confederate cause, and Shirley's business interest were ruined by the constant attacks of both military forces. In an effort to save his family, Shirley moved them to a farm in Scyene, Texas, just southeast of Dallas.

In Texas, other members of Quantrill's Gang had also sought to escape the pursuit of Union forces. The Younger brothers and James brothers were visitors in their home along with another Missouri neighbor, James C. Reed. Reed had been a childhood acquaintance of May, and the two began a romance, culminating with their marriage on November 1, 1866. May was eighteen, and Reed was twenty. Reed was not yet wanted in Missouri, so they traveled back. Two children were born the following years. May became known as an unusually talented woman, riding sidesaddle on the best horses and in the best clothes. Reed failed as a farmer and began associating with a new friend Tom Starr. The gang would race horses, gamble, and hide out on the Starrs' ranch in the Indian Territory (Oklahoma), just west of Fort Smith, Arkansas. When Reed became wanted in Missouri, the family temporarily moved to California. Reed found work in a gambling house in Los Angeles.

In California, Reed was accused of using counterfeit money. To escape arrest, he moved with the family back to Texas. Their attempts at farming failed once again, and Reed turned to robbery and murder. He needed to escape the warrant and reward on him, so once again they moved back to the Starr ranch in the Indian Territory. Growing concerned about Reed's selfishness and lack of concern for his family, May moved with the children to her parents' home in Texas. Betrayed by an undercover law official, Reed was shot and killed.

In 1879, May joined with Bruce Younger in the mining town of Galena, Kansas. The two were a strange couple, even by Western standards. Bruce was a foul-mouthed gambler, and May was a well-dressed woman with an educated manner of speaking. It is uncertain if the pair actually married, but their association did not last very long. May returned to Starr's ranch in the Indian Territory. She met the three-quarters Cherokee son of Tom Starr, Sam Starr. They were married on June 1, 1880 in a special Cherokee ceremony. It was then that May changed her name to "Belle Starr."

They cleared land and built a cabin on Younger's Bend, on the Canadian River about seventy miles southwest of Fort Smith. They remained quiet for about two years. In 1882, they were accused of horse stealing. On November 7, 1882, they were both brought before the District Court in Fort Smith. A grand jury ruled against them. They posted bail and returned to Indian Territory to await trial.

A four-day trial was held in early March, 1883, in Fort Smith before "Hanging Judge" Isaac C. Parker. An unusually lenient Judge Parker sentenced Sam to twelve months hard labor and Belle to two six-month terms in the House of Corrections in Detroit, Michigan. They both served only nine months because of their good behavior.

In December, 1884, the Starrs hosted John Middleton, a notorious murderer. With law officials hot on his trail, the Starrs and Middleton decided to take a trip. With a horse, later discovered to have been stolen, the party ran into trouble. Middleton supposedly drowned in a river crossing. Sam, under pursuit, was arrested by lawman Frank West. He escaped but was later cornered again by West, and both died in an ensuing gunfight.

Belle returned to their home in Indian Territory, only to discover that the property was no longer hers since Sam, her American Indian husband, was dead. Belle took up with an adopted son of Tom Starr named Jim July Starr. This allowed her to stay on the land. She wanted to live out a peaceful life and refused to use her house as a refuge for criminals. She began to lease out some of her land. One renter was a man named Edgar Watson, who claimed to be from Arkansas. Belle discovered from Watson's wife that he was in fact a criminal charged with murder in Florida. Belle threatened to tell the authorities of his identity if he did not move off her land. He reluctantly agreed and found land nearby.

Once again Belle and Jim were accused of horse stealing. On February 2, 1889, Jim July left to go to Fort Smith to deal with the charges. Belle rode partway with him. On her return trip home, she stopped at a friend's house and discovered the presence of Edgar Watson. Later, when Belle left the house, Watson also disappeared. On February 3, 1889, as she rode near the Watson cabin, a shogun fired buckshot in her back and neck. She fell off the horse, and another shot was fired point blank at shoulder and face. Over sixty shots had been fired. Although Watson was charged with the crime, a not guilty verdict was rendered because of no witness and circumstantial evidence.

The women of the community, who had benefitted from Belle's kindnesses, prepared Belle's body for burial. There was no preacher and no prayer at her funeral service. She was buried on her ranch near today's Eufala Dam in Oklahoma. Her grave was just a few steps away from the entrance to her cabin.

Like other western outlaws. Belle became legendary. In 1889, a book was written, *Belle Starr, Bandit Queen and The Female Jesse James*, by reporter Richard K. Fox. Film and television movies were made of her life with embellished legends. A biography of some note was written by Glenn Shirley, *Belle Starr and Her Times: The Literature, Facts, and the Legends*. A year before her death, she told a reported for the *Fort Smith Elevator*, "I regard myself as a woman who has seen much of life." On her grave marker was written, "Shed not for her the bitter tear nor give the heart to vain regret, 'tis but the casket that lies here, the gem that fills it sparkles yet."

Belle Starr began what could and should have been a wonderful life in Missouri. Like so many families of the area, the Civil War and community divisions led to a change of heart and life's purpose.

Sacred Sun
Saline County
American Indian

She was a Native American from Missouri who found celebrity in Europe in the early 1800s. She gave birth to twins in a hotel room in Belgium. Only the generosity of the Marquis de Lafayette allowed her to return to her home.

Sacred Sun (Mohongo) was born around 1809, in the area of what became Saline County on the Missouri River among the Osage Indian tribe. Her father was Little Chief, leader of the nomadic tribe of fur hunters. In 1803, the United States purchased the vast Louisiana Territory from France, which included the Osage tribal lands. With the purchase, Sacred Sun and the Osage tribe would experience the arrival of settlers and forts in the nearby land.

They had traded for many years with the French fur traders. Some of the Osage Indians in previous generations had been able to travel to France and meet with French King Louis XV. Little Chief had a strong desire to visit France. For months, the tribe stockpiled furs to be used to finance a trip to France for tribal members.

In 1827, Sacred Sun and eleven others from the tribe loaded a raft with their goods to travel the Missouri River to St. Louis. Just before arrival, their raft overturned and all of the furs were lost. Half of the party returned home: Little Chief; his wife, Hawk Woman; Sacred Sun;

and her husband, Black Bird. Minckhatahooh and Big Soldier continued on foot to St. Louis.

In St. Louis, they met an acquaintance, David Delaunay, a Frenchman and experienced traveler. Delaunay surmised that the appearances and shows performed by the Indians would cover the expense of the trip. Delaunay traveled ahead to prepare for their arrival and alert the press. The Indians all left on board a steamboat called *Commerce* and traveled down the Mississippi River to New Orleans. They then boarded a ship named *New England* and sailed for France.

They arrived in Le Havre, France, on July 27, 1827. Delaunay had done a good job promoting their arrival. They were greeted by a crowd of thousands curious to see and meet the American Indians. The French were excited by the appearances of the visitors. Their bronze skin, colorful clothing, and face paintings were viewed with awe. The guests were treated as royalty. They were called the "Missourian Majesties." They stayed in nice hotels, were served exquisite French meals, and were honored guests at local cultural events. They were even granted an audience with French King Charles X at his palace.

The expenses of the trip and the lavish lifestyle in France was a strain on the Delaunay account. He began to charge for tickets for personal appearances and performances of American Indian dances. After a while, the French had lost interest in the guests and additional income in support of the American Indians dried up.

Several events created turmoil with the traveling Osage party. First, David Delaunay was arrested for some outstanding debts and charged as a swindler. The Indians were on their own. Second, Sacred Sun was pregnant and desired to go back home to give birth to her child. The American Indians began extensive travels to other neighboring European countries in an attempt to raise funds. On February 10, 1828, Sacred Sun gave birth to twin daughters in a hotel room in Liege, Belgium. Local church women helped her with the delivery. Perhaps for financial assistance, one daughter was given to a wealthy Belgium woman. That child would die within the year.

The American Indians continued traveling around Europe in Holland, Belgium, Germany, Switzerland, France, and Italy for the next two years. They would often have to beg for food and lodging. Concern was raised back in the United States about their welfare. The group of six divided into two groups. European newspapers wrote of their plight.

Word reached the attention of American friend and Revolutionary War hero, French General Marquis de LaFayette. In 1829, he arranged for the American Indians to sail back to the United States. On the return trip, Black Bird and Minckhatahooh died of smallpox on the boat. The first group arrived in Norfolk, Virginia, in late 1829. Superintendent of the Bureau of Indian Affairs, Thomas McKenney, provided care for the group while they waited for the arrival of the remaining Indians. The Osage were reunited in Washington, D. C. While there, McKenney arranged for Sacred Sun and her baby to have their portrait painted by Charles Bird King. Their portrait would hang in the National Indian Portrait Gallery until it was destroyed by a fire in 1865.

On May 6, 1830, the group left Washington, D. C., and traveled by stagecoach to St. Louis, Missouri. The tired group returned to meet their ancestral tribal members, only to discover that they had been forced to leave their homeland and move to the Indian Territory. Sacred Sun and her family lived with the Osage tribe, located near Fort Gibson on the Neosho River, in what is today northeast Oklahoma. The last mention of her was in 1833. It was assumed she died around 1836.

Sacred Sun was an adventurous and brave young woman with roots in Missouri well before it was a state. She was a unique representative of the American Indian culture put on display throughout Europe. She experienced a difficult life in Europe as well as upon her return the United States.

Other Missouri Innovators

Charles "Pretty Boy" Floyd • *Kansas City* • outlaw

Tom Horn • *Scotland County* • lawman

James Earl Ray • *Ewing* • assassin

Conclusion

Missouri is called the 'Show Me State.' It was not only for others to show us proof of better things. It is also important to recognize that many Missourians have and are showing the world better things. Missourians have proven to be innovators in many of the important fields of national and international history. Both men and women have led the way as those innovators.

We have explored many areas of innovation and creativity in a number of important fields. Our state has offered unique leaders in entertainment, fine arts, education and literature, business, science and technology, politics and military, sports, and other fields. There are certainly many other fields not highlighted in this book.

Most of these innovators have been important figures in our past history. But what about our leadership in innovative roles today and in the future? We have the great challenge to provide for educational and occupational opportunities for research and development of new processes and products to improve our lives. Our state must advance the cause of educating our children, youth, and adults to reach beyond the minimal skills for survival. We must provide the financial and leadership abilities to "Show Me" a better way of life.

Resources and References

Chapter One

Josephine Baker

Books
Baker, J., and J. Bouillon. *Josephine Baker*. New York: Marlow and
  Company, 1995

Brown, John. *Missouri Legends: Famous People from the Show-Me State*.
  Reedy Press: St. Louis, Missouri, 2008

Hammond, Bryan, and Patrick O'Connor. *Josephine Baker*. Boston: Little
  Brown, 1993

Haney, Lynn. *Naked at the Feast: The Biography of Josephine Baker*.
  Robson Books Ltd: XX, XX, 1995

Lahs-Gonzales, O. *Josephine Baker: Image and Icon*. St. Louis: Reedy
  Press, 2006

Mellberg, Robert William. *Missouri Proud*. Xlibris Corporation, 2007

Merkel, Jim. *The Colorful Characters of St. Louis*. Reedy Press: St. Louis,
  Missouri, 2016

Reese, Alice Anna. *Show Me Famous Missourians*. Compass Compass
  Flower Press, 2014

Thompson, Bernice. *Famous Missourians*. Carlton Press, Inc.: New York,
  New York, 1992

Wood, E. *The Josephine Baker Story*. United Kingdom: Sanctuary
  Publishing, 2000

Websites
britannica.com/Josephine-Baker
cmgww.com/stars/baker/about/biography.html
imdb.com/name/nm0001927/bio
noteablebiohraphies.com/Ba-Be/Baker-Josephine.html
thoughtco.com/Josephine-baker-3528473

Photo Credit
Wikimedia Commons. Josephine Baker in Banana Skirt from the Folies
  Bergère production "Un Vent de Folie", Photo by Lucien Walery, 1927.

Linda Bloodworth-Thomason

Websites
imdb.com/name/nm0089124/

tcm.com/tcmdb/person/7504900/Linda-Bloodworth-Thomason/
thefullwiki.org/Linda_Bloodworth-Thomason
wow.com/wiki/Linda_Bloodworth_Thomason
Photo Credit
yahoo.com

Molly Brown

Books

Iverson, Kristen. *Molly Brown: Unraveling the Myth*. Boulder: Johnson
   Books, 1999

Landau, Elaine. *Heroine of the Titanic: The Real Unsinkable Molly Brown*.
   New York: Clarion Books, 2001

Mellberg, Robert William. *Missouri Proud*, Xlibris Corporation, 2007

Websites

biography.com/people/molly-brown-20638583#!

Britannica.com/print/article/81595

mollybrown.org/about-molly-brown/

shsmo.org/historicmissourians/name/b/brownmt/

thefamouspeople.com/profiles/molly-brown-3392-php

Photo Credit

Wilimedia Commons. Mrs. James J. "Molly" Brown, ca. 1890-1920.

Walt Disney

Books

Barrier, M.,- and B. Thomas. *Disney's Art of Animation: From Mickey
   Mouse to the Beast*. New York: Hyperion, 1999

Brown, John. *Missouri Legends: Famous People from the Show-Me State*.
   Reedy Press: St. Louis, Missouri, 2008

Mellberg, Robert William. *Missouri Proud*. Xlibris Corporation, 2007

Reese, Alice Anna. *Show Me Famous Missourians*. Compass Flower
   Press, 2014

Thompson, Bernice. *Famous Missourians*. Carlton Press, Inc.: New York,
   New York, 1992

Watts, S. *The Magic Kingdom: Walt Disney and the American Way of Life*.
   Boston: Houghton Mifflin, 1997

Websites

biography.com/people/walt-disney-9275533

brainyquotes.com/quotes/authors/w/walt_disney.html

imdb.com/name/nm0000370/bio

justdisney.com/walt_disney/biography/long_bio.html

Other

Missouri Life Magazine, Robin Seaton Jefferson, "Marceline," September, 2017, pages 45-51

Photo Credit

Wikimedia Commons. Publicity photo of Walt Disney from the Boy Scouts of America, 17 May 1946.

Emmett Kelly

Books

Mellberg, Robert William. *Missouri Proud*. Xlibris Corporation, 2007

Websites

britannica.com/biography/Emmett-Kelly

imdb.com/name/nm0446374

joeykelly.com/emmett.html

Site Visit

Emmett Kelly Park, Houston, Missouri

Photo Credit

Wikimedia Commons. Emmett Kelly, 1953.

Sally Rand

Books

Knox, Holly. *From Films to Fans*. Maverick Publications, ISBN 0-89288-172-0, 1988

Merkel, Jim. *The Colorful Characters of St. Louis*. Reedy Press: St. Louis, Missouri, 2016

Websites

cemeteryguide.com/gotw-rand.html

lamorguefiles.blogspot.com/2015/08/burlesque-dancer-actress-sally-rand.html

yodaslair.com/dumboozle/sally/sallydex.html

Photo Credit

cemeteryguide.com/gotw-rand.html

Ginger Rogers

Books

Mellberg, Robert William. *Missouri Proud*. Xlibris Corporation, 2007

Thompson, Bernice. *Famous Missourians*. Carlton Press, Inc.: New York, New York, 1992

Websites

britannica.com/biography/Ginger-Rogers
gingerrogers.com/about/biography.html
imdb.com/name/nm0001677/bio
reelclassics.com/Actress/Ginger/ginger-bio.html
thefamouspeople.com/profiles/ginger-1527.pho

Photo Credit

yahoo.com

Dick Van Dyke

Books

Mellberg, Robert William. *Missouri Proud*. Xlibris Corporation, 2007
Thompson, Bernice. *Famous Missourians*. Carlton Press, Inc.: New York, New York, 1992
Van Dyke. Dick. *Faith, Hope and Hilarity and Those Funny Kids: A Treasury of Classroom Laughter*, 1970
Van Dyke, Dick. *My Lucky Life In ad Out of Show Business.*

Websites

biography.com/people/dick-van-dyke-9515591
fandango.com/people/dick-van-dyke-692765/biography
officialdickvandyke.com/biography/
tvguide.com/celebrities/dick-van-dyke/bio/147391/

Photo Credit

yahoo.com

Chapter Two

Thomas Hart Benton

Books

Brown, John. *Missouri Legends: Famous People from the Show-Me State*. Reedy Press: St. Louis, Missouri, 2008
Burroughs, Polly. *Thomas Hart Benton, a portrait.*
Gruber, J. Richard. *Thomas Hart Benton and the American South*. Augusta, GA: Morris Museum of Art, 1998
Mellberg, Robert William. *Missouri Proud*. Xlibris Corporation, 2007
Thompson, Bernice. *Famous Missourians*. Carlton Press, Inc.: New York, New York, 1992

benton.truman.edu/artist.html

biography.com/people/Thomas-hart-benton-9208158

imdb.com/name/nm0072973/bio

theartstory.org/artist-benton-thomas-hart.html

thefamouspeople.com/profiles/Thomas-hart-benton-5383.php

thomashartbenton.org/ index.html

Other

"Ken Burns' American Stories: Thomas Hart Benton," PBS, 1988

Site Visit

Truman Presidential Library, Independence, Missouri, Lobby mural

Photo Credit

Wikimedia Commons. Thomas Hart Benton, painter. Photo by Carl Van
Vechten, 16 April 1935.

Chuck Berry

Books

Berry, Chuck. *The Autobiography*. New York: Random House, 1989

Brown, John. *Missouri Legends: Famous People from the Show-Me State*.
Reedy Press: St. Louis, Missouri, 2008

Mellberg, Robert William. *Missouri Proud*. Xlibris Corporation, 2007

Pegg, B. *Brown Eyed Handsome Man: The Life and Times of Chuck Berry*.
London: Routledge, 2002

Thompson, Bernice. *Famous Missourians*. Carlton Press, Inc.: New York,
New York, 1992

Websites

biography.com/people/chuck-berry-9210488

chuckberry.com/biography

nbcnews.com/pop-culture/celebrity/chuck-berry-father-rock-n-roll-
dies-90-missouri-police-n699311

Photo Credit

Wikimedia Commons. Publicity photo of Chuck Berry, ca. 1957.

Carl and Robert Boller

Books

Soren, Noelle. *The Missouri Theater, Columbia, Missouri (Part III)*.
Columbia: University of Missouri Art History Dept., c. 1975. [REF
H056.23 So68]

Windows to Wonderland: Cinespace Creations of the Boller Brothers,
    Atchitects. Tucson, AZ: MGP Publishing, 1999. [REF F529 So68]
Websites
    courtlistener.com/opinion/4068857/billings-v-boller/
    kshs.org/kansasapdeia/carl-and-robert-boller/19726
    shsmo.org/historicmissourians/name/b/boller/index.html
    wow.com/wiki/Boller_Brothers
Photo Credit
    shsmo.org/historicmissourians/name/b/boller/index.html

Grace Bumbry
Books
    Mellberg, Robert William. *Missouri Proud.* Xlibris Corporation, 2007
    Story, Rosalyn. *And So I Sing: African American Divas of Opera and*
      Concert. Warner Brothers, 1990
    Thompson, Bernice. *Famous Missourians.* Carlton Press, Inc.: New York,
      New York, 1992
Websites
    biography.com/people/grace-bumbry-21088649
    blackpast.org/aah/bumbry-grace-1937
    gracebumbry.com/biography/ (David Lee Brewer, Brewer International,
      Berlin, Germany)
    musicianguide.com/biographies/1608000604/grace-bumbry.html
Photo Credit
    blackpast.org/aah/bumbry-grace-1937

Walter Cronkite
Books
    Brown, John. *Missouri Legends: Famous People from the Show-Me State.*
      Reedy Press: St. Louis, Missouri, 2008
    Cronkite, Walter. *A Reporter's Life.* 1996
    Mellberg, Robert William. *Missouri Proud.* Xlibris Corporation, 2007
    Thompson, Bernice. *Famous Missourians.* Carlton Press, Inc.: New York,
      New York, 1992
Websites
    biography.com/people/walter-cronkite-9262057
    cbsnews.com/news/walter-cronkite-dies/
    cronkite.asu.edu/about/walter-cronkite-and-asu/walter-cronkite-biography

great-quotes.com/quotes/author/Walter/Cronkite

thinkexist.com/quotes/walyer_cronkite/2.html

<u>Other</u>

Rottenberg, D. "And that's the Way It Is," *American Journalism Review*, College Park, Maryland, 1994

<u>Photo Credit</u>

Wikimedia Commons. Legendary CBS newsman Walter Cronkite speaks at a ceremony at the National Air and Space Museum in Washington celebrating the 35th anniversary of Apollo 11 in 2004. Photo by NASA/Bill Ingalls.

Scott Joplin

<u>Books</u>

Berlin, Edward A. *King of Ragtime: Scott Joplin and His Era*. New York: Oxford University Press, 1994 [REF F508.1 J747be]

Brown, John. *Missouri Legends: Famous People from the Show-Me State*. Reedy Press: St. Louis, Missouri, 2008

Curtis, S. *Dancing to a Black Man's Tune; A Life of Scott Joplin*. Columbia: University of Missouri Press, 2004

Frew, Timothy. *Scott Joplin & the Age of Ragtime*.

Mellberg, Robert William. *Missouri Proud*. Xlibris Corporation, 2007

Mitchell, Barbara. *Raggin'; A Story About Scott Joplin*. Minneapolis: Carolhoda Books, 1987 (IJ M692r)

Thompson, Bernice. *Famous Missourians*. Carlton Press, Inc.: New York, New York, 1992

<u>Websites</u>

biography.com/people/scott-joplin-9357953

lsjunction.com/people/Joplin.html

mfiles.co.uk/composers/Scott-Joplin.html

thefamouspeople.com/profiles/scott-joplin-347.php

shsmo.org/historicmissourians/name/j/joplin/

<u>Photo Credit</u>

Wikimedia Commons. Portrait of Scott Joplin, first published in the St. Louis Globe-Democrat newspaper, 7 June 1903.

Bill Mauldin

Books

Mauldin, Bill. *Bill Mauldin's Army*. 1951; Ballantine Books, Inc., April 1983

Mauldin, Bill. *The Brass Ring*. New York: W. W. Norton, 1971

Mauldin, Bill. *Up Front*. Cleveland and New York: World Publishing, 1945; Norton, W.W. & Company, Inc., November 2000

Mauldin, Bill. *A Sort of Saga*. New York: William Sloane Associates Publishers, 1949

Mauldin, Bill. *Star Spangled Banter by Sgt. Bill Mauldin*. Washington, D.C.: Army Times Publishing Co., 1944

Mellberg, Robert William. *Missouri Proud*. Xlibris Corporation, 2007

Merkel, Jim. *The Colorful Characters of St. Louis*. Reedy Press: St. Louis, Missouri, 2016

Websites

encyclopedia.com/people/literature-and-arts/American-art-biographies/bill-mauldin

imdb.com/name/nm-560887/bio

jeanalbanogallery.com/artists-a-m/bill-mauldin

loc.gov/rr/print/swann/mauldin/mauldin-atwar.html

stripes.com/news/cartoonist-bill-mauldin-friend of gis-creator-of-willie-and-joe-dies-at-81-1.1473#WSwj5TOZOb8

Photo Credit

Wikimedia Commons. Pulitzer Prize-winning cartoonist Bill Mauldin, with sketch pad, Photo by Fred Palumbo, 1945.

Charlie "Bird" Parker

Books

Mellberg, Robert William. *Missouri Proud*. Xlibris Corporation,2007

Websites

allmusic.com/artist/charlie-parker-mn0000211758/biography

biography.com/people/charlie-parker-9433413

cmgww.com/music/parker/about/biography.html

findagrave.com/cgi-bin/fg.cgi?page=gr&Grid=1426

nypost.com/2017/02/05/charlie-parkers-heroin-addiction-helped-make-him-a-genius/

Photo Credit

Wikimedia Commons. Portrait of Charlie Parker in the Three Deuces of New York (NY), August 1947. Photo by William Gottlieb.

Joseph Pulitzer

Books

Barrett, James Wyman. *Joseph Pulitzer and his World*. New York: Vanguard Press, 1941 [REF 920 P966b]

Ireland, Alleyne. *Joseph Pulitzer: Reminiscences of a Secretary*. New York: Mitchell Kennerly, 1914 [F508.1 P966i]

Mellberg, Robert William. *Missouri Proud*. Xlibris Corporation, 2007

Seitz, Don Carlos. *Joseph Pulitzer, His Life & Letters*. New York: Simon and Schuster, 1924 [F508.1 P966s]

Thompson, Bernice. *Famous Missourians*. Carlton Press, Inc.: New York, New York, 1992

Websites

britannica.com/biography/Joseph-Pulitzer-Jr

pulitzer.org/page/biography-joseph-pulitzer

shsmo.org/historicmissourians/name/p/pulitzer/

Photo Credit

Wikimedia Commons. Joseph Pulitzer, ca. early 1900s.

Chapter Three

Maya Angelou

Books

Angelou, Maya. *I Know Why the Caged Bird Sings*. 1969

Angelou, Maya. *All God's Children Need Traveling Shoes*. 1986

Angelou, Maya. *A Song Flung Up to Heaven*. 2002

Angelou, Maya. *Hallelujah! The Welcome Table: A Lifetime of Memories With Recipes*. 2005

Angelou, Maya. *Letter to My Daughter*. 2008

Kite, L. Patricia. *Maya Angelou*. Minneapolis: Lemer Publications, 1999

Loos, Pamela. *Maya Angelou*. Philadelphia: Chelsea House, 2000

Mellberg, Robert William. *Missouri Proud*. Xlibris Corporation, 2007

Websites

biography.com/people/maya-angelou-9185388

datesandevents.org/people-timeline/19-maya-angelou-timeline.html

dicksters.com/biography/authors/mayaangelou.php

biographyonline.net/writers/maya-angelou.html

imdb.com/name/nm0029723/bio

notablebiographies.com/An-Ba/Angelou-Maya.html

poemhunter.com/maya-angelou/biography/

Photo Credit

Wikimedia Commons. Maya Angelou reciting her poem "On the Pulse of Morning" at President Bill Clinton's inauguration, January 1993. Courtesy, William J. Clinton Presidential Library.

Susan Blow

Books

Blow, Susan E. *Symbolic Education.* 1894

Blow, Susan E. *Letters to a Mother on the Philosophy of Froebel.* 1899

Blow, Susan E. *Kindergarten Education.* 1900

Blow, Susan E. *Educational Issues in the Kindergarten.* New York: D. Appleton, 1908

Brown, John. *Missouri Legends: Famous People from the Show-Me State.* Reedy Press: St. Louis, Missouri, 2008

Mellberg, Robert William. *Missouri Proud.* Xlibris Corporation, 2007

Menius, Joseph M. *Susan Blow.* St. Clair. MO: Page One Publishing, 1993 [ref f508.1 B623m]

Thompson, Bernice. *Famous Missourians.* Carlton Press, Inc.: New York, New York, 1992

Websites

findagrave.com/cgi-bin/fg.cgi?page=gr&GRid=9316

froebelweb.org/images/blow.html

shsmo.org/historicmissourians/name/b/blow/index.html

historyhappenshere.org/node/6931

myhero.com/hero.asp?hero=S_Blow_moran_ms_2008

neworldencyclopedia.org/entry/Susan_Blow

Other

Nicole Heisick. *Missouri Life Magazine.* "10 Top Women Who Changed Missouri: Susan Blow." March 5, 2013

Photo Credit

shsmo.org/historicmissourians/name/b/blow/index.html

Dale Carnegie

Books

Brown, John. *Missouri Legends: Famous People from the Show-Me State.* Reedy Press: St. Louis, Missouri, 2008

Carnegie, Dale. *How to Win Friends and Influence People.* 1931

Carnegie, Dale. *Lincoln the Unknown*. 1932

Carnegie, Dale. *Little Known Facts About Well Known People*. 1934

Carnegie, Dale. *Biographical Roundup*. 1945

Carnegie, Dale. *How to Stop Worrying and Start Living*. 1945

Kemp, G., and E. Claflin. *Dale Carnegie: The Man Who Influenced Millions*. New York: St. Martin's Press, 1989

Mellberg, Robert William. *Missouri Proud*. Xlibris Corporation, 2007

Watts, Steven. *Self-Help Messiah: Dale Carnegie and Success in Modern America*. New York: Other Press, 2013 [REF F508.1 C215]

Websites

biography.com/people/dale-carnegie-9238769

famousauthors.org/dale-carnegie

imdb.com/name/nm013646/bio

nytimes.com/learning/general/onthisday/bday/1124.html

shsmo.org/historicmissourians/name/c/carnegie/

Photo Credit

famousauthors.org/dale-carnegie

Samuel Clemens (Mark Twain)

Books

Brown, John. *Missouri Legends: Famous People from the Show-Me State*. Reedy Press: St. Louis, Missouri, 2008

Gold, C. *Mark Twain's Road to Bankruptcy*. Columbia: University of Missouri Press, 2003

Kirk, Connie Anne. *Mark Twain: A Biography*. Westport, CT: Greenwood Press, 2004 [REF IC591 Bkir]

Mellberg, Robert William. *Missouri Proud*. Xlibris Corporation, 2007

Reese, Alice Anna. *Show Me Famous Missourians*. Compass Flower Press, 2014

Tenney, T. *Mark Twain: A Reference Guide*. Boston: G. K. Hall, 1977

Thompson, Bernice. *Famous Missourians*. Carlton Press, Inc.: New York, New York, 1992

Twain, Mark. *The Adventures of Tom Sawyer*. 1876

Twain, Mark. *The Prince and the Pauper*. 1881

Twain, Mark. *Life on the Mississippi*. 1883

Twain, Mark. *Adventures of Huckleberry Finn*. 1884

Twain, Mark. *A Connecticut Yankee in King Arthur's Court*. 1889

Twain, Mark. *The Tragedy of Pudd'nhead Wilson*. 1894

Twain, Mark. *Letters from the Earth*. 1909

Ward, Geoffrey C., Dayton Duncan, and Ken Burns, *Mark Twain [An Illustrated Biography]*, New York: Alfred A. Knopf, 2001 [REF IC591 Bwar]

Websites

biography.com/people/mark-twain-9512564

geni.com/people/Mark-Twain/4239183543700124287

goodreads.com/quotes/tag/mark-twain

marktwainhouse.org/man/biography_main.php

pbs.org/weta/thewest/people/a_c/Clemens.html

shsmo.org/hostoricmissourians/name/c/Clemens

Site Visit

Becky Thatcher Home, Hannibal, Missouri

Photo Credit

Wikimedia Commons. Mark Twain photo portrait. Photo by Matthew Brady, 7 February 1871.

T. S. Eliot

Books

Brown, John. *Missouri Legends: Famous People from the Show-Me State*. Reedy Press: St. Louis, Missouri, 2008

Eliot, T. S. *The Waste Land*. 1922

Eliot. T. S. *Old Possum's Book of Practical Cats*. 1939

Eliot, T. S. *Religious Drama: Mediaeval and Modern*. 1954

Lyndall, Gordon. *T. S. Eliot: An Imperfect Life*. New York: Norton, 1999

Mellberg, Robert William. *Missouri Proud*. Xlibris Corporation, 2007

Moody, D. *The Cambridge Guide to T. S. Eliot*. Cambridge: University Press, 1994

Thompson, Bernice. *Famous Missourians*. Carlton Press, Inc.: New York, New York, 1992

Websites

Bush, Ronald. "T. S. Eliot's Life and Career."english.illinois.edu/maps/poets/a_f/eliot/life.html

biography.com/people/ts-eliot-9286072

brainyquotes.com/quotes/authors/t/t_s_eliot.html

imdb.com/name/nm0253672/bio

nobelprize.org/nobel_prizes/literature/laureates/1948/eliot-bio.html

notablebiographies.com/Du0Fi/Eliot-T-S.html

poets.org/poetsorg/poet/t-s-eliot

thefamouspeople.com/profiles/t-s-eliot-33.pho

Photo Credit

Wikimedia Commons. T.S. Eliot, photographed one Sunday afternoon in 1923 by Lady Ottoline Morrell.

Langston Hughes

Books

Hughes, Langston. *The Weary Blues*. 1926

Hughes, Langston. *Fine Clothes to the Jews*. 1927

Hughes, Langston. *Not Without Laughter*. 1930

Hughes, Langston. *The Big Sea: An Autobiography*. New York: Alfred A. Knopf, 1940

Mellberg, Robert William. *Missouri Proud*. Xlibris Corporation, 2007

Reese, Alice Anna. *Show Me Famous Missourians*. Compass Flower Press, 2014

Thompson, Bernice. *Famous Missourians*. Carlton Press, Inc.: New York, New York, 1992

Walker, Alice. *Langston Hughes, American Poet*. New York: HarperCollins, 1889

Websites

biography.com/people/lamgston-hughes-9346313?_escaped_fragment

famouspoetsandpoems.com/poets/Langston_hughes/biography

imdb.com/name/nm0400745/bio

kansasheritage.org/crossingboundaries/pages6e1.html

noteablebiographies.com/Ho-Jo/Hughes-Langston.html

poemhunter.com/Langston-hughes/biography/

Photo Credit

Wikimedia Commons. Langston Hughes. Photo by Carl Van Vechten, 1936.

Reinhold Niebuhr

Books

Bingham, June. *Courage to Change: An Introduction to the Life and Thought of Reinhold Niebuhr*. 1961

Brown, Charles C. *Niebuhr and His Age: Niebuhr's Prophetic Role in the Twentieth Century*. 1992

Mellberg, Robert William. *Missouri Proud*. Xlibris Corporation, 2007

Niebuhr, Reinhold. *Moral man and Immoral Society: A Study in Ethics and Politics*. 1932

Stone, Ronald H. *Reinhold Niebuhr: Prophet to Politicians*. Washington, D. C.: University Press of America, 1981

Websites

Dorrien, Gary. "Irony Repeats Itself: Reconsidering Reinhold Niebuhr in the Trump Era." religiondispatches.org/irony-repeats-itself-reconsidering-reinhold-niebuhr-in-the-trump-era

Schlesinger, Jr., Arthur. "Forgetting Reinhold Niebuhr." nytimes.cpm/2005/09/18/books/review/forgetting-reinhold-niebuhr.html?_r=0

christianitytoday.com/ct/2017/may-web-only/why reinhold-niebuhr-still-haunts-american-politics.html

conservapedia.com/Reinhold_Niebuhr

motivational-quotes-sayings.com/reinhold-niebuhr/

newworldencyclopedia.org/entry/Reinhold_ Niebuhr

Photo Credit

Wikimedia Commons. Reinhold Niebuhr, date unknown.

Marlin Perkins

Books

Brown, John. *Missouri Legends: Famous People from the Show-Me State*. Reedy Press: St. Louis, Missouri, 2008

Mellberg, Robert William. *Missouri Proud*. Xlibris Corporation, 2007

Merkel, Jim. *The Colorful Characters of St. Louis*. Reedy Press: St. Louis, Missouri, 2016

Perkins, Marlin. *My Wild Kingdom*. 1982

Websites

Boorstein, Robert O. "R. Marlin Perkins, TV Host for Decades on 'Wild Kingdom,'" nytimes.com/1986/06/15/obituaries/r-marlin-perkins-tv-host-for-decades-on-wild-kingdom.html

biography.com/people/marlin-perkins--41716

famousbirthdays.com/people/marlin-perkins.html

fampeople.com/cat-marlin-perkins

findagrave.com/cgi-bin/fg.cgi?page=gr&Grid=7947131

imdb.com/name/nm0674002/

robinsonlibrary.com/science/zoology/biography/perkins.html

Photo Credit

Wikimedia Commons. Marlin Perkins bottle-feeding a young kangaroo from the television program Wild Kingdom. NBC Television photo ca. 1962-1971.

Laura Ingalls Wilder

Books

Anderson, William. *Laura Ingalls Wilder: A Biography*. New York: HarperCollins, 1992

Brown, John. *Missouri Legends: Famous People from the Show-Me State*. Reedy Press: St. Louis, Missouri, 2008

Mellberg, Robert William. *Missouri Proud*. Xlibris Corporation, 2007

Miller, John E. *Becoming Laura Ingalls Wilder: The Woman Behind the Legacy*. Columbia: University of Missouri Press, 1998

Reese, Alice Anna. *Show Me Famous Missourians*. Compass Flower Press, 2014

Thompson, Bernice. *Famous Missourians*. Carlton Press, Inc.: New York, New York, 1992

Wadsworth, Ginger. *Laura Ingalls Wilder: Storyteller of the Prairie*. Minneapolis: Lerner, 1997

Wilder, Laura Ingalls. *Little House in the Big Woods*. 1932

Wilder, Laura Ingalls. *The Long Winter*. 1940

Wilder, Laura Ingalls. *On the Way Home*. 1962

Wilder, Laura Ingalls. *West From Home: Letters of Laura Ingalls Wilder to Almanzo*. Edited by R. L. MacBride. New York: Harper, 1974

Zochert, Donald. *Laura: The Life of Laura Ingalls Wilder*. Chicago: Regnery, 1976

Websites

biography.com/people/laura-ingalls-wilder-9531246

enotes.com/topics/laura-ingalls-wilder

lauraingallswilderhome.com/

littlehouseontheprairie.com/about-us/laura-ingalls-wilder-documentary

noteablebiographies.com/We-Z/Wilder-Lauta-Ingalls.html

who2.com/laura-ingalls-wilder/

Site Visit

Laura Ingalls Wilder Museum and Homes, Manfield, Missouri

Photo Credit

Wikimedia Commons. Laura Ingalls Wilder, ca. 1885.

Tennessee Williams

Books

Brown, John. *Missouri Legends: Famous People from the Show-Me State.* Reedy Press: St. Louis, Missouri, 2008

Crandell, G. *Tennessee Williams: A Descriptive Bibliography.* Pittsburgh: University of Pittsburgh Press, 1995

Holditch, Kenneth W. and Richard Freeman Leavitt. *Tennessee Williams and the South.* April, 2002

Mellberg, Robert William. *Missouri Proud.* Xlibris Corporation, 2007

Websites

biography.com/people/tennessee-williams-9532952??escaped_ fragment+=

enotes.com/topics/tennessee-williams

famourauthors.org/tennessee-williams

imdb.com.name/nm0931783/bio

olemiss.edu/dir/Williams-tennessee/index.html

pbs.org/wnet/americanmasters/Tennessee-williams-about-tennessee-williams/737/

Photo Credit

Wikimedia Commons. Tennessee Williams, American playwright. Photo by Orlando Fernandez, World Telegram, 1965.

Walter Williams

Books

Brown, John. *Missouri Legends: Famous People from the Show-Me State.* Reedy Press: St. Louis, Missouri, 2008

Farrar, Ronald T. *A Creed for My Profession: Walter Williams, Journalist to the World.* Columbia: University of Missouri Press, 1998. [REFF508.1 W676fa]

Merkel, Jim. *The Colorful Characters of St. Louis.* Reedy Press

Rucker, Frank W. *Walter Williams.* Columbia: Missourian Publishing Association, 1964 [REF F508.1 W676r]

Weinberg, Steve. *A Journalism of Humanity: A Candid History of the First Journalism School.* Columbia: University of Missouri Press, 2008 [REF UMC 378.778 Z122]

Websites

journalism.missouri.edu/jschool/

muarchives.missouri.edu/exh_mu_cenetery_williams.html

muarchives.missouri.edu/c-rg1-s5.html

shsmo.org/historicmissourians/name/w/Williams.index.html

Photo Credit

Wikimedia Commons. American journalist and educator Walter
Williams. U.S. Department of Transportation photo.

Chapter Four

Henry and Richard Bloch

Books

Bloch, Henry W. (with Michael Shook) *H&R Block's Tax Relief*, 1995

Websites

newsroom.hrblock.com/henry-w-bloch/

nndb.com/people/574/000207950/

smei.org/page/henry_bloch

Other

"Henry W. Bloch & Richard A. Bloch, H&R Block." The Curators of the
University of Missouri, 2009

"Leadership: Henry W. Bloch," 2005, from H&R Block

Photo Credit

yahoo.com

Adolphus Busch

Books

Brown, John. *Missouri Legends: Famous People from the Show-Me State.*
Reedy Press: St. Louis, Missouri, 2008

Hernon, Peter, and Terry Ganey. *Under the Influence: The Unauthorized Story
of the Anheuser-Busch Dynasty.* New York: Simon and Schuster, 1991

Mellberg, Robert William. *Missouri Proud.* Xlibris Corporation, 2007

Thompson, Bernice. *Famous Missourians.* Carlton Press, Inc.: New York,
New York, 1992

Wilson, R. G. and T. R. Gouvish, ed. *The Dynamics of the International
Brewing Industry Since 1800.* London, New York: Routledge, 1998

Websites

anheuser-busch.com/about/heritage.html

beerhistory.com/library/holdings/kingofbeer1.shtml

shsmo.org/historicmissourians/name/b/busch/

Photo Credit
Wikimedia Commons. Adolphus Busch, co-founder of Anheuser-
Busch, ca. before 1913.

James Buchanan Eads
Books
Brown, John. *Missouri Legends: Famous People from the Show-Me State.*
Reedy Press: St. Louis, Missouri, 2008
Dorsey, Florence L. *Road to the Sea: The Story of James B. Eads and the
Mississippi River.* 1947
Mellberg, Robert William. *Missouri Proud.* Xlibris Corporation, 2007
Miller, H., and Q. Scott. *The Eads Bridge.* St. Louis: Missouri Historical
Society Press, 1999.
Orrmont, Arthur. James Buchanan Eads: *The Man Who Mastered the
Mississippi.* Englewood Cliffs, NJ: Prentice Hall, 1970 [REF F508.1
Ea25or]
Scott, Quinta and Howard S. Miller. *The Eads Bridge.* Columbia:
University of Missouri Press, 1979 [REFH235.21 Sco85 1999]
Thompson, Bernice. *Famous Missourians.* Carlton Press, Inc.: New York,
New York, 1992
Websites
"James B. Eads, American Engineer" Walter Harry Green Armytage,
2-2-2017, britannica.com/biography/James-B-Eads
archives@mohistory.org A0427 James Buchanan Eads Collection, 1776-1974
missourilegends.com/business-and-technology/james-buchanan-eads/
museum.state.il.us/RiverWeb/landings/Ambot/TECH/TECH20.htm
shsmo.org/historicmissourians/name/e/eads/
Other
"James B. Eads and His Amazing Bridge at St. Louis." *Museum Gazette,*
January 2001. National Park Service, U.S. Department of the Interior
Photo Credit
Wikimedia Commons. James Buchanan Eads. Photo by Brady-Handy,
ca. 1865-1880.

Joyce Hall
Books
Hall, Joyce C. *When You Care Enough.* Kansas City, MO: Hallmark
Cards, 1993

Mellberg, Robert William. *Missouri Proud.* Xlibris Corporation, 2007

Websites

emotionalcards.com/museum/joycehall.html

entrepreneur.com/article/197552

famouspeople.com/cat-joyce-hall

house.mo.gov/famous.aspx?fm=18

nytimes.com/1982/10/30/obituaries/jc-hall-hallmark-founder-is-dead.html

referenceforbusiness.com/businesses/G-L/Hall-Joyce-C.html

Photo Credit

yahoo.com

Ewing Kauffman

Books

Brown, John. *Missouri Legends: Famous People from the Show-Me State.* Reedy Press: St. Louis, Missouri, 2008

Mellberg, Robert William. *Missouri Proud.* Xlibris Corporation, 2007

Morgan, Anne. Prescription for Success: *The Life and Values of Ewing Marion Kauffman.* Andrews McMeel, 1995

Websites

kansascity.royals.mlb.com/kc/hall_of_fame/member.
    jsp?name=EKauffman

kauffman.org/who-we-are/our-founder-ewing-kauffman

kauffman.org/who-we-are/Kauffman-foundation-conference-center

philanthropyroundtable.org/almanac/hall_of_fame/ewing_kauffman

nytimes.com/1993/08/02/obituaries/ewing-m-kauffman-76-owner-of-
    kansas-city-baseball-team.html

wow.com/wiki/Ewing_Kauffman

Site Visit

Kauffman Center, Kansas City, Missouri

Photo Credit

Wikimedia Commons. Kansas City Royals owner Ewing Kauffman, 1968.

Johnny Morris

Books

Brown, John. *Missouri Legends: Famous People from the Show-Me State.* Reedy Press: St. Louis, Missouri, 2008

Reese, Alice Anna. *Show Me Famous Missourians.* Compass

<u>Websites</u>

417mag.com/417-Magazine/November-2014/The-Johnny-Morris-Story/
basspro.com/webapp/wcs/stores/servlet/CFPPagesC?st051&angld=1&p
   ageID=5483&cm_sp=JLMBsCnOct2016_RD&affcode_c=
igfa.org/Museum/HOF-Morris.aspx
missourilegends.com/business-and-technology/johnny-morris
<u>Site Visit</u>
Bass Pro Shop, Springfield, Missouri
Top of the Rock, Missouri
<u>Photo Credit</u>
Wikimedia Commons. John Morris, founder of Bass Pro Shops. U.S.
   Fish and Wildlife Service photo, 3 June 2013.

James Cash Penney

<u>Books</u>
Brown, John. *Missouri Legends: Famous People from the Show-Me State.*
   Reedy Press: St. Louis, Missouri, 2008
Bruere, Robert W. J. C. Penney: *The Man With A Thousand Partners.*
   New York: Harper & Brothers, 1931[REF F508.1 P383pj]
Curry, Mary Elizabeth. *Creating An American Institution: The
   Merchandising Genius of J. C. Penney.* New York: Garland Publishing,
   1993 [REF F508.1 P383cu]
Mellberg, Robert William. *Missouri Proud.* Xlibris Corporation, 2007
Penney, J.C. *My Experience With the Golden Rule.* Kansas City: Frank
   Glenn Publishing, 1949 [REF F508.1 P383pm]
Reese, Alice Anna. *Show Me Famous Missourians.* Compass Flower
   Press, 2014
Thompson, Bernice. *Famous Missourians.* Carlton Press, Inc.: New York,
   New York, 1992
Tibbetts, Orlando L. The Spiritual Journey of J. C. Penney. Rutledge Books
<u>Websites</u>
biography.com/people/jc-penney-38638
britannica.com/biography/J-C-Penney
christianity.com/church/church-history/timeline/1901-2000/jc-
   penney-11630672.html
shsmo.org/historicmissourians/name/p/penney/
<u>Photo Credit</u>
yahoo.com

Sam Walton

Books

Mellberg, Robert William. *Missouri Proud*. Xlibris Corporation, 2007

Scott, R., and S. Vance. *Wal-Mart: A History of Sam Walton's Retail Phenomenon*. New York: Twayne, 1994

Websites

biography.com/people/sam-walton-9523270

brainyquotes.com/quotes/authors/s/sam_walton.html

entreprepneur.com/article/197560

thefamouspeople.com/profiles/sam-walton-209.php

Photo Credit

yahoo.com

Chapter Five

George Washington Carver

Books

Brown, John. *Missouri Legends: Famous People from the Show-Me State*. Reedy Press: St. Louis, Missouri, 2008

Gray, James Marion. *George Washington Carver*. Englewood Cliffs, NJ: Silver Burdett Press, 1991

Holt, Rackham. *George Washington Carver: An American Biography*. Rev. ed. Garden City, NY: Doubleday, 1963

Kremer, Gary R. *George Washington Carver in His Own Words*, 1987

McKissack, Pat and Frederick. *George Washington Carver: The Peanut Scientist*. Rev. ed. Berkeley Heights, NJ: Enslow Publishers, 2002

McMurry, Linda O. *George Washington Carver: Scientist and Symbol*, 1981

Mellberg, Robert William. *Missouri Proud*. Xlibris Corporation, 2007

Moore, Eva. *The Story of George Washington Carver*. New York: Scholastic, 1995

Reese, Alice Anna. *Show Me Famous Missourians*. Compass Flower Press, 2014

Thompson, Bernice. *Famous Missourians*. Carlton Press, Inc.: New York, New York, 1992

Websites

biography.com/people/George-washington-carver-9240299

britannica.com/biography/George-Washington-Carver

duckster.com/biography/george_washington_carver.php

history.com/topics/black-history/George-washington-carver

livescience.com/41780-george-washington-carver.html

noteablebiographies.com/Ca-Ch/Carver-George-Washington.html

Other

Printed information from the George Washington Carver

Visitor's Center, Diamond, Missouri, 2017, National Park Service, U.S.
   Department of the Interior

Site Visit

George Washington Carver National Monument, Diamond, Missouri

Photo Credit

Wikimedia Commons. Botanist George Washington Carver, ca. 1910.

Thomas Anthony Dooley

Books

Dooley, Thomas A. *Dr. Tom Dooley's Three Great Books: Deliver Us
   from Evil, The Edge of Tomorrow [and] The Night They Burned the
   Mountain.* New York: Farrar, Straus and Cudahy, 1960 [REF 921
   D72d]

Fisher, James T. *Dr. America: The Lives of Thomas A Dooley, 1927-1961.*
   Amherst: University of Massachusetts Press, 1997 [REF 921 D72f]

Mellberg, Robert William. *Missouri Proud.* Xlibris Corporation,2007

Thompson, Bernice. *Famous Missourians.* Carlton Press, Inc.: New York,
   New York, 1992

Websites

findagrave.com/cgi-bin/fg.cgi?page=gr&Grid=290

shsmo.org/historicmissourians/name/d/dooley/index.html

Photo Credit

findagrave.com/cgi-bin/fg.cgi?page=gr&id=290

Charles Stark Draper

Books

Mellberg, Robert William. *Missouri Proud.* Xlibris Corporation, 2007

Reese, Alice Anna. *Show Me Famous Missourians.* Compass Flower
   Press, 2014

Websites

authors.library.caltech.edu/5456/1/hrst.mit.edu/apollo/
   public/people/csdraper.html

Britannica.com/biography/Charles-Stark-Draper
draper.com/news/equipping-insects-special-service
lemelson.mit.edu/resources/charles-stark-draper
madehow.com/inventorbios/15/Charles-Stark-Draper.html
nmspacemuseum.org/halloffame/detail.php?id=6
nytimes.com/1987/07/27/obituaries/Charles-s-draper-engineer-guided-
    astronauts-to-moon.html

Other

Duffy, Robert A. "Charles Stark Draper, 1901-1987, A Biographical
    Memoir." Washington, D.C.: National Academy of Sciences, 1994

Photo Credit

Robert Duffy, Biographical Memoir, 1994, National Academy of
    Sciences, Washington, D.C.

James Fergason

Books

Brown, John. *Missouri Legends: Famous People from the Show-Me State.*
    Reedy Press: St. Louis, Missouri, 2008

Mellberg, Robert William. *Missouri Proud.* Xlibris Corporation, 2007

Websites

almanacnews.com/news/2008/12/30/obituary-james-l-fergason-
    pioneer-in-liquid-crystal-display
infoplease.com/science-health/national-inventors-hall-of-fame/james-l-
    fergason
lemelson.mit.edu/winners/james-fergason-O
missourilegends.com/business-and-technology/james-fergason
ohiohistorycentral.org/w/James_L._Fergason
osa.org/en-us/about_osa/newsroom/obituaries/earlier/jamesfergason/
spie.org/about-spie/press-room/spie-member-news/fergason-
    obit-12/16/08

Other

Sparavigna, Amelia Carolina. "James Fergason, a Pioneer in Advancing
    of Liquid Crystal Technology." Department of Applied Science and
    Technology, Politecnico di Torino, Torino, Italy

Photo Credit

almanacnews.com/news/2008/12/30/obituary

Leonard Goodall

Websites:

bolivarmonews.com/neighbors/mozarks-moments-these-missou...er/
  article_21b83b80-5126-11e7-bbe4-3f61f4970834/html?mode=print
gasenginemagazine.com/print?printid={DA6D2BFF-2D92-4E28-8AF2-
  0148DBB80F1B}
lawnandlandscape.com/article/coming-of-age—history-of-mowers/
mytractorforum.com/155-walk-behindmowers/392161-discussion-
  rotary-power-mower-rpm-company-history-1946=1952-a.html
smokstak.com/forum/showthread.php?t=22678&page=2
swnewsmedia.com/eden_prairie_news/business/rotar...manufacturing/
  article_7ce90777-533a-5e97-a8df-d4e14fe4458e.html

Photo Credit

bolivarmonews.com/neighbors/mozarks-moments

Edwin Hubble

Books

Brown, John. *Missouri Legends: Famous People from the Show-Me State.*
  Reedy Press: St. Louis, Missouri, 2008
Hubble, Edwin. *The Realm of the Nebulae.* Yale University Press, 1936
Mellberg, Robert William. *Missouri Proud.* Xlibris Corporation, 2007
Reese, Alice Anna. *Show Me Famous Missourians.* Compass Flower
  Press, 2014

Websites

asd.gsfc.nasa.gov/archive/hubble/overview/hubble_bio.html
biography.com/people/Edwin-hubble-9345936
biography.com/news/edwon-hubble-biography-facts#!
edwinhubble.com/
famousscientists.org/edwin-hubble/
hubblesite.org/the_telescope/hubble_essentials/edwin_hubble.php
nasa.gov/mission_pages/hubble/story/the_story.html
physicssoftheuniverse.com/scientists_hubble.html
sciencedaily.com/terms/Edwin_hubble.html
space.com/15665-edwin-powell-hubble.html
spacetelescope.org/about/history/the-man-behind-the-name/

Photo Credit

space.com/15665-edwin-powell-hubble.html

Jack Kilby

Books

Mellberg, Robert William. *Missouri Proud*. Xlibris Corporation, 2007

Reid, T.R. *The Chip: How Two Americans Invented the Microchip and Launched a Revolution*. Random House paperback, 2001

Websites

biography.com/people/jack-kilby-40499

britannica.com/biography/Jack-Kilby

gardenofpraise.com/ibdkilby.html

ideafinder.com/history/inventors/kilby.html

nobelprize.org/nobel_prizes/physics/laureates/2000/kilby-facts.html

nndb.com/people/041/000027957/

nytimes.com/2005/06/22/business/jack-s-kilby-an-inventor-of-the-microchip-is-dead-at 81.html

thoughtco.com/jack-kilby-father-of-the-microchip-1992042

ti.com/corp/docs/kilbyctr/jackbuilt.shtml

Photo Credit

gardenofpraise.com/ibdkilby.html

William Lear

Books

Boesen, V. *They Said It Couldn't Be Done: The Incredible Story of Bill Lear*. Garden City, NY: Doubleday, 1971

Brown, John. *Missouri Legends: Famous People from the Show-Me State*. Reedy Press: St. Louis, Missouri, 2008

Mellberg, Robert William. *Missouri Proud*. Xlibris Corporation, 2007

Rashke, R. *Stormy Genius: The Life of Aviation's Maverick Bill Lear*. Boston: Houghton Mifflin, 1985

Websites

britannica.com/biography/William-P-Lear

davison.com/blog/2013/06/24/inventor-monday-william-lear/

missourilegends.com/business-and-technology/william-powell-lear

nndb.com/people/990/000113651/

omni.media/bill-lear-interview

people.com/archive/the-widow-of-the-learjet-is-getting-her-husbands-last-design-ff-the-ground-vol-14-no-18/

todayinsci.com/L/Lear_William/Lear_William.html

uh.edu/engines/epi2767.html

Wikimedia Commons. William P. Lear with turbine engine, ca. 1972.

Chapter Six

Omar Bradley

Books

Bradley, Omar Nelson. _A Soldier's Story_. 1951

Bradley, Omar Nelson, and Clay Blair. _A General's Life_. 1983

Brown, John. _Missouri Legends: Famous People from the Show-Me State_. Reedy Press: St. Louis, Missouri, 2008

Mellberg, Robert William. _Missouri Proud_. Xlibris Corporation, 2007

Thompson, Bernice. _Famous Missourians_. Carlton Press, Inc.: New York, New York, 1992

Websites

arlingtoncemtery.net/omarnels.html

biography.com/people/omar-bradley-922368

brainyquote.com/quotes/authors/omar_n_bradlry.html

history.army.mil/brochures/bradley/bradley.html

indb.com/name/nm0103357/bio

thoughtco.com/world-war-ii-general-omar-bradley-2360152

Photo Credit

Wikimedia Commons. U.S. General of the Army Omar Bradley, first Chairman of the Joint Chiefs of Staff.

William Clark and Meriwether Lewis

Books

Bakeless, John. _Lewis and Clark: Partners in Discovery_. New York: William Morrow and Co., 1947

Dansi, Thomas, and John C. Jackson. _Uncovering the Truth about Meriwether Lewis_. Amherst, NY: Prometheus Books, 2012 [REF F508.1 L587 da2]

Jackson, Donald, ed. _Letters of Lewis and Clark Expedition with Related Documents_. Urbana, IL.: University of Illinois Press, 1962

Jones, Landon Y., ed. _The Essential Lewis and Clark_. New York: Ecco Press, 2000 [REF 917.8 J72]

Mellberg, Robert William. _Missouri Proud_. Xlibris Corporation, 2007

Steffen, Jerome. *William Clark: Jeffersonian Man on the Frontier.*
   Norman, OK.: University of Oklahoma Press, 1977
Thompson, Bernice. *Famous Missourians.* Carlton Press, Inc.: New York,
   New York, 1992
Websites
   2.vcdh.virginia.edu/lewisandclark/biddle/biographies_html/clark.html
   biography.com/people/william-clark-954620
   lewisclark.net/biogrpahy
   scienceviews.com/historical/williamclark.html
   shsmo.org/historicmissourians/name/l/lewisclark/
Photo Credit
   William Clark: Wikimedia Commons. Painting by Charles Willson
   Peale, 1810.

Enoch H. Crowder

Books
   Lockmiller. David A. *Enoch Crowder: Soldier, Lawyer, and Statesman.*
   Columbia: University of Missouri Studies, 1955. [REF F508.1 C885L]
   Mellberg, Robert William. *Missouri Proud.* Xlibris Corporation, 2007
Websites
   arlingtoncemetery.net/ehcrowder.html
   cdm.sos.mo.gov/cdm/ref/collection/overthere/id10577
   revolvy.com/topic/Enoch%20Crowder
   shsmo.org/historicmissourians/name/c/crowder/
Photo Credit
   Wikimedia Commons. Major General Enoch Herbert Crowder, Provost
   Marshal General of the U.S. Army, May 1917-July 1919.

Ulysses S. Grant

Books
   Mellberg, Robert William. *Missouri Proud.* Xlibris Corporation, 2007
   Thompson, Bernice. *Famous Missourians.* Carlton Press, Inc.: New York,
   New York, 1992
Websites
   biography.com/people/ullsses-s-grant-9318285?_escaped_fragment_=
   brainyquote.com/quoates/authors/u/Ulysses_s_grant.html\
   goodreads.com/author/quotes/6926.Ulysses_S_Grant
   granthomepage.com/grantchronology.html

history.com/topics/us-presidents/Ulysses-s-grant

historynet.com/Uuysses-s-grant

Photo Credit

Wikimedia Commons. The 18th President of the United States Ulysses S. Grant. Photo by Brady-Handy ca. 1870-1880.

Carrie Nation

Books

Beals, Careton. *Cyclone Carrie: The Story of Carrie Nation.* 1962

Mellberg, Robert William. *Missouri Proud.* Xlibris Corporation, 2007

Nation, Carry A. *The Use and Need of the Life of Carry A. Nation.* 1904

Taylor, Robert Lewis. *Vessel of Wrath: The Life and Times of Carry Nation.* 1966

Websites

alcoholproblemsandsolutions.org/carry-nation-biography-carrie-nation/

azquotes.com/author/24362-Carrie_Nation

biographybase.com/biography/Nation_Carry.html

browsebiography.com/bio-carry_nation.html

imdb.com/name/nm1534284/bio

thoughtco.com/carrie-nation-biography-3530547

Photo Credit

Wikimedia Commons. Carrie Nation. Photo by Philipp Kester, 1910.

Tom Pendergast

Books

Brown, John. *Missouri Legends: Famous People from the Show-Me State.* Reedy Press: St. Louis, Missouri, 2008

Dorsett, Lyle. W. *The Pendergast Machine.* New York: Oxford University Press, 1968 [REF H128.74 D738]

Larsen, Lawrence H., and Nancy J. Hulston. *Pendergast!* Columbia: University of Missouri Press, 1997 [REFF508.1 P373l]

McLachlan, Sean. *Outlaw Tales of Missouri.* Guilford, CT: Morris Book Publishing, 2009

Reddig, William M. *Tom's Town: Kansas City and the Pendergast Legend.* New York: Lippincott, 1947

Websites

shsmo.org/historicmissourians/name/p/pendergast/

vintagekansascity.com/menwhomadekc/pendergast_thomas_j.html

Photo Credit
yahoo.com

John J. Pershing
Books

Bass, Paul William. *The History of Fort Leonard Wood, Missouri.* Sikeston, MO.: Acclaim Press, 2016

Brown, John. Missouri Legends: *Famous People from the Show-Me State.* Reedy Press: St. Louis, Missouri, 2008

Mellberg, Robert William. *Missouri Proud.* Xlibris Corporation, 2007

Smith, G. *Until the Last Trumpet Sounds: The Life of General of the Army John J. Pershing.* New York: Wiley, 1998

Thompson, Bernice. *Famous Missourians.* Carlton Press, Inc.: New York, New York, 1992

Websites

biography.com/people/john-j-pershing#!
history.com/topics/world-war-i/john-j-pershing
shsmo.org/historicmissourians/namep/pershing/

Photo Credit

Wikimedia Commons. General John Joseph "Black Jack" Pershing.

Phyllis Schlafly
Books

Critchlow, Donald T. *Phyllis Schalfly and Grassroots Conservatism*, 2006

Felsenthal, Carol. *The Sweetheart of the Silent Majority*, 1981

Mellberg, Robert William. *Missouri Proud.* Xlibris Corporation, 2007

Schlafly, Phyllis. *A Choice Not an Echo.* 1964

Schlafly, Phyllis. *The Power of the Christian Woman.* 1981

Schlafly, Phyllis. *Who Killed the American Family?* 2014

Schlafly, Phyllis. *How the Republican Party Became Pro-Life.* 2016

Websites

imdb.com/name/nm0772067/bio
nwhm.org/education-resources/biography/biographies/phyllis-schlafly
nytimes.com/2016/09/06/obituaries/phyllis-schlafly-conservative-leader-and-foe-of-ers-dies-at-92.html
rawstory.com/2016/09/anti-feminist-phyllis-schlaflys-philosophy-perfectly-captured-in-15-disturbing-quotes/
thoughtco.com/Phyllis-schlafly-anti-feminist-3529774

Photo Credit

nwhm.org/education-resources/biography/ biographies/Phyllis-schafly/

Dred Scott

Books

Ehrlich, Walter. _They Have No Rights: Dred Scott's Struggle for Freedom._ Westport, CT: Greenwood Press, 1979 [REF552 Eh89]

Ferenbacher, Don E. _The Dred Scott Case: Its Significance in American Law and Politics._ New York: Oxford University Press, 1978 [REF F552 F322]

Latham, Frank Brown. _The Dred Scott Decision, March 6, 1857: Slavery and the Supreme Court's Self-Inflicted Wound._ New York: F. Watts, 1968 [REF IJ L347d]

Maltz, Earl. _Dred Scott and the Politics of Slavery._ Lawrence, KS." University of Kansas Press, 2007 [REF F552 M299]

Mellberg, Robert William. _Missouri Proud._ Xlibris Corporation, 2007

Thompson, Bernice. _Famous Missourians._ Carlton Press, Inc.: New York, New York, 1992

Websites

american-historama.org/1850-1860-secession-era/dred-scott-decision.html

biography.com/people/dred-scott-9477240#!

britannica.com/events/Dred-Scott-decision

pbs.org/wgbh/aia/part4/4p2932.html

shsmo.org/historicmissourians/name/s/scottd/

sos.mo.gov/archives/respurces/africanamerican.scott/scott.asp

thedredscotttfoundation.org/dshf/index.php?option=com_contents&view=article&id=50&ltemid-55

u-s-history.com/pages/h88.html

Photo Credit

Wikimedia Commons. Dred Scott, ca. 1857.

Harry S Truman

Books

Bass, Paul William. _Fellow Dreamers._ Stillwater, OK: New Forums Press, 2008

Brown, John. _Missouri Legends: Famous People from the Show-Me State._ Reedy Press: St. Louis, Missouri, 2008

Donovan, R. *Conflict and Crisis: The Presidency of Harry S Truman, 1945-1948.* New York: Norton, 1977

Ferrell, R. H. *Harry S. Truman: A Life.* Columbia: University of Missouri Press, 1996

McCullough, David. *Truman.* New York: Simon & Schuster, 1992

Mellberg, Robert William. *Missouri Proud.* Xlibris Corporation, 2007.

Reese, Alice Anna. *Show Me Famous Missourians.* Compass Flower Press, 2014.

Thompson, Bernice. *Famous Missourians.* Carlton Press, Inc.: New York, New York, 1992.

Websites

datesandevents.org/American-timelines/harry-s-truman-timeline.html

history.com/topics/us-presidents/harry-truman

nps.gov/hstr/index/html

google.com/site/harrystrumanthe33president/fun-facts

totallyhistory.com/harry-s-truman/

trumanlittlewhitehouse.com/key-west/president-truman-biography.html

whitehouse.gov/1600/presidents/harrystruman

yahoo.com/news/10-fascinating-facts-president-harry-truman-102056313.html

Site Visit

Truman Presidential Library, Independence, Missouri

Truman Home, Independence, Missouri

Truman Birthplace, Lamar, Missouri

Photo Credit

Wikimedia Commons. Harry S Truman, President of the USA in 1945.

Chapter Seven

Henry Armstrong

Books

Armstrong, Henry. *Gloves, Glory and God.* 1956

Mellberg, Robert William. *Missouri Proud.* Xlibris Corporation, 2007

Thompson, Bernice. *Famous Missourians.* Carlton Press, Inc.: New York, New York, 1992

Websites

biography.com/people/henry-armstrong-918829? *escapedfragment_=*

britannica.com/biography/Henry-Armstrong

espn.go.com/sportscentury/features/00014077.html

henryarmstrong.net/BIOGRAPHY.html

mytimes.com/1988/10/25/obituaries/henry-armstrong-boxing-
champion-dead-at-75.html

Photo Credit

Wikimedia Commons. Portrait of Henry Armstrong. Photo by Carl
Van Vechten, 15 July 1937.

Yogi Berra

Books

Berra, Yogi, and Ed Fitzgerald. *Yogi: The Autobiography of a Professional
Baseball Player.* Garden City, NY: Doubleday, 1961 [REFIJ B458y]

Berra, Yogi. *The Yogi Book: I Really Didn't Say Everything I Said.*
Workman, 1962

Berra, Yogi, and Tom Horton. *It Ain't Over...*New York: McGraw-Hill,
1989 [REFF508.1 B4583b3]

Berra, Yogi, and Dave Kaplan. *Ten Rings: My Championship Seasons.*
New York: HarperCollins, 2003 [REF F508.1 B4583b 2005]

Berra, Yogi, and Dave Kaplan. *You Can Observe a Lot by Watching.*
Hoboken, NJ: John Wiley & Sons, Inc. 2008 [REF F508.1 B4583b2]

Devito, Carlo. *Yogi: The Life and Times of an American Original.*
Chicago: Triumph Books, 2008 [REF F508.1 B4583]

Mellberg, Robert William. *Missouri Proud.* Xlibris Corporation, 2007

Merkel, Jim. *The Colorful Characters of St. Louis.* Reedy Press: St. Louis,
Missouri, 2016

Robinson, Ray. *The Greatest Yankee of Them All.* New York: Putnam,
1969 [REF LJ R566g]

Websites

biography.com/people/yogi-berra-9210325?_escaped_fragment_=

encyclopedia.com/people/sports-and-games/sports-biographies/yogi-
berra

espn.com/mlb/player/bio/_/id/19152/yogi-berra

ftw.usatoday.com/2015/15/09/the-50-greatest-yogi-berra-quotes

imdb.com/name/nm007286/bio

shsmo.org/historicmissourians/name/b/berra/

thefamouspeople.com/profiles/yogi-berra-2115.php

yogi-berra.com/

Photo Credit

yahoo.com

Bob Costas

Books

Costas, Bob. Fair Ball: *A Fan's Case for Baseball*. 2000

Mellberg, Robert William. *Missouri Proud*. Xlibris Corporation, 2007

Websites

ans-wer.com/biography/bob-costas-plastic-surgery-toupee-and-salary.html

biographyarchive.com/biograohy-of-bob-costas.html

biography.com/people/bob-costas-071216imdb.com/name/nm0182471/
bio

fandango.com/people/bob-costas-137784/biography

filmreference.com/film/66/Bob-Costas.html

tvguide/com/celebrities/bob-costas/bio/195051/

washingtonspeakers/biography.cfm?SpeakerID=874

Photo Credit

biographyarchive.com/biography-of-bob-costas.html

Joe Garagiola

Books

Brown, John. *Missouri Legends: Famous People from the Show-Me State*.
Reedy Press: St. Louis, Missouri, 2008

Garagiola, Joe. *Baseball Is A Funny Game*. 1960

Garagiola. Joe. *It's Anybody's Ballgame*. New York: Berkley Publishing,
1980

Garagiola, Joe. *Just Play Ball*. 2007

Mellberg, Robert William. *Missouri Proud*. Xlibris Corporation, 2007

Merkel, Jim. *The Colorful Characters of St. Louis*. Reedy Press: St. Louis,
Missouri, 2016

Thompson, Bernice. *Famous Missourians*. Carlton Press, Inc.: New York,
New York, 1992

Websites

baseballhall.org/discover/short-stops/garagiola-baseball-humor-book

espn.com/blog/sweetspot/post/_/id/69111/joe-garagiola-sr-was-part-of-
growing-up-a-baseball-fan-for-many

foxnews.com/us/2016/03/23/hall-fame-sportscaster-mlb-catcher-joe-
garagiola-dead at-90/html

imdb.com/name/nm0304792/bio

washingtonpost.com/sports/joe-garagiola-ballplayer-w...4-f132-11e5-
a61f-e9c95c06edca_story.html?utm_term=.4b7be3787457

yahoo.com/news/joe-garagiola-ends-broadcast-career-58-
years-002559020—mlb.html

Photo Credit

Wikimedia Commons. St. Louis Cardinals catcher Joe Garagiola in a
June 1951 issue of Baseball Digest.

Stan Musial

Books

Giglio, James N. *Musial: From Stash to Stan the Man.* Columbia:
University of Missouri Press, 2001 [REF F508.1 M973gi]

Mellberg, Robert William. *Missouri Proud.* Xlibris Corporation, 2007

Musial, Stan, and Bob Broeg. *Stan Musial: "The Man's" Own Story, as
Told to Bob Broeg.* New York: Doubleday, 1964

Robinson, Ray. *Stan Musial: Baseball's Durable "Man."* New York:
Putnam, 1963 [REF lJ R566s]

Schoor, Gene, with Henry Gilfond. *The Stan Musial Story.* New York: J.
Messner, 1955 [REF F508.1 M973s]

Thompson, Bernice. *Famous Missourians.* Carlton Press, Inc.: New York,
New York, 1992

Vecsey, George. *Stan Musial: An American Life.* New York: Ballantine
Books, 2011 [REF F508.1 M973v]

Websites

anb.org/articles/19/19-01019-article.html

baseballhall.org/hof/musial-stan

blog.aarp.org/2013/01/20/stan-musial-10-fascinating-facts-about-stan-
the-man/

cnn.com/2013/01/19/sports/Missouri-musial-obit/index.html

encyclopedia.com/people/sports-and-games/sports-biographies.stanley-
frank-musial

hardballtimes.com/stan-musial-an-american-life

imdb.com/name/nm0615705/bio

shsmo.org/historicmissourians/name/m/musial/

stlouis.cardinals.mlb.com/stl/fan_forum/stan_musial.jsp?loc=bio

Photo Credit

Wikimedia Commons. St. Louis Cardinals Hall of Famer Stan Musial
from his 1953 Bowman baseball trading card, ca. 1953.

Satchel Paige

Books

Fox, William Price. *Satchel Paige's America*. Fire Ant Books, 2005

Mellberg, Robert William. *Missouri Proud*. Xlibris Corporation, 2007

Paige, Satchel, and David Lipman. *Maybe I'll Pitch Forever: A Great Baseball Tells the Hilarious Story Behind the Legend. Player* University Of Nebraska Press, 1993

Paige, Satchel, and Hal Lebovitz. *Pitchin' Man: Satchel Paige's Own Story*. Westport, CT: Meckler, 1992

Reese, Alice Anna. *Show Me Famous Missourians*. Compass Flower Press, 2014

Ribowsky, Mark. *Don't Look Back: Satchel Paige in the Shadows of Baseball*. New York: Da Capo Press, 1994

Websites

biography.com/people/satchel-paige-9431917?_escaped_fragment_=

baseballhall.org/hof/paige-stachel

newworldencyclopedia.org/entry/Satchel_Paige

quotationspage.com/quotes/Satchel_Paige/

sabr.org/bioproj/person/c33afddd

u-s-history.com/pages/h3777.html

Photo Credit

en.wkipedia.org/wiki/Satchel_Paige

Casey Stengel

Books

Allen, Maury. *You Could Look It Up: The Life of Casey Stengel*. Times Books, 1979

Bak, Richard. *Casey Stengel—A Splendid Baseball Life*. Taylor Publishing Co., 1997

Berklow, I., and J. Kaplan. *The Gospel According to Casey: Casey Stengel's Inimitable, Instructional, Historical Baseball Book*. New York: St. Martin's Press, 1992

Brown, John. *Missouri Legends: Famous People from the Show-Me State*. Reedy Press: St. Louis, Missouri, 2008

Creamer, Robert W. *Stengel: His Life and Times*. University of Nebraska Press, 1984

Mellberg, Robert William. *Missouri Proud*. Xlibris Corporation, 2007

Websites

baseball-almanac.com/quotes/quosteng.shtml

baseballhall.org/hof/stengel-casey

caseystengel.com/biography/

findagrave.com/cgi-bin/fg.cgi?page=gr&Grid=980

sabr.org/bioproj/person/bd6a83d8

shsmo.org/historicmissourians/name/s/Stengel/

Photo Credit

Wikimedia Commons. New York Yankees manager Casey Stengel in a October 1953 issue of Baseball Digest.

Helen Stephens

Books

Hanson, Sharon Kinney. *The Life of Helen Stephens: The Fulton Flash.* Carbondale: Southern Illinois University Press, 2004 [REF F508.1 St439]

Mellberg, Robert William. *Missouri Proud.* Xlibris Corporation, 2007

Reese, Alice Anna. *Show Me Famous Missourians.* Compass Flower Press, 2014

Websites

callway.dbrl.org/history/callaway-biographies/helen-stephens

missourilife.com/life/top-10-women-who changed-missouri-helen-stephens/

nytimes.com/1994/01/19/obituaries/Helen-stephens-75-Olympic-medalist-in-1936-at-berlin.html

shsmo.org/historicmissourians/name/s/stephens/

sports-reference.com/olympics/athletes/st/Helen-stephens-1.html

Photo Credit

missourilife.com/life/top-10-women-who-changed-missouri-Helen-stephens/

Chapter Eight

Daniel Boone

Books

Bakeless, *John. Daniel Boone.* 1939

Draper, Lyman C. *The Life of Daniel Boone.* Mechanicsburg, PA: Stackpole Books, 1988

Elliott, Lawrence. *The Long Hunter: A New Life of Daniel Boone*. 1976

Faragher, John Mack. *The Life and Legend of an American Pioneer*. New
York: Holt, 1992

Mellberg, Robert William. *Missouri Proud*. Xlibris Corporation, 2007

Thompson, Bernice. *Famous Missourians*. Carlton Press, Inc.: New York,
New York, 1992

Websites

biography.com/people/Daniel-boone-9219543?_escaped_fragment_=

danielboone.org/

greatriverroad.com/stcharles/boonehome.html

history.com/topics/daniel-boone

notablebiographies.com/Be-Br/Boone-Daniel.html

sccmo.org/1701/The-Historic-Daniel-Boone-Home

Photo Credit

Wikimedia Commons. Engraving of Daniel Boone by Alonzo Chappel,
ca. 1861.

Kit Carson

Books

Carson, Kit. *Kit Carson's Autobiography*. Chicago: R.R. Donnelly & Sons
Co., 1935

Carter, Harvey L. *Old Kit: The Historical Christopher Carson*. Norman:
Iniversity of Oklahoma Press, 1968

Ellis, Edward Sylvester. *The Life of Kit Carson*. Lake Wales, FL: Lost
Classics Book Co., 1998

Gliester, Jan, and Kathleen Thompson. *Kit Carson*. Milwaukee: Raintree
Childrens Books, 1987

Reese, Alice Anna. *Show Me Famous Missourians*. Compass Flower
Press, 2014

Thompson, Bernice. *Famous Missourians*. Carlton Press, Inc.: New York,
New York, 1992

Websites

biography.com/people/kit-carson-9239728

browsebiography.com/bio-kit-carson.html

legendsofamerica.com/nm-kitcarson.html

notablebiographies.com/Ca-Ch/Carson-Kit.html

pbs.org/weta/thewest/people/a_c/carson.html

Photo Credit

Wikimedia Commons. Kit Carson, American Explorer, ca. 1860-1875.

Jesse and Frank James

Books

Brant, M. *Jesse James: The Man and The Myth*. New York: Berkley Publishing Group, 1998

Brown, John. *Missouri Legends: Famous People from the Show-Me State*. Reedy Press: St. Louis, Missouri, 2008

Dyer, R. *Jesse James and the Civil War*. Columbia: University of Missouri Press, 1994

McLachlan, Sean. *Outlaw Tales of Missouri*. Guilford, CT: Morris Book Publishing, 2009

Reese, Alice Anna. *Show Me Famous Missourians*. Compass Flower Press, 2014

Stiles, T. *Jesse James: Last Rebel of the Civil War*. New York: Knopf, 2002

Wood, Larry. *Murder and Mayhem in Missouri*. Charleston, SC: The History Press, 2013

Websites

biography.com/jesse-james-9352646?_escaped_fragment_=

history.com/news/history-lists/7-things-you-might-know-about-jesse-james

legendsofamerica.com/we-jessejames.html

Photo Credit

Jessie James: Wikimedia Commons. Portrait of Jesse James, ca. 1876-1882. Frank James: Wikimedia Commons. Alexander Franklin James, an American outlaw. Photo by Guerin, St. Louis, 1898.

Calamity Jane

Books

Horan, James D. *Desperate Women*. 1952

Jennewein, John Leonard. *Calamity Jane of the Western Trails*. 1953

Mumey, Nolie. *Calamity Jane, 1852-1903: A History of Her Life and Adventures in the West*. 1950

Reese, Alice Anna. *Show Me Famous Missourians*. Compass Flower Press, 2014

Websites

biography.com/people/calamity-jane9234950?_escaped_fragment_=

biographybase.com/biography/Jane_Calamity.html

encyclopedia.com/people/history/us-history-biographies/calamity-jane

history.com/this-day-in-history/calamity-jane-is-born

thefamouspeople.com/profiles/calamity-jane-3699.php

thoughtco.com/calamity-janebiography-353703

Photo Credit

Wikimedia Commons. Calamity Jane, Gen. Crook's Scout, ca. 1880s.

Charles Lindbergh

Books

Berg, A. Scott. *Lindbergh*. New York: G. P. Putnam's Sons, 1998

Cole, Wayne S. *Charles A. Lindbergh and the Battle Against American Intervention in World War II*. New York: Harcourt Brace Jovanovich, 1974

Gilbin, James. *Charles A. Lindbergh: A Human Hero*. New York: Clarion Books, 1997

Gill, Brendan. *Lindbergh Alone*. New York: Harcourt Brace Jovanovich, 1977

Kent, Zachary. *Charles Lindbergh and the Spirit of St. Louis*. Parsippany, NJ: New Discovery Books, 1998

Lindbergh, Charles. *We*. New York: Grosset & Dunlap Publishers, 1927

Lindbergh, Charles. *Of Flight and Life*. 1948

Linbergh, Charles. *The Spirit of St. Louis*. 1953

Mellberg, Robert William. *Missouri Proud*. Xlibris Corporation, 2007

Milton, Joyce. *Loss of Eden: A Biography of Charles and Anne Morrow Lindbergh*. New York: Harper Collins, 1993

Mosley, Leonard. *Lindbergh: A Biography*. New York: Doubleday and Company, 1976

Websites

biography.com/people/Charles-lindbergh-9382609?_esacped_fragment_=

charleslindbergh.com/history/

history.com/news/history-lists/10-fascinatng-facts-about-charles-lindbergh

history.com/topics/charles-a-lindbergh

newworldencyclopedia.org/entry/Charles_Lindbergh

notablebiographies.com/Ki-Lo/Lindbergh-Charles.html

shsmo.org/historicmissourians/name/l/Lindbergh/index.html

Photo Credit

Wikimedia Commons. Charles Lindbergh, with the Spirit of St. Louis in the background.

William Quantrill

Books

Castel, Albert E. *William Clarke Quantrill, His Life and Times.* Norman: University of Oklahoma Press, 1999

Connelley, William E. *Quantrill and the Border Wars.* Cedar Rapids, IA: The Torch Press, 1910

Leslie, Edward E. *The Devil Knows How to Ride: The Story of William Clarke Quantrill and His Confederate Raiders.* New York: Random House, 1996

McLachlan, Sean. *Outlaw Tales of Missouri.* Guilford, CT: Morris Book Publishing, 2009

Schultz, Duane. *Quantrill's Wars: The Life and Times of William Clarke Quantrill, 1837-1865.* New York: St. Martin's Press, 1996

Websites

civilwaronthewesternborder.org/encyclopedia/quantrill-william-clarke

civilwarsaga.com/William-qntrills-three-graves/

geni.com/people/William Quantrill/6000000012667141672

history.com/this-day-in-hiastory/William-Quantrill-killed-by-union-soldiers

legendsofamerica.com/mo-quantrill.html

nndb.com/people/977/000165482/

thoughtco.com/William-quantrill-soldier-or-murderer-104550

Other

Green, Rodney J., "The Man Who Killed Quantrill." *Missouri Life* magazine, June 1, 2017

Photo Credit

yahoo.com

Belle Starr

Books

Burton, Rascoe. *Belle Starr: The Bandit Queen.* Lincoln, NE: Bison Books, 2004

McLachlan, Sean. *Outlaw Tales of Missouri.* Guilford, CT: Morris Book Publishing, 2009

Shirley, Glenn. *Belle Starr and Her Times: The Literature, Facts, and the Legends.* Norman: University of Oklahoma Press, 1990

Websites

biography.com/people/belle-starr-9492533?_escaped_fragment_=

encyclopediaofarkansas.net/encyclopedia/entry-detail.
    aspx?entryID=2406
genealogytrails.com/oka/muskogee/bio_bellestarr.html
history.com/this-day-in-history/belle-starr-murdered-in-oklahoma
history.net/com/belle-starr.html
legendsofamerica.com/we-bellestarr.html
newworldencyclopedia.org/entry/Belle_Starr
nndb.com/people/881/000206263/
Photo Credit

Wikimedia Commons. A studio portrait of Belle Starr probably taken at
Fort Smith in the early 1880s.

Sacred Sun

Books

McMillen, Margot Ford, and Heather Roberson. *Called to Courage: Four
    Missouri Women*. Columbia: University of Missouri Press, 2002 (REF
    F508 M228]
Reese, Alice Anna. *Show Me Famous Missourians*. Compass Flower
    Press, 2014

Websites

columbia-mo.aauw.net/notablewomen/womenos/sacred-sun/
shsmo.org/historicmissourians/name/s/sacredsun/

Photo Credit

Wikimedia Commons. Sacred Sun and her child, from the University
of California McKenney-Hall Collection, "The History of the Indian
Tribes of North America" by Thomas L. McKenney and James Hall,
1870.

About the Author

Paul William Bass was born in Independence, Missouri. He graduated from William Chrisman High School, Southwest Baptist College, and Midwestern Baptist Theological Seminary. He married Jan Smashey in 1969. He served in full-time church staff positions for nineteen years in Arkansas, Alabama, and Missouri. From 1990–2007, he served at Ouachita Baptist University in Arkadelphia, Arkansas, as director of student activities and held various adjunct teaching positions. He became the intercollegiate debate coach, with OBU debaters winning three national championships. He took early retirement in 2007 and, in that year, received the Isocrates Distinguished Debate Coach Award from the International Public Debate Association. During that time in Arkansas, he served in several interim pastor positions and became a bivocational pastor at Anchor Baptist Church for twelve years.

He began his writing career in 2007 with publication of *No Little Dreams: Henry Garland Bennett, Educator and Statesman*. He received the Henry Bennett Distinguished Fellow Award from Oklahoma State University. In 2008, his second book in the Bennett trilogy, *Fellow Dreamers: Oklahoma, Education and the World*, was published. The third book in the Bennett trilogy, *Touching the Dream: Point Four*, was published in 2009. That year he was commissioned by Oklahoma State University to write a history of their School of International Studies, entitled *Legacy, Leadership and Learning*. In 2011, he published two religious works from his pastoral experience, *In Jesus' Names* and *Minor Characters of the Bible*. In 2012, he published *Robert S. Kerr: Oklahoma's Pioneer King*. For the Kerr book, he received the 2013 Missouri Writer's Guild First Place President's Award and the 2013 Walter Williams Major Work Award. In 2013, he published *Grace through Tolerance*. In 2014, he completed the autobiographical work of *Me and Church*.

In 2015, a four-year project was published as *The History of Fort Leonard Wood, Missouri*. In May 2017, the Missouri Writers Guild awarded *The History of Fort Leonard Wood, Missouri* the **2017 First Prize Walter Williams Major Work Award**. That same year his commissioned work from Oklahoma State University, *Legacy, Leadership and Learning*, was published.

Published in the fall of 2017, the latest book is *Pioneer Churches in Springfield, Missouri*. All profits and royalties are given to a local women's shelter and food bank. *Missouri Innovators* will be the first in a series of neighboring state innovator books he is considering for the immediate future. In addition to his writing, the last few years he has been teaching college-level Bible classes at the Mercy School of Nursing in Springfield, Missouri, in cooperation with Southwest Baptist University.

Paul and his wife, Jan, are retired and living in Willard, Missouri. His email address is bassp@obu.edu.

Index